£8·99

Social Work and the

```
C000078605
```

Social Work and the Legacy of Freud

Psychoanalysis and its Uses

Edited by

Geoffrey Pearson

Judith Treseder

Margaret Yelloly

**MACMILLAN
EDUCATION**

First published 1988

Published by
MACMILLAN EDUCATION LTD
Houndmills, Basingstoke, Hampshire RG21 2XS
and London
Companies and representatives
throughout the world

Printed in Hong Kong

British Library Cataloguing in Publication Data
Social work and the legacy of Freud:
psychoanalysis and its uses.
1. Great Britain. Welfare work. Influence
of psychoanalysis
I. Pearson, Geoffrey   II. Treseder, Judith
III. Yelloly, Margaret
361'.941
ISBN 0–333–39781–9 (hardcover)
ISBN 0–333–39782–7 (paperback)

Contents

Notes on the Contributors

Roger Bacon took a Degree in Sociology at the University of Cambridge, and then a PhD after research on attempted suicide by drug-overdosing. He then undertook a research project for the Association of British Adoption and Fostering Agencies on the management of resources for fostering and adoption in five local authorities. From 1976 to 1982 he was research officer in the Child Care and Development Group at the University of Cambridge, working for the DHSS on research into various aspects of child abuse. In 1983 he completed a training in psychoanalytical psychotherapy and has since then been working full-time as a psychotherapist in private practice. He is the author of a number of articles on the problem of child abuse.

Robert Bocock is Senior Lecturer in Sociology at the Open University, having previously held a Lectureship at Brunel University. He is also a consultant Lecturer in sociology and psycho-social studies at the Richmond Fellowship College, London. He is the author of *Sigmund Freud* (1983), *Religion and Ideology* (1985) and *Hegemony* (1986).

Catherine Crowther was, at the time of writing, a Senior Social Worker for the London Borough of Southwark in the Department of Child and Adolescent psychiatry of the Maudsley Hospital, London, where she had worked for nine years. She now works as a counsellor at the Westminster Pastoral Foundation, London, and as a freelance individual and family therapist. She is training to be a Jungian analyst at the Society of Analytical Psychology, London.

Mira Dana was born in Israel, where she did her first degree in psychology and worked in a psychiatric hospital with drug addicts. Her interest in eating problems has developed since coming to England eight years ago, and she wrote her MA thesis on the links between anorexia and compulsive eating. She works as a psychotherapist at the Women's Therapy Centre in London, where she coordinates the work on eating problems. Her own work is mainly with compulsive eaters and bulimic women, running groups, workshops, training and supervision.

Celia Downes is a Lecturer in Social Work at the University of York. She has practised as a social worker in area teams and acted as a consultant to social workers. With a practitioner colleague she has developed an advanced course in supervision and consultancy for experienced social workers.

Marilyn Lawrence trained as a psychiatric social worker and began working with anorexic and bulimic women in 1973. In 1978 she co-founded the Anorexia Counselling Service in Leeds and since 1981 she has had close links with the Women's Therapy Centre in London. She works as a Senior Lecturer in Social Work at the West London Institute of Higher Education, having previously held a lectureship at the University of Bradford. She is the author of *The Anorexic Experience* (1984) and the editor of *Fed Up and Hungry* (1987).

Geoffrey Pearson is Professor of Social Work at Middlesex Polytechnic. Educated at the Universities of Cambridge and Sheffield and at the London School of Economics, where he trained as a psychiatric social worker, he taught formerly at University College, Cardiff, and at the University of Bradford, where he was Reader in Applied Social Studies. His published work includes *The Deviant Imagination* (1975), *Working Class Youth Culture* (1976), *Hooligan: A History of Respectable Fears* (1983), *Young People and Heroin* (1986) and *The New Heroin Users* (1987).

Janet Sayers is a Lecturer in Psychology on the MA in Social Work at the University of Kent. She also does some sessional work as a Clinical Psychologist, and is currently doing research on psychoanalytical and feminist perspectives on childbirth. Her publications include *Biological Politics* (1982) and *Sexual Contradictions* (1986).

Laurence Spurling has been a social worker since 1975. He is now a freelance psychotherapist, and also a consultant to a social services department and lecturer on both a counselling and a social work course. He is the author of *Phenomenology and the Social World* (1977), editor of *Critical Assessments on Freud* (1988) and co-editor of *On Becoming a Psychotherapist* (1988).

John Simmonds, after social work experience in child care and a specialist agency working with adolescents, joined the staff of

Goldsmiths' College, University of London. His major interests are in the principles and practice of social work, the application of psychodynamic concepts to social work and social work organisations, and latterly new developments in child care thinking. He maintains an active interest in the practice of social work through various consultancies in both residential and fieldwork settings.

Judith Treseder is Social Work Coordinator, based at St Thomas's Hospital in London, for the group of hospitals in the West Lambeth Health Authority. After reading history at St Anne's College, Oxford, she took the Diploma in Social Administration at Barnet House, Oxford, and later the Certificate in Mental Health at the London School of Economics. For the large part of her career she has worked in adult and child psychiatry settings, and for twelve years she was Principal Social Worker in the Department of Child and Adolescent Psychiatry at the Maudsley Hospital. During this time she served on the editorial board of the *British Journal of Social Work*, and she was recently Chair of the Association of Child Psychology and Psychiatry. Her published work includes papers on the treatment of school refusal and aspects of childcare.

Stephen Wilson received his medical education at the Royal Free Hospital, London. He specialised in psychiatry at Fulbourn Hospital, Cambridge and went on to hold a Research Fellowship in the sociology of medicine at Bedford College, London and subsequently Merton College, Oxford. He trained as an analyst at the Institute of Psychoanalysis in London, and is also a Fellow of the Royal College of Psychiatrists. He is now Clinical Lecturer in the Department of Psychiatry, University of Oxford, and Consultant Psychiatrist, Littlemore Hospital. He has contributed widely to journals and has a psychotherapeutic practice in the city of Oxford.

Margaret Yelloly is Professor of Social Work and Director of Social Work Education at the University of Stirling, having moved there in 1986 from Goldsmith's College, University of London. She trained as a social worker at Liverpool University and the Tavistock Clinic, and her practice experience has been largely with children and families. For a number of years she served as Editor of the *British Journal of Social Work*. She is author of *Social Work and Psychoanalysis* (1980), a major study of the influence of psychoanalysis on social work in Britain, and one of her central interests is the contribution of psychodynamic thinking to the understanding of the group and organisational context of social work practice.

The editors also wish to acknowledge the contribution of **Ved Varma**, who played an important role in helping to establish the original idea for this book, although he was unfortunately unable to become involved in the actual planning of its form and content.

Introduction: Social Work and the Legacy of Freud

The aim of this book is to re-state the claims of psychoanalysis, together with some of its attendant difficulties, after a period of time in which Freud's work and that of his successors has been largely neglected within social work. This neglect has been almost a complete reversal of social work's earlier enchantment with psychoanalytical ideas during the 1950s and 1960s when, as Eileen Younghusband recalled, the 'heady wine' of Freudian theory had been a dominant influence within the education and training of social workers, and in their examination scripts 'psychoanalytical theory tripped relevantly or irrelevantly off their pens' (Younghusband, 1978, p. 41).

It is easy to overstate the extent to which social work once depended on psychoanalytical theory, although it would not be an overstatement to say that since the early 1970s psychoanalysis has been almost entirely forgotten within social work. But if it has been forgotten (and it should be remembered that Freud himself had a great deal to say about the process of forgetting), it is important to ask why, and also what has been forgotten. Because psychoanalysis has certainly not been forgotten elsewhere. On the contrary, major developments have taken place within psychoanalytical theory and its theory and its applications in recent years, including not only developments which have helped to advance the psychoanalytical project, but also a number of critiques which challenge the entire basis of the Freudian legacy.

In the essays collected together in this volume, the authors address a number of practical and theoretical issues as these relate to social work and psychoanalysis. It is a common view that psychoanalysis is no more than a method of treatment – the client on the couch, the world safely locked outside the analyst's consulting room during the 'fifty minute' hour of the analytic session. If this were true, then social work might well have been justified in forgetting psychoanalysis. The problems which the clients of social workers typically face refuse such a neat compartmentalisation – the world is constantly banging on the door. However, this a misrepresentation of what psychoanalysis places on offer. A more faithful account of Freud's own views, for

1

example, would be that he was quite hostile to the idea that psychoanalysis was no more than a system of therapy, in that he hoped to have offered an approach to human self-understanding which had a much wider relevance. We have attempted to reflect this broader appreciation of psychoanalysis here, so that while some chapters are concerned with therapeutic considerations, others are not. In our introduction, also, we will address a number of questions with far-reaching implications: such as the scientific status of psychoanalysis, and whether it is even useful to think of psychoanalysis as a 'science'; a consideration of attempts to reconcile psychoanalytic understanding with different bodies of theory and evidence from sociology and anthropology, including the ambitious project to bring about a marriage of Freud and Marx; and finally the vexed question of Freud and feminism. First, however, in order to lay the ground for these broader discussions, we will adopt a narrower focus on influence of psychoanalysis within social work and the distinctive contribution of the 'British School' of psychoanalysis flowing from the work of Anna Freud, Melanie Klein, Donald Winnicott, John Bowlby, Wilfred Bion and others.

The influence of psychoanalysis on social work

Psychoanalysis is a living tradition, which was born but did not die with Freud. When his revolutionary ideas first began to evolve towards the end of the nineteenth century, Freud had already made a successful career as a neurologist. Medical psychiatry at this time, of course, was beginning to put together its modern systems of diagnostic classification, and its practice was dominated by the growth of the asylum which is now well documented (cf. Rothman, 1971; Scull, 1979 & 1981; Barham, 1985; MacDonald, 1981; Foucault, 1967). Freud's early work, involving experiments with hypnosis, nevertheless formed part of a growing interest in the idea of 'repression' and an 'unconscious' in late-nineteenth-century traditions of German and French psychology and philosophy, where the work of Pierre Janet who had begun to use emotional 'catharsis' as a treatment method was particularly influential (cf. Dalbiez, 1941; Ellenberger, 1970). Janet's work, however, was soon to be eclipsed by that of Freud and his followers.

Accounts of how psychoanalysis began to gain influence in Europe and North America are often tainted by heroic versions of Freud's lonely descent into the unconscious, and in tracing these developments we are handicapped by not having an adequate social history of the psychoanalytical movement. What can be said with confidence, however, is that Freud's ideas were to have a considerable impact within social work, particularly in the United States after his successful lecturing tours early in the twentieth century (cf. Castel *et al.*, 1982; Woodroofe, 1962). This was itself part of a more widespread process by which psychoanalysis was received into the culture of Europe and North America, and put to any number of uses. The advertising industry had also been quick to sense the possibilities in Freud's work, as when he was asked for his advice on how to encourage women to smoke by appealing to their unconscious desires (cf. Castel *et al.*, 1982, p. 32). However, the influence of psychoanalysis upon social work was particularly dramatic, so that within the space of a few years whereas social work had been previously concerned largely with matters such as the relief of poverty, as early as the 1920s in North America it was swept by what Katherine Woodroofe has called a 'psychiatric deluge'.

It would seem that Freud was not unaware of the influence of his ideas within social work, and in the conclusion to *The Question of Lay Analysis* which first appeared in 1926, he allowed himself a joke to the effect that perhaps 'an American may hit on the idea of spending a little money to get the "social workers" of his country trained analytically and to turn them into a band of helpers for combating the neuroses of civilisation' (cf. Freud, 1962, p. 170). The impact of psychoanalysis upon British social work was to come later, of course, and it was also to be less dramatic than in the United States. Nevertheless, it remains true that psychoanalytic ideas have been an integral part of the intellectual heritage of social work for most of the twentieth century, with an influence that is both ideological and practical. Its influence is ideological in that it creates a particular stance towards and conceptualisation of day to day professional situations – a stance characterised by an emphasis on the therapeutic role of the social worker, an individualistic and deeply personal approach to human problems, and an alertness to the unconscious and latent levels of feeling and communication in human interactions. Its influence is also practical, shaping the social worker's understanding and assessment of the problems which he or she encounters, and the kind of help which may be offered. Social workers have always directed their attention to both practical and emotional problems, to the situation as well as the person, but it is the understanding of the person as moulded and shaped by his or her particular life experiences and interpersonal relationships that has been the special concern of the psychodynamically-oriented worker; psychoanalysis has its own particular ways of understanding human predicaments.

The influence of psychoanalysis on the developing social work profession in Britain has been explored in detail elsewhere (Yelloly, 1980); and while the extent of this influence has probably been overstated in some accounts of social works' history, it was undoubtedly among the most significant theoretical underpinnings of social work as it developed as a profession through the 1950s and 1960s. Psychoanalytic language, concepts, and its fundamental premise of unconscious but dynamic mental processes, have become part of the intellectual culture of Europe and North America generally in the course of the twentieth century – indeed in certain respects terms such as the 'unconscious', 'fixation', 'Freudian slip' or 'phallic symbol' have entered into everyday speech – but psychoanalysis nevertheless came to play an especially important role in the professional culture of social work. We have already noted how psychoanalytical ideas, or what was often known as the 'new psychology', had been readily accepted into social work in North America during the 1920s (cf. Robinson, 1930). This is for a number of reasons. First, the association between North American social work with psychiatry and the 'mental hygiene' movement was a channel for the transmission of psychoanalytic ideas, just as American social work theories were to become a strong influence on the new developments in British education and training which began with the first generic course established at the London School of Economics in 1954. Second, the diffusion of psychodynamic theories coincided with the professionalisation of social work and its need for an acceptable and distinctive theoretical base to support its aspirations to professional status.

From the early 1950s there were a number of explorations in Britain, particularly from within psychiatric social work, of the applicability of psychodynamic theories, as these related to the use of the client–worker relationship and the concept of 'transference' (cf. Irvine, 1952 & 1956; Goldberg, 1953; Ferard & Hunnybun, 1962). In this period the influential work of the Family Discussion Bureau, also began to develop its distinctive approach to questions such as 'neurotic collusion' in marital difficulties (cf. Family Discussion Bureau, 1955 & 1962; Pincus, 1960; Dicks, 1967). But it never even approached a psychoanalytic takeover; British social work was too firmly rooted in the Tawney tradition of democratic socialism for that to be a possibility. Even such psychoanalytic ideas as were incorporated were modified and adapted, in the characteristic spirit of British eclecticism. This was equally true of one of the major sources of indigenous influence – the Tavistock Clinic – whose stance towards psychoanalysis was (at least until the Second World War) one of cautious eclecticism rather than committed adherence.

Psychoanalysis nevertheless became particularly influential within British social work during the 1950s and early 1960s, although since that time it has been generally more common for new developments in social work theory to have reacted against psychodynamic theory, so that a random glance at discussions of theory for social work such as those of Hardiker and Barker (1981), Herbert (1981) and Bailey and Lee (1982) will reveal only the barest mentions of psychodynamic theories. It is interesting to speculate on why this should have happened. A major reason is probably the emphasis placed by earlier generations of analytically-oriented social workers on the social worker as therapist. Such a role model has come to seem remote from the day to day realities of social work tasks, and impossible to achieve within the busy and pressured life of local authority social work. Increasingly social workers have found their actions both directed and constrained by legislation, while also often having to cope with the casualties of a political and social context in which a therapeutic role has seemed peripheral and barely relevant. Psychoanalysis came to be seen within social work's 'radical' critique from the late 1960s and through the early 1970s as part of the 'case con' which deflected attention away from what were defined as the more significant material difficulties experienced by clients, such as poverty and poor housing. It became fashionable to knock psychoanalysis within this context, although what was 'knocked' was often only a pale shadow of what psychoanalysis had to offer. Indeed, it was one of the ironies of this 'radical' rejection of psychoanalysis within social work that it coincided with a renewal of interest in psychoanalysis within the broader 'New Left' and 'counter-cultural' movements which were to be counted as an important part of the inspirations for social work's own 'radicalism' (cf. Pearson, 1975, p. 142).

If social work has seemed largely uninterested in psychoanalysis since the mid-1970s, then it must seem even more extraordinary that this again contradicts the more general tendency for an enthusiastic re-appraisal of the Freudian tradition across a range of activities. This is exemplified most vividly perhaps within the sphere of women's studies where psychoanalysis has inspired a number of varied developments of feminist theory and practice (cf. Mitchell, 1974; Rose, 1978; Gallop, 1982; Eichenbaum & Orbach, 1982 & 1985; Bernheimer & Kahane, 1985). Other developments have included a significant renewal of psychoanalytical applications within the study of art and literature, together with psychoanalytical explorations of the failings of contemporary culture and the 'modern' personality such as Christopher Lasch's provocative writings on 'narcissism' (cf. Eagleton, 1983; Lasch, 1979 & 1985). The emergence of a distinctively French purchase on psychoanalysis has been another recent development, which has begun to alter the contours of theoretical debate whether in the form of Lacan's deployment of structural linguistics to the unconscious, in the development of a 'Freudo-Marxist' approach such as that offered by Deleuze and Guattari in *L'Anti-Oedipe* and other works where a fusion between Freud and Marx is attempted, or in Janine Chasseguet-Smirgel's re-assessments of fundamental theoretical constructs within Freud's own work, including the understanding of female sexuality (cf. Turkle, 1978; Chasseguet-Smirgel, 1985a & 1985b; Chasseguet-Smirgel *et al.*, 1985; Chasseguet-Smirgel & Grunberger, 1986; Deleuze & Guattari, 1974; Guattari, 1984; Lacan, 1977 & 1979). What was to prove to be the final phase of Michel Foucault's work, before his untimely death in 1984, could also be read as a prolonged dialogue with Freud, particularly with regard to Freud's views on sexuality and repression (cf. Foucault, 1979, 1980, 1984a & b).

However, these different lines of development have not been grappled with by social workers, even those who might have retained an interest in psychoanalysis, so that much of the social work literature seems strangely dated. Introductory texts in general use still tend to focus on the classical theories of Freud, as if the psychoanalytic tradition had been frozen in time. However, as Mitchell (1986) has described it, 'Psychoanalysis starts but does not end with Freud', and one aim of the present publication is to remain faithful to psychoanalysis as an active tradition by encompassing some of those changes which are continuing within psychoanalysis, particularly those which seem to be of special relevance for social work theory and practice.

Major streams of psychoanalytic thought in Britain

Psychoanalysis has attracted to itself an enormous literature – expository, historical and critical as well as clinical. There are also considerable divergences between different traditions within the psychoanalytical movement: for example, the work of Lacan in France, of ego psychology in the USA, and of Klein in the UK. Besides those authors who are clearly within the psychoanalytic tradition proper (i.e. for our purposes those orientations represented within the Institute of Psychoanalysis), there are many other schools which ultimately derive from the work of Freud, though their subsequent development may show marked divergence. Among them are those who owe particular debt to Carl Jung, to Adler, to the existentialist wing of psychoanalysis represented by Rollo May and Victor Frankl, as well as a vast army of analytically-oriented writers who owe allegiance to no particular school but use theories and ideas culled from a number of psychodynamic sources. Some of the differences, while important to practising therapists, concern clinical debates which are of little interest to those who are not directly involved in therapeutic practice. It is certainly doubtful if many social workers are either interested in or informed about them. Furthermore, social work has been selective in what it has taken from psychoanalysis; what has seemed relevant is not any simple coherent and monolothic body of theory but a perspective and range of concepts which help to illuminate the contradictions and perplexities of human behaviour. The everyday tasks of social workers involve dealing with loss, bereavement, separation, emotional distress and conflict of all kinds. This too is the bread and butter of psychoanalysis, and this community of interest has fostered fruitful interchange. For the purposes of this book, therefore, 'psychoanalysis' is taken in a broad sense to include not only a narrowly defined psychoanalytical orthodoxy, but also theories and therapeutic approaches which ultimately derive from Freud, and which Rycroft would term 'psychodynamic'. The justification for this broad and inclusive rather than exclusive definition is that our primary purpose is to show how ideas born of psychoanalysis can be used to illuminate and guide a range of activities that are incorporated within social work practice. The label a practitioner bears, or the training she or he has had, bears no necessary relationship to her approach in practice, and for the social worker the theoretical disputes within psychoanalysis are sometimes much less important than what they have in common. Nevertheless, we will at a later point discuss a number of theoretical disputes which seem most relevant to social work – including attempts to integrate psychoanalysis with social theory, and in particular attempts to reconcile Freud and Marx; recent debates on the question of feminism and psychoanalysis, and the prospects of a 'feminist therapy'; the conflict between those who stress the importance of 'outer' environmental influences on personal development as against those who emphasise the primacy of 'inner' experience and unconscious phantasy; and also controversies surrounding the status of psychoanalysis and its 'scientific' credentials.

First, however, we will introduce a more focused set of questions concerning the development of psychoanalysis in Britain. Two distinct traditions can be discerned within British writing, both built on object relations theory associated particularly with Klein, Fairbairn and Winnicott. Object relations theory involves a primary focus on the development of the capacity for relationship as a fundamental need both in childhood and in adult life; clinically, investigation has been particularly concerned with the ways in which this process can undergo distortion, thereby profoundly inhibiting the capacity for mature relationship. The first of these traditions is epitomised by the work of Bowlby on attachment and loss; the second draws on the work of Melanie Klein and W. R. Bion.

The tradition associated with Bowlby follows Freud in seeing psychoanalysis as a natural science, and seeks to test psychoanalytic hypotheses and refine its theory on the basis of empirical research, particularly in the field of child development. Scientific research into psychoanalysis is, on this view, not irrelevant, but just more difficult to conduct because of the distinctive nature of the data. This tradition eschews parochialism, and seeks to develop theory along a broad front which establishes linkages between different scientific disciplines such as developmental psychology, ethology, and anthropology, for example. Bowlby describes as characteristic of his research orientation a prospective approach, a focus on a pathogen and its sequelae, direct observation of young children, the use of animal data, and a new model of instinct behaviour. His work is firmly anchored, therefore, in natural science methodology, although the hypotheses he examines are the outcome of clinical analytic experience so that his work derives from and extends object-relations theory (Bowlby 1969, pp. 3–23). This work has been a strong influence in social work, particularly on child care practice, and is territory which is covered in a number of publications. The work of Bowlby's close associate James Robertson, using the medium of film for the direct observation of young children – at first studying children's experiences of separation from their parents during hospitalisation, and later in both foster care and residential nurseries – has also been fundamentally important in changing child care practices (cf. Robertson, 1952, 1958 & 1962; Robertson & Robertson, 1967–73 & 1971).

The second tradition is sometimes referred to as 'the British School', and departs in major ways from the classical theories of Freud, and from the work of his daughter and associate Anna Freud. This parting of the ways gave rise to separate systems of psychoanalytical training within the Institute of Psychoanalysis – the A group (Freudian), the B group (Kleinian) and the 'Middle Group', this final grouping being those analysts who wished to adopt neither label and who subsequently came to be know from 1973 as the 'Independent Group' (cf. Kohon, 1986). Whilst the Institute of Psychoanalysis incorporates each of these approaches, the Kleinian tendency is particularly strongly represented in the Tavistock Clinic (a major source of psychoanalytic training and acculturation of social workers) and has therefore been particularly influential; it is therefore no accident that a number of the contributions in the book reflect the Kleinian perspective. A succinct account of Kleinian object-relations can be found in Bacon (chapter 9) and the reader wishing a fuller introduction to her ideas is referred to Hanna Segal's *Introduction to the Work of Melanie Klein* or *The Selected Melanie Klein* by Juliet Mitchell. Briefly, however, the most important aspects taken from Kleinian theory are her views on the nature of anxiety, and the mechanisms for dealing with it – splitting, projection, introjection and projective identification. This work, dealing as it does with the earliest months of infant life and the passage through the splitting and paranoid-schizoid to the depressive position, is inevitably more speculative and less easy to substantiate through empirical work than is Bowlby's attachment theory.

Klein's work has been extended by W. R. Bion, a highly original thinker and a strong influence within British psychoanalysis. Some of his concepts have seemed particularly illuminating to social workers, notably the idea of 'containing' mental pain, and they have also been used to provide a model for the learning process within social work education (Barker, 1982). Bion's particular contribution to psychoanalytic development has been his concern with thought and

thinking – the capacity to reflect on and learn from experience in a
way which changes the learner. This emphasis is sharply distinct from
the traditional focus on the emotional roots of behaviour (Meltzer,
1978). Bion's work must however often seem quite remote and
exceptionally difficult to understand – he himself said that his work
on learning could only be understood by the practising analyst – and
it is specifically concerned with the particular learning which goes.on
in the analytic situation. Care therefore has to be taken in applying
Bion's ideas to spheres of activity to which they were never intended
to refer. The validity of concepts advanced by both Klein and Bion is
correspondingly particularly difficult to establish through conventional scientific methods, and generally the clinical situation is the major
testing ground; for this reason, much remains speculative. Their
appeal to many social workers, however, may lie in the fact that they
give an account which seems to make sense of their own or their
clients' puzzling and emotionally charged experience. By giving shape
and meaning to often painful or deeply distressing experience they
make it more amenable to rational control and the sphere of the ego,
opening the way to more constructive, less defensive modes of
response. It may be noted here that natural science is not the only
approach to epistemology, and if psychoanalysis is viewed as a
hermeneutic (or interpretative) activity rather than as a natural
science questions of validity become less central, or at the least lead
to different sets of questions, formulated on the basis on different
criteria (cf. Steele, 1982). These arguments will be further developed
in the following section of the status of psychoanalysis.

  Possibly the most unique contribution within the 'British School' of
psychoanalysis was that of Donald Winnicott who was also responsible for the vast popularisation of psychoanalytical ideas of infancy
and childhood through the series of radio talks which he gave in the
1940s which were subsequently published as *The Child, the Family
and the Outside World*. Winnicott is also one of the few analysts to
have directly addressed the concerns of social workers, as in papers
on such subjects as casework and depression, or casework with the
mentally ill where he took care to distinguish between the concerns of
psychoanalysts and those of social workers (cf. Winnicott, 1963a &
1964a). As well as leaving some vivid accounts of the process of
psychoanalysis with young children, such as in his book *The Piggle,*
his work included a number of important theoretical and observatio-
nal studies. He developed a rich and insightful account, for example,
of the tendency for little children to form such powerful attachments

to 'transitional objects' such as pieces of blanket or rag or a 'teddy' which they carry with them everywhere (cf. Winnicott, 1953) and his notion of 'good enough' mothering is one which helps to avoid what can otherwise be highly idealised portrayals of the functions of motherhood. Winnicott has recently been described by John Bowlby, in not unfriendly terms, as 'a very intuitive chap' who 'used poetic metaphors' (cf. Bowlby *et al.*, 1986, p. 61). Winnicott was preoccupied with many of the same issues as those investigated by Bowlby and his colleagues, although in a manner which was quite different from Bowlby's attempt to develop psychoanalysis on the grounds of formal scientific enquiry. His work nevertheless seems quite indispensable to child care, in whatever setting it is practised.

Another of the most fruitful extensions of psychoanalytic work in the postwar years (from the point of view of social work) has been in relation to the functioning of groups and organisations (cf. De Board, 1978). Of particular importance is the work of Miller and Rice (1967) at the Tavistock who devised a socio-technical model of organisational functioning which drew upon Bion's work, psychoanalytical object-relations theory, as well as other group and organisational theories, and which was also influential in forms of 'group dynamics' experiential learning for the development of interpersonal skills in management and leadershop (cf. Rice, 1965; Menzies Lyth, 1986). An early contribution to this tradition by Isabel Menzies (1960), which seems particularly important in terms of the demands made upon social workers today, had explored the ways in which the organisation of hospital nursing services functions as a defence against intolerable levels of anxiety and stress which are associated with nursing the sick. The use of psychoanalytic theory to illuminate group and organisational dynamics is well illustrated in chapter 8 by Roger Bacon who examines how anxiety is managed in the context of child abuse case conferences and in chapter 9 by John Simmonds who explores the impact of unconscious levels of group life on a staff group's handling of sexuality in residential care.

A further promising development is the integration of psychoanalytic and systems concepts in the field of family therapy. A large amount of the original impetus for family therapy came from within the child guidance movement where psychoanalytical ideas and methods of working had always been highly influential (cf. Ackerman, 1958; Ackerman *et al.*, 1961). But although some forms of family therapy remained close to psychoanalysis, undoubtedly the major impetus was from the quite different spheres of communications theory and systems theory (cf. Ruesch & Bateson, 1951; Jackson, 1968; Watzlawick *et al.*, 1968; Minuchin, 1974; Pearson, 1974). Correspondingly, the two approaches of family therapy and psychoanalysis could sometimes be quite sharply opposed (cf. Walrond-Skinner, 1976, ch. 3). Nevertheless, although some family therapists make much more extensive use of psychoanalytic concepts than do others (e.g. Dare, 1981) many therapists, and social workers adopting a family therapy approach, make use of analytic concepts within a systemic model. Within developing fields of application outside the clinical situation, an eclectic approach in which psychoanalytic and other theories are used flexibly is increasingly common, and the theoretical boundaries are, in practice often blurred.

The status of psychoanalysis: 'science' or 'conversation'?

We now turn to some more general questions. It is reasonable to ask of psychoanalysis at the outset, for example, what its current standing is within the overall range of the human sciences. But although this might seem a simple enough question to answer, it raises a number of difficult problems which can be briefly reviewed.

The status of psychoanalysis has been a hotly contested issue since Freud's work first appeared, when it met with a strange mixture of intellectual acclaim, mild disbelief and even a sense of outrage and scandal. One form of objection that is commonly encountered, particularly from within the field of experimental psychology, is that Freud's work is 'unscientific'. What is meant by this is that it does not yield explanations which offer the possibilities of the prediction and control of human behaviour, and is without any testable empirical evidence to support it. An alternative view would then be that it is mistaken to apply such criteria to psychoanalysis which is concerned with interpretation rather than explanation, and with assisting communication and self-reflection rather than prediction and control.

There is not a great deal of love lost between these two traditional forms of response to the status of psychoanalysis, and any attempt to arbitrate between them is likely to be found wanting by one side of the argument, if not by both sides. They are opposing views which rest on quite different assumptions about the philosophy of science, and how the scientific status of the human sciences should be addressed. On the one hand is the view that the human sciences should attempt to emulate the natural sciences, striving for explanation, prediction and control. On the other hand, is a 'hermeneutic' view which describes the aim of the human sciences as one to achieve understanding rather than explanation.

These are arguments which are not confined to the status of psychoanalysis, however, and they properly belong to how we understand the social sciences or human sciences in their entirety (cf. Winch, 1958; Rorty, 1982). So that when psychoanalysis is defamed in these terms because of its 'unscientific' character, it is important to recognise that far-reaching philosophical disputes are touched upon across the whole range of different fields of human enquiry. The status of psychoanalysis, nevertheless, can sometimes be seen as a special case within these wider debates, in that Freud himself was often given to the belief that psychoanalysis should be understood as one of the natural sciences rooted in biology – something which can either be viewed as a basic fault of mechanical determinism in the whole psychoanalytical project, as it is within humanistic critiques of Freud's work (cf. Matson, 1964) or which can be represented as a self-misunderstanding on Freud's part in the nature of his enterprise (e.g. Habermas, 1972). The struggle over how one should read and interpret Freud is still an active one, however, so that it remains possible to claim Freud for scientific biology as Frank Sulloway does in his book, *Freud, Biologist of the Mind,* or to offer an equally spirited argument such as Bruno Bettelheim's *Freud and Man's Soul,* which claims Freud for humanism (cf. Sulloway, 1979; Bettelheim, 1983). These are arguments, recently reviewed in a most useful summary by Robert Young (1986), which simply refuse to lie down.

Nevertheless, perhaps an even more enduring difficulty in assessing the status of psychoanalysis is that it is no one single thing. To describe how psychoanalysis is received and understood within medical psychiatry, for example, would be quite different from an appraisal of how derivations from Freud's work have been deployed within the advertising industry in order to promote different products. Arguments within the academic discipline of psychology on Freud's contribution to our understanding of dreams will similarly have a quite different character from the ways in which psychoanalysis has been employed within powerful traditions of literary criticism, film criticism and cultural criticism more generally (cf. Eagleton, 1983; Moretti, 1983). Or, to give one final contrasting argument, the uses to which Talcott Parsons put psychoanalysis within his overall scheme of social theory bears little or no relation to recent appreciations of the possible usages of psychoanalysis within feminist thought.

One reason for this vast diversity in the reception and deployment of psychoanalysis is the tendency within the psychoanalytical movement itself to schism and conflict. Sometimes more or less friendly relations are observed between different schools of thought – as between the Freudians in Britain today as against those who subscribe to the work of Melanie Klein or the 'independent' group associated with the work of Donald Winnicott and others – but this has not always been the case (cf. Bowlby *et al.*, 1986; Kohon, 1986, pp. 24–50). The tendency towards schism was there almost from the beginning, with a fierce and irreparable split betwen Freud and Adler (one of his closest associates) as early as 1911. The final break with Jung came only two years later, and the ensuing professional feuds around this and other breaks were often conducted with exceptional bitterness and hostility, as described by Erich Fromm (1963) in his essay, 'Psychoanalysis – Science or Party Line?'. Among the innumerable schools of thought to have emerged, some such as the wayward genius of Wilhelm Reich were originally very much part of mainstream psychoanalysis, whereas theoretical departures such as Ludwig Binswanger's 'existential analysis' are very difficult to place, even though constantly returning to Freud as the initial inspiration (cf. Needleman, 1963). But others are related to psychoanalysis only as distant cousins, such as the various encounter groups or gestalt therapies, although they are often nevertheless connected at a root source in the notion of the unconscious and face-to-face work with a therapist as a means of addressing a variety of personal issues and troubles. Some of these psychotherapeutic movements have departed so far from the psychoanalytical mainstream that they would not be acknowledged by psychoanalysis as being in any way associated, and might themselves deny any correspondence between their own work and that of Freud, or even express some animosity towards the Freudian tradition. Nevertheless, a more distanced non-participative judgement might see clear historical connections which originate from the 'point source' of Freudian vision. And the nature of this 'point source' is probably best defined in therapeutic terms as the discipline of self-scrutiny – or what was described by Philip Rieff (1959) as the method of 'ruthless talk' by which a person attempts to overhaul the basis of motivation, feeling and action in his or her life.

To go one step further is then to recognise that these splits and divisions are larger than any simple competition between different 'brand-name' therapies. Because there was from the outset an active confusion in Freud's own work as to what he was about. On the one hand, he offered a set of prescriptions for a theory of therapeutic practice, which have been handed down and modified across half a century of psychoanalytical practice in different cultures and contexts. But there was more to Freud than a therapy. Indeed, he expressed the fear in his lectures on *The Question of Lay Analysis* that psychoanalysis might be 'swallowed up by medicine' and 'find its last resting-place in a textbook of psychiatry under the heading "Methods of Treatment"'. Moreover, the learning and knowledge base which Freud recommended for analytical practice was not narrowly therapeutic. The analyst, he thought, needed to study 'the history of civilisation, mythology, the psychology of religion and the science of literature. Unless he is well at home in these subjects, analysts can make nothing of a large amount of his material' (Freud, 1962, pp. 165, 167). Near the end of his life, Freud again returned to his fear of the 'tendency to turn psychoanalysis into a mere housemaid of psychiatry' which he thought was particularly strong within the reception of his work in North America (quoted in Chasseguet-Smirgel & Grunberger, 1986, p. 28). In summary, as he described his ambition in a 'Postscript' to *The Question of Lay Analysis*, this was not so much 'to help suffering humanity' but 'to understand something of the riddles of the world in which we live' (Freud, 1927b, p. 253).

Accordingly, after the appearance of the early papers in which he developed the theory of childhood sexuality and the theory of dreams, Freud's own published work was arguably only marginally connected with therapy. What he attempted to offer was something more complete, as a means to offer a better understanding of art, literature, civilisation and the cultural ordering of our affairs. Among those various dimensions of human experience which he tried to elucidate were the formation and structuring of human sexuality and gender; human aggression, the origins of war and fascism; the basis on which we might understand everyday slips of the tongue and moments of unaccountable forgetfulness; an interrogation of jokes, fairy stories and mythology; the basis of religious belief; etc.

We can see then how Freud's initial inspiration could lend itself to such a diverse range of intellectual activity, other than clinical and therapeutic developments − such as the work of Wilhelm Reich, which attempted an amalgamation of psychoanalysis and Marxism, leading to a theory of authoritarianism and fascism which preceded that of Erich Fromm, later squandering its talents in obscure bio-electric theories; Geza Roheim's attempts to apply psychoanalysis to the understanding of distant cultures through an anthropological method; the work of the Frankfurt School, first in the writings of Horkheimer and Adorno in the 1930s, and later in the more widely known work of Herbert Marcuse; Erik Erikson's studies of child-rearing in different cultures and excursions into psychoanalytical biography such as *Young Man Luther*; Ronald Laing's early psychoanalytical accounts of schizoid states later to evolve into the wholly unorthodox stance of 'anti-psychiatry'; in Christopher Lasch's explorations of the 'narcissisistic' dissolution of the modern self; or finally Norman O. Brown's provocative interventions into 'psycho-history' (cf. Reich, 1933; Fromm, 1942; Roheim, 1950 & 1955; Erikson, 1950 & 1958; Laing, 1965, 1967 & 1969; Brown,1966 & 1968; Marcuse, 1955; Jay, 1973; Robinson, 1972; Lasch, 1979 & 1985).

Quite apart from these varied developments within social theory, some of which we will discuss in a little more detail subsequently, psychoanalysis has also been a major source of inspiration for literary and artistic developments in the West in the twentieth century. Around the time of the First World War, for example, the Dada movement in Berlin included among its inspirations some of the earliest derivations from psychoanalysis, and some of Freud's work, such as the theory of dreams and his accounts of the unconscious and concealed motivations were also formative influences upon surreal-ism (cf. Mitzman, 1977; Breton, 1978). One might almost say that if creative and intellectual developments in the twentieth century were not in some way influenced by psychoanalysis, then they were intended as oppositional to psychoanalysis. Nothing, or almost nothing, in the cultural development of the twentieth century was indifferent to Freud's work and influence (cf. Gellner, 1985).

In the light of this broad sweep of the scope of psychoanalysis, it can be readily appreciated that discussions of the influence of psychoanalysis upon social work can sometimes be too insular, as if this influence were somehow odd or exceptional in the case of social work. This is clearly not so. The influence of psychoanalysis on the culture of Europe and North America is endemic. If psychoanalysis has influenced social work, then this simply reflects the fact that social work is a child of its culture. Although, the issue requires a more detailed analysis, in that it is only certain highly selective parts of the psychoanalytical tradition which have had a major influence on social work. Notably, it was the neo-Freudian revisions of 'ego psychology' which weighed most heavily in what was imported into British social work through the United States (cf. Yelloly, 1980). Which is not to say that the reception of psychoanalytical ideas into social work was entirely consensual. For more than twenty years, a sharp rivalry divided North American social casework between the Freudian 'Diagnostic School' as against the 'Functionalist School' which drew upon the work of Otto Rank whose ideas on the 'birth trauma' and 'brief therapy' had led to a break with Freud in the 1920s (cf. Taft, 1933; Kasius, 1950; Rank, 1945) – although this was a factional dispute which is now hardly remembered within social work, and which made little impact in Britain. Indeed, on any reckoning the reception of psychoanalysis within British social work never even began to compare with the American flood-tide of the 'psychiatric deluge' (cf. Woodroofe, 1962, ch. 6).

This last point alerts us to one final aspect of the diverse and uneven nature of the reception of Freud's work, in that psychoanalysis has made very different kinds of impact at different times in different societies. The impact has been almost entirely confined to Europe and North America, moreover, with considerably less influence in Latin America and virtually none whatsoever in South East Asia and China (cf. Tseng & Wu, 1985). These cultural variations offer what is perhaps the most persuasive indication that something other than its scientific credentials have been at stake in determining the influence of psychoanalysis. In the USA, for example, although there was opposition in some quarters psychoanalysis began to take root very soon after Freud's visit in 1909, and North America was eventually to become the power-base of the psychoanalytical movement with a burgeoning growth of professional therapists of different descriptions. Psychoanalytical theory also assumed specific forms in North America, principally in the shape of the already mentioned 'ego psychologies', in such a way that it is possible to speak of an 'Americanisation of the unconscious' (cf. Castel *et al.*, 1982; Jacoby, 1975).

In France, by contrast, Freud's work made very little headway for fifty years. French psychiatry had been dominated by neurology, although more generally France has been described as an 'anti-psychoanalytical culture' and it was not really until after 1968 that psychoanalytic thought made any impact there. Whereupon, of course, psychoanalysis once again developed a highly specific form in the work of the school of Jacques Lacan, the so-called 'return to Freud' represented in the work of Janine Chasseguet-Smirgel and others, and the intellectual fireworks of 'Freudo-Marxists' such as Gilles Deleuze and Félix Guattari (cf. Turkle, 1978). Finally, in Britain, although there had been some interest in Freud's ideas in the 1920s and 1930s, the most notable developments were to come in the postwar years. And although the availability of psychoanalytical therapy did not even remotely approach the situation in North America, there would be a number of significant theoretical and therapeutic innovations: first through the separate and distinctive traditions developed by Anna Freud and Melanie Klein, then through the work of John Bowlby, the influence of Ronald Fairbairn's 'object relations' theory, and finally the quite unique contribution to therapy made by Donald Winnicott in the postwar years (cf. Kohon, 1986, pp. 24–50).

If we then return to the question of the status of psychoanalysis, what can we say other than that it is vast? Questions of its scientific status seem almost irrelevant in the face of its influence. Scurrilous attacks on Freud's work, such as the recent suggestion by Thornton (1986) that the whole edifice of psychoanalysis is merely the product of his over-indulgence with cocaine in the late nineteenth century, seem even worse than irrelevant: the important question, if the allegation were true, would be why and how the twentieth century has been bewitched by drugged fantasies?

Nevertheless, the interrogation of the scientific credentials of psychoanalysis should not be dismissed so lightly. Whenever psychoanalytical theory and therapy has been put to the test of experimental scrutiny, for example, it tends not to fare very well (cf.Sears, 1943; Lee & Herbert, 1970; Fisher & Greenberg, 1977). Can this mean that, for all its influence in so many different spheres of human activity, psychoanalysis is scientifically worthless? Or, as Sir Peter Medawar (1975) has described it, that psychoanalysis is 'the most stupendous intellectual confidence trick of the twentieth century'?

An exceptionally bitter version of such an argument is to be found in Hans Eysenck's *Decline and Fall of the Freudian Empire*, which, although it does not dispute the wide sphere of influence of psychoanalysis, calls into question the entirety of its scientific basis. Eysenck's preference, of course, is for a behaviourist experimental psychology, and in spite of attempts to reconcile psychoanalysis with learning theory (e.g. Dollard & Miller, 1950) it is hardly surprising that he finds little of scientific value in Freud's work when measured against his own experimentalist assumptions as to what constitutes 'scientific' authenticity. (What is altogether surprising in this context, however, is that the founder of 'behaviourism', J. B. Watson, was himself an early enthusiast of Freud's work who advocated that public servants in high office should be obliged to undergo psychoanalysis. Cf. Castel *et al.*, 1982, p. 51).

Eysenck's critique runs along familiar lines which subject psychoanalysis to the requirements of a natural science – that is one which yields explanatory variables, offering prediction and control over events, and the testability of its propositions – thus by-passing those long-standing controversies in the philosophy of science which have been already mentioned, and which suggest an alternative basis for the validity of the human sciences in terms of their 'interpretative' or 'hermeneutic' value (cf. Winch, 1958). Eysenck does at one point briefly entertain such a possibility that the value of psychoanalysis might be precisely in its ability to yield 'interpretations' or 'insights' into human conduct which would necessarily elude the 'explanatory' scientific model of behaviourism. But immediately, faced with the existence of a number of different schools of thought within psychoanalysis, he wants to know 'how are we to tell which of these interpretations is right?' Because, Eysenck argues, 'even if we accept the hermeneutic approach, we still need criteria for deciding about the truth and falsity of given interpretations' (Eysenck, 1986, p. 195).

This seems a straightforward enough requirement. Nevertheless, it is not, and in order to see why it is not the argument should be returned to those complexities in the philosophy of science which Eysenck fails either to acknowledge or to understand. One form of response is provided by the highly innovative work of Richard Rorty, which turns on how to develop a theory of knowledge which is adequate to the human sciences, given all the philosophical difficulties which stand in the way of representations of 'truth' and what is 'real' (cf. Rorty, 1979 & 1982). Rorty's answer to Eysenck's question would be to suggest that it is badly phrased, and that blunt queries about 'truth' should be replaced by asking whether an interpretation is 'helpful'. So that the question becomes not whether Freud's theories are 'true' but rather, whether they offer forms of self-description of human beings and human motives which are found to be useful when applied to ourselves and to other human beings. And when those criteria, essentially in Rorty's terms the criteria of pragmatism, are used to assess Freud's contribution to human self-understanding, then the resounding conclusion is that Freud's descriptions are among those which have been found to be supremely relevant to the human condition as it is experienced in Europe and North America in the twentieth century. It has allowed forms of interrogation of this experience, and conversations between different varieties of this experience, which could otherwise not have been possible. Or at least, they are the actual forms which human self-interrogation have taken in the twentieth century. In other words, we might say that whether or not Freud supplied the 'right' answers, it would seem that he was asking the right questions.

Rorty's work seems to have the edge on other philosophical responses to these dilemmas, because he does not claim that the 'interpretative' or 'hermeneutic' approach to the human sciences is the only one that is valid, or necessarily the most appropriate for all human purposes. So that he would also allow, for other purposes, the value of a behaviourist approach grounded in 'prediction' or 'explanation' such as that favoured by Eysenck. Thus he describes the conflict between 'explanation' and 'understanding' in the following terms:

> This contrast is real enough. But it is not an issue to be resolved, only a difference to be lived with. The idea that explanation and understanding are opposed ways of doing social science is as misguided as the notion that microscopic and macroscopic descriptions of organisms are opposed ways of doing biology. There are lots of things you want to do with bacteria and cows for which it is very useful to have biochemical descriptions of them; there are lots of things you want to do with them for which such descriptions would be merely a nuisance. Similarly, there are lots of things you want to do with human beings for which descriptions of them in non-evaluative, 'inhuman' terms are very useful; there are others (e.g., thinking of them as your fellow-citizens) in which such descriptions are not. 'Explanation' is merely the sort of understanding one looks for when one wants to predict and control. It does not contrast with something else called 'understanding' as the abstract contrasts with the concrete, or the artificial with the natural, or the 'repressive' with the 'liberating'. To say that something is better 'understood' in one vocabulary than another is always an ellipsis for the claim that a description in

the preferred vocabulary is more useful for a certain purpose. If the purpose is prediction, then one will want one sort of vocabulary. If it is evaluation, one may or may not want a different sort of vocabulary. In the case of evaluating artillery fire, for example, the predictive vocabulary of ballistics will do nicely. In the case of evaluating human character, the vocabulary of stimulus and response is beside the point (Rorty, 1982, p. 197).

To say that Freud's psychoanalysis has offered a form of 'understanding' which has enjoyed a wide sphere of influence which outstrips that claimed by the 'understanding' offered by behaviourism is thus not to say that it is more or less 'scientific'. We return to the fact that whatever scientific status one might wish to afford to psychoanalysis, Freud's project has provided a vocabulary which has proved immensely agreeable to our form of civilisation. If, as Eysenck and others suggest, psychoanalysis is merely a pseudo-science akin to astrology or witchcraft, then the important question becomes why our civilisation has been be-witched in this particular way and not in other ways? Or if, as Medawar insists, psychoanalysis is merely a 'confidence trick', why have we been conned by this and not some other system of belief? And the answer then must be, for whatever reasons, Freud's vision is one which offers a self-ratifying system of exploration within our particular cultural horizons. In the most general terms, it addresses questions of human motivation which do not always seem clear (either to ourselves or to others) by offering forms of description within which we can sometimes (but not always) recognise ourselves and others. It is above all a disquieting form of description. The theory of the unconscious, as Freud (1917, p. 143) described it, is one which insists that 'the ego is not master in its own house'. This, he suggested, was the 'third blow' to human narcissism that had been delivered by science: the first having been Copernicus's revelation that the earth was not the centre of the solar system, and the second Darwin's assertion that human beings were of animal descent. In this sense, Freud's work was a continuation of the humbling experience of modernity and rational enquiry – whereby the process of scientific Enlightenment stripped humankind of its naive illusion that it stood at the centre of the universe.

It seems wholly inappropriate to describe such a venture as a 'confidence trick'. Indeed, the very expression would imply that something had been offered which proved to be false coin, and this is quite unfaithful to either the actual relationships between psychoanalysis and the wider culture, or the actual form of the reception of psychoanalysis within that culture. Because although we have described Freud's work as 'immensely agreeable' to our form of civilisation, this is only half of the picture. It would be equally true to say that Freud's work has often been described (and for any number of different reasons) as immensely disagreeable, and continues to be regarded in some quarters as disagreeable. What Freud's psychoanalysis did, when one takes into account both the favourable responses to his project and those which have been unfavourable, was not to supply answers that could be regarded as satisfactory answers from every standpoint. Rather, what the new vocabulary which he supplied did was to allow new forms of *controversy*. So that instead of seeing Freud as supplying answers, and then asking whether these are right or wrong, we should perhaps view his work as something which allows a new field of human controversy to take shape. And within this controversy, then Freud might be seen to have facilitated different kinds of *conversation* between different viewpoints. And within these controversies and conversations, Freud's new vocabulary allowed new kinds of questions to be asked, while also allowing certain things to be said which could not be said before – and indeed which some people wished had remained unsaid!

If one takes such a stance towards Freud, then it is not necessary to agree with psychoanalytical orthodoxy in its entirety to see its importance within our culture. Rather, it simply becomes necessary to admit the possibilities of conversation – although a more serious difficulty, given the widespread reception of Freud's ideas into the culture, would be actually trying to avoid the conversation. And for those who wish to shout down this conversation, by proscribing it as 'unscientific' or a 'confidence trick', then the ground has shifted appreciably. Because one might even allow that Freud's work was unscientific, and yet still the conversation would go on – arguably one of the most important conversations of the modern age.

Psychoanalysis and social theory: 'pessimism' and 'optimism'

If one is not merely to approach psychoanalysis as a form of therapy, but also as a contribution to human self-understanding which might illuminate some of the 'riddles of the world' as Freud himself put it, then a crucial question must be its relationships to other systems of social theory. Various attempts have been made either to utilise psychoanalysis within a theory of society, or to integrate psychoanalysis with different forms of sociological or political theory. The underlying moral and political implications of Freud's work have also been a matter for controversy and debate (cf. Rieff, 1959 & 1966; Roazen, 1970; Chasseguet-Smirgel & Grunberger, 1968). Freud had devised his own theories of social organisation, of course, in works such as *Totem and Taboo* (1912) where he advanced a theory of primitive society, *Group Psychology and the Analysis of the Ego* (1921) which dealt with the psychology of the crowd and leadership, *The Future of an Illusion* (1927) which offered a penetrating critique of the origins of religion, and what is often seen as the crowning pessimism of one of his last major works *Civilisation and Its Discontents* (1930) which addressed the central question of why human happiness was so difficult to secure, suggesting that there would be inevitable and irreconcilable tensions and conflicts between human desire and any form of civilisation.

As far as Freud's views on the origins of society are concerned, these have been generally rejected by social anthropologists as nothing less that fanciful, and it was indeed his misfortune that the older traditions of speculative anthropology which had guided him (such as those of Frazer and Robertson-Smith) were being supplanted by the new social anthropology of the twentieth century which was based on rigorous and systematic fieldwork. Among the early indications of this new approach was Malinowski's *Sex and Repression in Savage Society* (1927) which directly addressed the contribution of psychoanalysis to anthropology. In spite of considerable initial sympathy towards psychoanalytical interpretations of myth and kinship, Malinowski found no hint of father–son Oedipal conflicts among the people of the Trobriand Islands in Melanesia where the family structure was radically different from that of Western Europe, in that it was organised on matrilineal grounds and did not recognise the role of the father in procreation. There was also little if any inhibition of sexual play and exploration among children who were allowed a large amount of freedom from adult control, living and playing for much of the time in what Malinowski described as a sort of 'juvenile republic'. Nevertheless, a severe taboo did exist against brother–sister incest, and Malinowski found that such incestuous phantasies formed the content of one of the typical dreams of the Trobriand people, 'occurring frequently, and one which haunts and disturbs the dreamer' (ibid., p. 96). Malinowski therefore proposed that what Freud took to be the universal phenomenon of the Oedipal conflict was a product of the specific configuration of Western family relations which was 'displaced' into a different form within the non-patriarchal kinship arrangements of the Trobriand Islanders, so that he finally came to disagree entirely with Freud's own anthropological assertions on the origins of civilisation in *Totem and Taboo* as quite unfounded.

Malinowski's approach had nevertheless been unusually sympathetic towards Freud's work. More typical was the view expressed by Evans-Pritchard (1965, p. 42) in his *Theories of Primitive Religion* where he was utterly dismissive of Freud's *Totem and Taboo*, barely mentioning Freud's work and when he did accusing him of telling a 'fairy story'. These are the works of Freud which stir perhaps the most controversy, and which are sometimes rejected as mere speculation even by those who otherwise adhere to the general principles of psychoanalysis, although arguments have also been advanced that these writings must be centrally addressed for a true appreciation of Freud's achievement (cf. Bocock, 1976; Chasseguet-Smirgel & Grunberger, 1986). Indeed, one must admit some sympathy with the view of Chasseguet-Smirgel and Grunberger (1986, pp. 144 ff.) that whereas Malinowski depicted the Trobriand Island culture as one which allowed a free expression of infantile sexuality, for the part played by the father in procreation to be 'unknown' an equally weighty form of sexual repression might be thought to be operating – an argument which had been first advanced by Ernest Jones (1925) in a review of Malinowski's work.

In general terms, however, psychoanalysis can be said to have had little impact upon the development of social anthropology in the twentieth century. Indeed, the only sustained attempt to develop a psychoanalytical anthropology has been that of Geza Roheim, and even then his approach belonged much more to the 'folklore' tradition of the nineteenth century than it did to that of the pioneers of modern anthropological fieldwork and theory such as Malinowski, Evans-Pritchard and Radcliffe-Brown (cf. Robinson, 1972; Roheim, 1950 & 1955). Nor have psychoanalytical ideas had much of an impact upon sociology, where in spite of the attempt by Talcott Parsons to incorporate psychoanalysis within his social theory by a series of modifications of Freud's work, there has been a persistent tendency to ignore or disparage the need for a theory or 'psychology' of the individual subject within the dominant intellectual traditions of 'functionalism' and 'structuralism' (cf. Parsons, 1951 & 1964; Parsons & Bales, 1956; Wrong, 1961; Giddens, 1979, ch. 1).

It is perhaps all the more surprising, then, given the overriding economic determinism of Marxism that this has undoubtedly been the major site upon which attempts have been made to reconcile psychoanalysis within a theory of social and economic formation, although there have often been tensions and various forms of ambivalence within this project to bring together Freud and Marx which must be briefly sketched in.

Something of this ambivalence could already be sensed in an often-quoted article from 1927 by Trotsky on 'Culture and 'Socialism' where he contrasted the approaches of Freud and Pavlov towards psychology. Both, as he described it were materialists, laying the basis for psychology in biology. But there the similarities stopped. Pavlov's methods, which were of course to become dominant within the officially sanctioned psychology of the Soviet Union, were based upon a painstaking experimental approach: 'Generalisations are won step by step: from the saliva of dogs to poetry ... though the paths that bring us to poetry have as yet not been revealed.' Whereas Freud took a different route, 'from above downwards, from the religious myth, the lyrical poem, or the dream straight to the physiological basis of the psyche.' And then, in an engaging metaphor, Trotsky described these two attempts to develop a materialist psychology in the following terms:

> The idealists tell us that the psyche is an independent entity, that the 'soul' is a bottomless well. Both Pavlov and Freud think that the bottom of the soul is physiology. But Pavlov, like a diver, descends to the bottom and laboriously investigates the well from there upwards; while Freud stands over the well and with penetrating gaze tries to pierce its ever shifting and troubled waters and to make out or guess the shape of things down below (Trotsky, 1927, pp. 312–13)

It would be too simplistic, Trotsky argued, 'to declare psychoanalysis "incompatible" with Marxism and simply turn one's back on Freudism'. Nevertheless, his even-handed appraisal of Freud was promptly superceded by a virtual suppression of psychoanalysis within the Soviet Union. One can sense from this article, however, that there must have been some popular interest in psychoanalytical ideas from the following comment in a footnote: 'This question has, of course, nothing in common with the cultivation of a sham Freudism as an erotic indulgence or piece of "naughtiness". Such claptrap has nothing to do with science and merely expresses decadent moods.' Whatever lay behind Trotsky's remarks, we know also that during the 1920s psychoanalytical ideas were associated in Left-wing bohemian circles in Berlin with 'café socialism', Dada experiments in art, and the use of cocaine (cf. Mitzman, 1977).

If Trotsky's response had been to identify Freud's psychoanalysis as a materialist psychology, then this judgement would be subsequently reversed in the mainstream of Marxist thought, both within the Soviet Union and elsewhere. It was precisely the charge of philosophical idealism which was brought against Freud by the British communist intellectual Christopher Caudwell in his *Studies in a Dying Culture* which appeared posthumously in 1938 after his death in action during the Spanish Civil War. For Caudwell, Freud was certain to be remembered as 'one of the pioneers of scientific psychology', although it would be much as Kepler is remembered 'as a scientist who discovered important empirical facts but was unable to synthesise these discoveries except in a primitive semi-magical framework' (Caudwell, 1965, p. 109). Freud's was irreducibly a 'bourgeois psychology', limited in its usefulness by its pessimism which portrayed the frustrated individual trammeled by an unchanging society, and yet which suffered from the illusion that one individual can cure another. 'But he cannot heal us,' Caudwell wrote, 'for he cannot teach us that first truth, that we must change the world in order to change ourselves' (ibid., p. 132)

This has emerged as undoubtedly the major tension within attempts to reconcile Marx and Freud, to recur in a variety of forms. So that in some of the most recent Marxist responses to psychoanalysis questions of whether it is sufficiently 'materialist' continue to loom large, as in Sebastiano Timpanaro's (1976) devastating critique of Freud's analysis of slips of the tongue; or Freud is charged with a 'liberal pessimism' as in Peter Leonard's (1984) recent attempt to devise a 'materialist understanding of the individual'. There is a significant element of contradiction between these two positions, however, in that asserting the need for a 'materialist' conception of a biologically rooted 'human nature' can easily lend itself to its own form of pessimism about the prospects for effecting changes in human affairs, or even to reactionary forms of belief such as racism. A useful discussion of these problems of materialism has been offered by Raymond Williams (1980) in response to Timpanaro's approach. Given that such a pessimism would relate to the prospects both for social *and* therapeutic change, this can be seen as a problem for both psychoanalysis *and* Marxism.

An alternative form of response, as represented in the work of the Frankfurt School, was to embrace the 'pessimism' of Freud's psychoanalysis partly as a means by which to explore their own pessimism about the prospects of social emancipation. The Frankfurt School was also increasingly disillusioned with mechanical Marxism which, lacking any adequate psychology, seemed unable to account for either those profound obstacles to social change which were of a non-economic character, or the emergence of authoritarian tendencies such as Stalinism and Nazism (cf. Billig, 1982, ch. 5). 'Hitler appealed to the unconscious in his audience', Max Horkheimer (1947, p. 120) wrote in *Eclipse of Reason,* and promised to release 'the repressed primitive urges of a superficially civilised people'. The Frankfurt School, accordingly, turned to psychoanalysis in order to attempt an explanation of the psychological dimensions of authoritarianism (cf. Adorno, 1951).

It was Erich Fromm who had taken the lead in the early 1930s in exploring the implications of an integration of Freud and Marx within the Frankfurt Institute's programme of work. Fromm's early writings ranged across a number of questions, including an appraisal of the theory of matriarchy or 'mother right', carrying the implication that psychoanalysis was only a relevant theory of patriarchal societies (cf. Fromm, 1934). However, as Fromm's work leaned increasingly towards neo-Freudian revisionism, serious differences came to separate Fromm and other members of the Frankfurt School. So that by the time that *Fear of Freedom* appeared in 1942, which as a timely and accessible analysis of authoritarianism and the psychology of Nazism was to be his best known work, they had already parted company (cf. Jay, 1973, ch. 3).

A major dispute between Fromm and the Frankfurt School centred around his growing rejection of Freudian 'pessimism', represented by Freud's emphasis in his later work on innate destructive impulses (the 'death instinct') together with Fromm's increasing departure from orthodox psychoanalysis towards a more sociological orientation such as that represented by Karen Horney and other 'neo-Freudian' revisionists. The Frankfurt School, as represented by Adorno and Horkheimer, was suspicious of these neo-Freudian revisions which were seen as softening the critical edge of Freud's work and accommodating it to the ideological imperatives of North American society (cf. Jacoby, 1975). Subsequent appraisals of psychoanalysis by the Frankfurt School stressed what might be described as Freud's 'revolutionary pessimism' and his representation of a fundamental opposition between human happiness and civilisation. For Theodor Adorno, attempts at a complete theoretical integration between sociology and psychology were both futile and wrong, in that these attempted a premature reconciliation of the actual conflicts between the individual and society. The value of a psychology such as Freud's was precisely its refusal to endorse such a reconcilation or to 'sociologise' the individual. 'A psychology which turns its back on society and idiosyncratically concentrates on the individual', Adorno (1967, p. 69–73) argued, 'says more about the hapless state of society than one which seeks by its "wholistic approach" or an inclusion of social "factors"' to pretend other than that the individual and society were in conflict: 'No future synthesis of the social sciences can unite what is inherently at odds with itself.'

Within this austere view, any attempt to suggest that the individual might aspire to happiness through conformity to the given social order (or through the development of more loving relationships, as in Fromm's later humanist work) was seen as a betrayal of the Freudian legacy (cf. Jacoby, 1975). As the debate between Fromm and the Frankfurt School became increasingly embittered, it fell to Herbert Marcuse in *Eros and Civilisation* which first appeared in 1955 to develop further the critique of neo-Freudian revisionism. The Fromm–Marcuse debate has been usefully summarised elsewhere (cf. Bocock, 1976, pp. 150 ff.; Jay, 1973, ch. 3; Billig, 1982, ch. 5; Jacoby, 1975) and is full of complexity. Marcuse, in Fromm's (1968, p. 9) terms, was a 'nihilist' and 'an alienated intellectual who presents his personal despair as a theory of radicalism'. And yet, such a judgement is difficult to reconcile with the fact that in contrast with the Frankfurt tradition, Marcuse's uses of psychoanalysis moved in an unusually optimistic direction, pointing the way towards the utopian possibilities of a 'non-repressive' society in which the 'pleasure principle' was re-asserted over and above the 'reality principle' (cf. Marcuse, 1955 & 1970). Marcuse thus saw in psychoanalysis the possibility of theorising a society in which human beings could enjoy 'happiness', rather than being merely 'productive'.

Such a view, of course, would have been quite unacceptable to Freud himself although he did concede in *Civilisation and its Discontents* that even though 'there are difficulties attaching to the nature of civilisation which will not yield to any attempt at reform', nevertheless one might 'expect gradually to carry through such alterations in our civilisation as will better satisfy our needs' (Freud, 1930, p. 52). Freud's cautious attitude towards the possibilities of social reform (or revolution) was quite typical. In so far as Marxism and communism were concerned, he had expressed the view in the last of the *New Introductory Lectures* (1933a, p. 181) that, 'We have to thank men of this kind [i.e. the Bolsheviks] for the fact that the tremendous experiment of producing a new order of this kind is now actually being carried out in Russia' which 'in spite of all its disagreeable details, seems none the less like the message of a better future'. The same unshakeable commitment to a detached scepticism was nevertheless there:

> Unluckily neither our scepticism nor the fanatical faith of the other side gives a hint as to how the experiment will turn out. The future will tell us; perhaps it will show that the experiment was undertaken prematurely, that a sweeping alteration of the social order has little prospect of success until new discoveries have increased our control over the forces of Nature and so made easier the satisfaction of our needs. Only then perhaps may it become possible for a new social order not only to put an end to the material need of the masses but also to give a hearing to the cultural demands of the individual. Even then, to be sure, we shall still have to struggle for an incalculable time with the difficulties which the untameable character of human nature presents to every kind of social community (ibid., pp. 180–1).

In his brief correspondence with Einstein, published in 1933 as 'Why War?', Freud returned once more to the ambitions of Marxists, and the view was perhaps even more explicit:

> It is a general principle, then, that conflicts of interest between men are settled by the use of violence. This is true of the whole animal kingdom, from which men have no business to exclude themselves.... For our immediate purpose then, this much follows from what has been said: there is no use trying to get rid of men's aggressive inclinations. We are told that in certain happy regions of the earth, where nature provides in abundance everything that man requires, there are races whose life is passed in tranquillity and who know neither coercion nor aggression. I can scarcely believe it and I should be glad to hear more of these fortunate beings. The

Russian Communists, too, hope to be able to cause human
aggressiveness to disappear by guaranteeing the satisfaction of all
material needs and by establishing equality in other respects among
all members of the community. That, in my opinion, is an
illusion . . . . In any case, as you yourself have remarked, there is no
question of getting rid entirely of human aggressive impulses; it is
enough to try to divert them to such an extent that they need not
find expression in war . . . . After all, it [war] seems to be quite a
natural thing, to have a good biological basis and in practice to be
scarcely avoidable' (Freud, 1933c, pp. 204–13).

A different form of utopianism to that envisaged by Marcuse was
the theory of 'sexual revolution' advanced by Wilhelm Reich. But
whereas Marcuse's *Eros and Civilisation,* which was subtitled 'A
Philosophical Enquiry into Freud', was a strictly theoretical undertaking, the work of Reich also involved him in various forms of
therapeutic and political intervention. Reich's work was not only the
most deliberate attempt to reconcile psychoanalysis with Marxism, it
was also the first. It is necessary to distinguish in this respect the work
of Wilhelm Reich in the 1920s and early 1930s from his later projects
which involved his infamous and wholly implausible experiments with
'orgone energy'. In the earlier phase, Reich had worked within a
fairly orthodox psychoanalytical framework, his intention to 'politi-
cise' psychoanalysis while at the same time 'psychoanalysing' politics
having been first declared in a pamphlet of 1929, *Dialectical
Materialism and Psychoanalysis.* This led subsequently to the
development of his 'Sex-Pol' movement in Germany which was
directed particulary towards the needs of working-class youth,
attempting to combine therapeutic interventions with sex education
and contraceptive advice, as well as campaigning on issues such as the
abortion laws and homelessness (cf. Reich, 1931; Reich & Teschitz,
1973). Reich came to understand sexual repression which resulted
from tyrannical fathers within patriarchal households as a powerful
source for the development of authoritarianism and fascism in
Germany, a thesis fully developed in *The Mass Psychology of
Fascism* which first appeared in 1933. This work has been widely
acknowledged, although not without controversy, as a landmark in
the development of 'Freudo-Marxist' theory which anticipated many
of the views later popularised by Erich Fromm and others. However,
as with all of Reich's work, great care must be taken in reading him
today because his writings went through many re-draftings and the

most easily available editions of his books tend to be later editions where the pseudo-scientific ramblings of his final years about bio-electric 'bions' and 'orgone energy' have been inserted (cf. Rieff, 1966, ch. 6; Robinson, 1972; Rycroft, 1971; Chasseguet-Smirgel & Grunberger, 1986).

Reich was certainly not the only member of the psychoanalytical fraternity to have sympathised with Marxism during the 1920s and early 1930s, in that there were a number of militant socialists and even ultra-leftists, including Fenichel, Rado, Ferenczi and Bernfeld. However, Reich succeeded in antagonising both Freudians and Marxists to such an extent that he was expelled from the German Communist Party in 1933, and then drummed out from the International Psychoanalytic Association in the following year. From then on, there was a steady progression in Reich's work towards the more fantastic eleborations of 'vegetotherapy' and the 'orgone' theory, which also evidenced increasing paranoid tendencies. Having gone into exile in the USA in 1938, he nevertheless enjoyed a large amount of success and attracted sufficient funds from his following to be able to pursue his 'orgone' research on an extensive scale. Before Reich's death in 1957, however, the sale of his 'orgone accumulators' had been legally prohibited, after some years of even more fantastic speculation and experimentation concerning extra-terrestial pheno-mena, the recommendation of a cure for cancer in 'orgonotherapy' and the disatrous 'Oranur' experiment with radioactive substances which was designed to avert the nuclear threat (cf. Robinson, 1972).

While it has usually been deemed convenient to separate Reich's work into two compartments – the early innovations of a psychoanalytical prodigy, as against the lunacies of his later years – Janine Chasseguet-Smirgel & Béla Grunberger (1986) have adv-anced the view in *Freud or Reich? Psychoanalysis and Illusion* that the continuities in Reich's work are equally important. The object of their critique, originally published in 1976, had been the resurgence of 'Freudo-Marxist' theory in France following the events of 1968 which had taken inspiration from Reich, most forcibly and popularly expressed in *L'Anti-Oedipe* by Gilles Deleuze and Félix Guattari (cf. Deleuze & Guattari, 1972 & 1977; Guattari, 1984; Turkle, 1978; Descombes, 1980). The argument of *Freud or Reich?* is that from the beginning Reich's work had departed significantly from psychoanaly-tical orthodoxy by stressing the origins of emotional difficulties and character deformations in the actualities of sexual frustration, rather than in unconscious phantasy. Freud himself had distinguished in his early work on the sexual theory between the psycho-neuroses and what he termed the 'actual neuroses' (Freud, 1984). The 'actual neuroses' were to be identified through symptoms of neurasthenia (headaches, fatigue, generalised and non-specific pain) and were regarded as resulting from actual problems in the discharge of sexual energy such as *coitus interruptus*. Whereas the 'psychoneuroses', which were Freud's primary interest, were exhibited through symptoms of hysteria, phobias and obsessional traits which resulted from the repression of infantile sexual wishes.

Reich's emphasis on actual sexual frustration as the root of psychological disturbance, expressed as early as 1927 in *The Function of the Orgasm* if not even earlier, was thus a clear departure from Freud's emphasis on the psychogenic origins of the neuroses. This initial departure from psychoanalytical orthodoxy was simply given further elaboration, according to Chasseguet-Smirgel and Grunberger, in Reich's subsequent attempt to weld together Marx and Freud. The development of a psychoanalytical theory of Nazism was fully justified in their view, given the inadequacies of purely economic explanations. Nevertheless, Reich's formulation of a 'sexual revolution' is described as an illusion which is based on an essentially anti-Freudian conception of sexuality which turns its back on the inescapable conflicts between human happiness and civilisation which had been revealed by psychoanalysis. The position adopted by Chasseguet-Smirgel and Grunberger can be recognised as one which stresses Freudian orthodoxy to the point of dogmatism. Nevertheless, whether one accepts the arguments of *Freud or Reich*? in their entirety or not, it is a work which sets out with immense clarity the obstacles which would lie in the path of any attempt to reconcile psychoanalysis with social theory.

The twists and turns of these different attempts to bring together psychoanalysis and social theory have been traced in some detail not only because they have often been over-simplified and vulgarised, as in the view that Freud was merely a 'reactionary', but also because they seem quite fundamental to any attempt to incorporate psychoanalysis within practical interventions such as social work. We have described the question of 'pessimism' in Freud's thought as one which provides a connecting thread through different attempts to reconcile psychoanalysis and Marxism, for example, and it is one which has also offered a back-drop to the uneasy relationships between psychoanalysis and social work in recent years. Wherever the prospects of social change or policy reform are relied upon to

ameliorate various human difficulties, then the resignation evident in
Freud's detached response to what were seen as inescapable sources
of human unhappiness is cold comfort.

The question of so-called 'pessimism' is informed by a fundamental difference of viewpoint on where the origins of emotional
difficulties lie, whether in the actual lived experiences of individuals
(within particular forms of society and family) or in terms of some
universal human conflicts which are experienced at the level of
phantasy irrespective of the individuals actual lived history (Oedipus
conflict, penis envy, primal scene, etc.). Freud's sexual theory
originated in a refusal of the former view (in the case of allegations of
rape and sexual interference by the fathers of neurotic young
women) towards the latter (the unconscious desire of the child itself
towards the parent of the opposite sex).

This question of the 'primacy of internal factors' (cf. Chasseguet-
Smirgel & Grunberger, 1986, chs 2 & 3) informs a number of
different theoretical and practical conflicts within psychoanalysis,
which do not necessarily assume either a 'political' or 'sociological'
form. For example, in the therapeutic sphere we have already noted
the potential for conflict between the individual orientation of
psychoanalysis as against the approach of family therapists. As
described by Sue Walrond-Skinner (1976, p. 27) this conflict is quite
fundamental: 'Whilst the psychoanalyst believes that it is possible for
an individual to change *in isolation* from his immediate psycho-social
environment, the systems theorist views lasting change as essentially
involving change within the client's significant others as a total
system. Psychoanalysis deals with the symbolic; family therapy with
the actual.' This emphasis on the actual environmental influences
bearing upon personal and pathological development has been given
a particularly vigorous expression in Morton Schatzman's re-
assessment of Freud's case study of Schreber's paranoia. Whereas
Freud interpreted the origin of Schreber's symptoms as a defence
against unconscious homosexual impulses, Schatzman suggests that
his symptoms corresponded precisely to the authoritarian and
persecutory child-rearing system advocated and practised by his
father (cf. Freud, 1911; Schatzman, 1973). The central thrust of a
large body of work on the origins of schizophrenia, including the
'anti-psychiatry' of Ronald Laing, moved of course in the same
direction by identifying patterns of distorted communication in the
so-called 'schizophrenogenic family' as the source of psychotic
difficulties (cf. Laing & Esterson, 1964; Lidz *et al.*, 1965; Wynne *et*

al., 1958). And it is perhaps important to emphasise, with the mention of Laing, that these disputes are not the same as those involved in attempts to reconcile Freud with Marx – because although Laing was briefly a celebrated figure on the Left, the relationship between his work and Marxism amounted to little more than rhetorical flourishes and gestures (cf. Sedgwick, 1982). What we wish to draw attention here, rather, is the way in which the conflict between the 'primacy of internal states' as against an attention to 'real life experiences' shows itself in different ways within psychoanalytical theory and its derivations.

It has also been a central assumption of John Bowlby's work on infancy and early childhood that one must attend to the 'real life experiences' which impinge upon people's emotional lives and development, rather than the 'internal states' of the child's unconscious phantasy – a departure from psychoanalytical orthodoxy which was viewed with considerable displeasure and even hostility by Freudian and Kleinian theorists when he first began to advance these views in the late 1950s (cf. Bowlby *et al.*, 1986). It is also at issue in the sharp attack recently issued by Jeffrey Masson (1985) on Freud's early work on childhood sexuality. Freud, it will be recalled, had first explained his female patients' hysterical symptoms as a result of their experiences of seduction by their fathers, although he quickly jettisoned this view in favour of the theory that these memories of seduction and sexual abuse were in fact 'screen memories' or phantasies, a form of 'wish fulfillment' originating in the daughter's unconscious desire for her father. This formulation of the problem eventually paved the way for the development of the theory of the Oedipus Complex which is so fundamental to psychoanalysis. Masson's thesis, which is that Freud intentionally suppressed the evidence of actual sexual assaults by fathers against daughters in order to avoid public infamy, would therefore imply that the whole basis of psychoanalytical theory demands a re-examination.

A difficulty with Masson's position, of course, is that if Freud had indeed abandoned the seduction theory in order to avoid public scandal, then it is odd that he went on to say equally outrageous things in this theory of infantile sexuality which took the place of the seduction theory. This challenge to childhood 'innocence' which is represented by Freud's views on infantile sexuality has itself recently come under attack by Alice Miller, in an argument very similar to Masson's although apparently developed quite independently. However, unlike Masson whose work is of an historical nature and involves a sifting of the Freud archive, Miller bases her arguments around her therapeutic experience as an analyst. Miller's argument initially took the form that systematic cruelties are involved in the process of child-rearing, whereby the child's spontaneity is crushed, although all recognition of such cruelty is kept hidden in the interests of parents as against children. The results of these wounding experiences, she suggested, were to be found a variety of character deformations, including authoritarianism (cf. Miller, 1983a & 1983b). The position is essentially 'Reichian', although she does not acknowledge the influence of Reich on her work. Later, Miller advanced a more specific accusation against the role of psychoanalytic practice in its conventional form, whereby these cruelties were kept hidden and also legitimised. She suggests that various forms of child abuse are much more prevalent than is usually assumed, and that Freud's work is guilty of collusion with an adult conspiracy to deny the harm done to children in the form of physical, sexual and psychological abuse (cf. Miller, 1985). Arguing that Freud's theory of infantile sexuality directs attention away from the possibilities of actual abuse where this is alleged, and into the realm of unconscious phantasy, on her account a more appropriate initial assumption would be that the child is always innocent.'

Wherever one might wish to strike the balance in such arguments (if there is a balance to be struck) the contest between the 'symbolic' and the 'actual', the 'inner' and the 'outer', seems unlikely to abate itself. It is of course one of fundamental importance to social workers, who define their professional sphere as one which addresses itself to both the emotional and the material difficulties of its clientele. Nevertheless, focused and determined strategies to bring together therapeutic interventions in tandem with action against material and environmental difficulties have only very rarely been attempted (cf. Holland & Holland, 1984; Hoggett & Lousada, 1985; Banton *et al.*, 1985; Pearson, 1988). There are, as we have already seen, formidable theoretical obstacles and objections to such ventures. Arguments such as those recently advanced by Jeffrey Masson and Alice Miller, although they do not deny the need for therapeutic interventions, are for these reasons likely to be found quite unacceptable to many therapists and counsellors. Even so, it seems likely that they will command increasing attention within British social work, given the imperative towards assuming a role in cases of suspected child abuse towards what is now commonly described as 'child protection'. The idea that the Freudian theory of childhood sexuality is a means of 'blaming the victim' of incestuous assault and rape, which is one way of describing Alice Miller's position, is also one that is favourably received in some radical feminist circles where Freud's views have always been regarded with the utmost suspicion (cf. Brownmiller, 1976). More generally, the conflict between the importance of 'real life experiences' as opposed to 'phantasy' has assumed significant proportions in psychoanalytical debates on feminism and the possibilities of developing a specifically 'feminist therapy', to which we shall now turn.

Freud, feminism and femininity: the 'dark continent'

The range of usages of psychoanalysis has been considerably enriched by the re-alignments that have taken place in recent years between Freud and feminism. Freudian theory had been traditionally re-garded from within the feminist movement as either unhelpful in that it neglected women's psychology, or even positively hostile in its emphasis on the inherent weakness and 'incompleteness' of women implied by key concepts such as 'penis envy'. Indeed, in one of the *New Introductory Lectures* on 'Femininity' Freud had said as much himself, admitting that what he had to say was 'certainly incomplete and fragmentary and does not always sound friendly' (Freud, 1933).

This position had been somewhat redressed during the 1920s and 1930s by the psychoanalytical contributions of Helene Deutsch, Karen Horney and Clara Thompson who had given more focused attention to questions of femininity, female sexuality and the specificities of women's psychology (cf. Deutsch, 1944 & 1945; Horney, 1967; Thompson, 1964). Substantial areas of disagreement were opened up within this body of theory, however, particularly on the familiar question of whether to place the emphasis on the biological or social roots of gender differentiation. Even so, there was no further development of these ideas for some years, and where women's issues were on the agenda Freud's work was still regarded with considerable suspicion. Simone de Beauvoir's vastly influential *The Second Sex* had rejected Freud's 'sexual monism' as dominated by masculine assumptions, and the early contributions to the new radical feminism to emerge from North America in the 1960s and early 1970s raised the hostilities to a new pitch (cf. de Beauvoir, 1974; Firestone, 1971; Greer, 1971; Millett, 1971). In Kate Millett's *Sexual Politics,* for example, psychoanalysis was condemned as reflecting a 'gross male-supremacist bias', a charge that was repeated in cavalier style by Germaine Greer in *The Female Eunuch*, whereas in Shulamith Firestone's *The Dialectic of Sex* Freud had been damned with faint praise, on the grounds that he was a misguided feminist.

The sea-change which was to overcome these embittered relations, first significantly registered in Juliet Mitchell's *Psychoanalysis and Feminism*, could hardly have been more of a surprise given what had gone before. Mitchell's work can be seen as a quite extraordinary achievement which simply took matters by the scruff of the neck and engaged in a radical overhaul of the basic assumptions of debate, through a detailed review and re-assessment of the Freudian theoretical tradition on sexuality, femininity and the family. Rather than seeing Freud as 'the enemy' who advocated a patriarchal arrangement of society, she argued that Freud's legacy should be sifted and re-appraised for its vital contribution to the understanding of women's oppression. While agreeing that popularised versions of Freudianism had indeed often been fundamentally reactionary, implying that 'women are inferior and that they can achieve true femininity only as wives and mothers', Mitchell rejected such bowdlerised interpretations of psychoanalysis as incompatible with a strict reading of the Freudian movement: 'However it may have been used, psychoanalysis is not a recommendation for a patriarchal society, but an analysis of one. If we are interested in understanding and challenging the oppression of women, we cannot afford to neglect it' (Mitchell, 1975, p. xv).

Mitchell's approach did not satisfy everyone, of course, and there are still echoes of the older suspicions and antagonisms in some feminist scholarship, such as Sheila Jeffreys' *The Spinster and Her Enemies*, which offers a provocative social history of responses to female sexuality, in Denis Riley's *War in the Nursery* with its highly critical account of the 'popularisation' of psychoanalysis by Bowlby and Winnicott immediately following the Second World War, or the recent collection of essays on Freud's celebrated case history of his hysterical patient 'Dora' (cf. Jeffreys, 1985; Riley, 1983; Bernheimer & Kahane, 1985). Nevertheless, the subsequent re-vitalisation of feminist interest in psychoanalysis gained significant theoretical authority and confidence from Juliet Mitchell's recovery of a critical edge within the Freudian tradition. There remained, however, much to argue about which can be conveniently grouped within the two main lines of growth within the past ten years – the development of a psychoanalytical theory offering a more adequate construction of femininity on the one hand, and the emergence of 'feminist therapy' on the other (cf. Ernst & Maguire, 1987).

These are of course not entirely separate enterprises, although some of the theoretical work has been concerned largely with a 'return to Freud' and what amounts essentially to a textual re-reading of his work which is not immediately interested in therapeutic considerations. This is especially so in those theoretical developments inspired by Lacan (e.g. Coward & Ellis, 1977; Gallop, 1982), and to a lesser extent in the theoretical re-working of Freudian texts as these bear upon sexual theory and femininity in the writings of Janine Chasseguet-Smirgel and her associates which are attracting increasing attention (Chasseguet-Smirgel, 1985 & 1986; Chasseguet-Smirgel *et al.*, 1985). Psychoanalysis has also made its own specific contribution to the renewed interest in the more general project of how to develop a more secure understanding of women's psychology, sexuality and mental health (cf. Baker-Miller, 1973 & 1978; Howell & Bayes, 1981).

In terms of therapeutic developments, some of the most influential forms of 'feminist therapy' which were developed from the early 1970s onwards were influenced less by psychoanalysis than other forms of theory and practice. They were more likely to involve adaptations of the so-called 'humanistic' psychologies and 'alternative therapies' such as encounter techniques which were closer to the feminist practices of 'consciousness-raising' groups. Feminist therapists also remained suspicious of the power relations implicit in psychoanalytical practice, preferring models of working which lent themselves to various forms of self-help (cf. Ernst & Goodison, 1981). Where psychoanalytical theory has become significant within the therapeutic sphere of British feminism, perhaps most influence has been drawn from the 'object relations' school of psychoanalysis associated with the work of Fairbairn, Guntrip and Winnicott (cf. Eichenbaum & Orbach, 1982 & 1985; Chodorow, 1978; Kohon, 1986). The work of the Lacanian school has made little impact in Britain to date in therapeutic terms, although it has come to be influential within some theoretical writing and in related spheres of women's studies such as history and literature (cf. Bernheimer & Kahane, 1985; Eagleton, 1983, ch. 5).

It is possible to juxtapose the 'return to Freud' theorists and the 'feminist therapists' as totally opposed, with a Freudian purism on the one hand disproving the possibility of a specifically feminist therapeutic practice in the same way that the marriage of Freudian and Marxist ideas and practices is refused by Freudian orthodoxy. Indeed, according to one rather severe and provocative reading of Freud owing some kind of debt to Lacan, the psychoanalytical understanding of the unconscious means that 'the individual can never again be at the centre of its experience' and so renders the prospect of a feminist therapy wholly problematical (cf. Lipshitz, 1978). If the ego is 'no longer master in its own house', as Freud had himself described the consequences of his theory of the unconscious, the notion of the 'personal' sphere so beloved of feminist therapy, and the slogan that 'the personal is the political' that had been promoted within feminist politics, was simply and irrelevance. Feminists must either engage in politics or in therapy, Susan Lipshitz appeared to be saying, but could not do both – since the grounds on which Freud had laid the basis for therapy robbed politics of its necessity of a conscious and autonomous ego. This, which is of course deeply reminiscent of the debates on Freud and Marx, remains an area of intense controversy.

The problem hinges once again on whether the origins of emotional difficulties are to be found in *real life experiences* or in *phantasy*. The work of John Bowlby is important in this regard, in that although he was trained within a Kleinian model where unconscious phantasy is held to be dominant, his own views diverged at an early point during the 1930s towards a stress on the importance of the child's early environment and in particular the consequences of the actual separation of the child from the parent (cf. Bowlby *et al.*, 1986). The focus on the actualities of broken or impaired relationships was also fundamentally important in the work of Anna Freud and Dorothy Burlingham at the Hampstead nursery during the second world war, as well as in Bowlby's own vastly influential work in the immediate postwar period on 'maternal deprivation' (Burlingham & Freud, 1944; Bowlby, 1951). This was, of course, subsequently elaborated to a degree of high sophistication and detail in Bowlby's later work which brought together psychoanalysis and ethological studies of human and animal behaviour (cf. Bowlby, 1971, 1975, 1979 & 1981).

This chapter in the development of psychoanalytical theory becomes relevant to feminist concerns largely around the question of the mother–daughter relationship and its implications for our understanding of women's psychology. Whether, in fact, the psychology of women is to be understood as interwoven with experiences of real deprivations in their early relationships with their mothers, or in the

'imagined' deprivations of unconscious phantasy. To describe deprivations as 'imagined' is not, of course, to deny their importance –
indeed, the strength of the Kleinian tradition is that it asserts the
importance of phantasy in early childhood and infancy as against
what might actually be happening in the 'real' world (cf. Sayers,
1984). Where feminist therapy affords central significance to
difficulties in the mother–daughter relationship, this is not
necessarily a major departure from orthodox psychoanalysis, in that
the successful resolution of the Oedipal conflict and the child's
dependence on its mother was traditionally recognised as quite
different for little girls than it was for little boys with the further
possibility that it was more hazardous and painful for women (cf.
Balint, 1973). What is new in the approach of feminist therapy is that
these difficulties are situated within an understanding of the
devaluation of femininity (and hence the woman's mother) within a
patriarchal society. Research from outside the psychoanalytical
tradition has also enlarged our understanding of the ways in which
motherhood impinges on the mental health of women. The sociological study of women's depression by George Brown and Tirril Harris
showed that among the 'vulnerability factors' increasing the likeli-
hood that a woman would become depressed were that she had the
responsibility for three or more children under the age of 15 years,
that she did not have a work role other than that of housewife and
mother, and that she had lost her own mother before the age of 11
years (cf. Brown & Harris, 1978; Brown, 1978).

But even when the importance of women's subordination within a
patriarchal society is centrally acknowledged, as it is in the feminist
therapy advocated by Luise Eichenbaum and Susie Orbach, a
fundamental recognition holds of the inescapably different childhood
experiences of little girls and boys. Both are dependent on mother in
their earliest years, but whereas for boys this involves an intimacy
with a member of the other sex, this is not so for the girl: 'The little
girl, being of the same gender as the mother, has not experienced
intimacy with an "other". Her original intimacy is homosexual'
(Eichenbaum & Orbach, 1985, pp. 21–2). The specific difficulties
experienced by daughters in their subsequent struggle for autonomy,
whereby the child separates itself from the early dependence on its
mother, had been earlier elaborated in a feminist context by Jane
Flax (1981) who suggested that women's experiences of low self-
esteem originated here. In one sense these attempts to situate
emotional development within an understanding of the patriarchal

family involve a significant innovation within psychoanalysis, while at the same time offering a line of continuity within the Freudian view that the resolution of the Oedipal conflict would be universally different for men and women, thus generating essentially different male and female psychologies and sexualities. The conflict between 'inner' and 'outer' upon which so many attempts to reconcile Freud and Marx have foundered seem more capable of resolution within the new departures of feminist therapy, possibly because there is already a wealth of clinical material upon which to build a new understanding of gender and sexuality. Indeed, whereas Freud confessed that female psychology was for him a largely unknown 'dark Continent', we seem to be fast approaching a situation where the question of masculinity will be less well understood than that of femininity. The achievements of feminist work in the past ten years have been so considerable, both in terms of theoretical and practical innovation, that this must be unhesitatingly identified as the growing edge within psychoanalysis.

Practice issues

The dilemmas which have arisen for the new 'feminist therapy' in its encounter with psychoanalysis are not dissimilar to those faced by social workers: how to attend to both the real life experiences and injuries suffered by clients, while remaining alert to the possibilities and actualities of unconscious motivation or unduly defended behaviour. There are of course many ways of coming at a client's difficulties, especially when these are multiple difficulties, and it would be wrong to take any view other than that psychoanalytical ideas offer only one way among many of approaching a client's problems. In the process by which social work turned away from psychoanalysis from the late 1960s onwards, questions such as these were very much at issue. Indeed, it became common to parody the 1950s and 1960s traditions of psychiatric social work, as ones which utterly neglected the material difficulties of clients and attended only to their inner worlds – so that if a depressed woman complained about her wretched house or flat, for example, this was to be regarded merely as an externalisation of her depression, with the sole focus for what was often called 'deep' casework defined as her relationship to her mother in infancy.

This was a parody, no doubt, although it did nevertheless reflect some of the possible ways in which power could be exercised within professional–client negotiations over the definitions of clients' difficulties (cf. Scheff, 1968). Moreover, it carried with it sufficient conviction for that generation of social workers who were being increasingly exposed not only to other theoretical models such as those from sociology or behavioural psychology, but also to the material hardship of clients within the unfolding crisis of the welfare state. It becomes necessary to ask, however, whether in reacting against psychodynamic ideas and the therapeutic role model so completely, the social work profession also lost out on those promising and relevant developments, some of which we have already outlined, within psychoanalysis itself?

Nevertheless, any attempt to re-evaluate the contribution of psychoanalysis to social work is faced with real obstacles. In the first place, despite new alignments between psychoanalysis and the political Left, represented most recently by the open encouragement to dialogue in the journal *Free Associations,* there has been an ideological swing away from the analytic perspective. In the second place, attacks on the value and effectiveness of analytic therapies have undermined the claims of psychodynamic theories as a basis for effective social work practice (e.g. Eysenck, 1986). Lastly, the whole status of psychoanalysis as a science has been called into question, and although we might not be happy with the terms on which this debate has been conducted, it has not been without influence.

Even so, there are many social workers who are not based in clinical settings and who maintain a firm identity as social workers rather than as therapists, and who nevertheless find that psychodynamic thinking informs their understanding of social work situations they encounter daily – for example, complex family problems, bereavement counselling, and work with people facing difficult life transitions. This is not a tradition, however, that has generated much in the way of a literature relating specifically to social work and psychoanalytic ideas – with the notable exceptions, such as the publications of the Institute of Marital Studies, Salzberger-Wittenberg's (1970) expository text on a Kleinian approach to social work, or the research study carried out by Mattinson and Sinclair and published as *Mate and Stalemate* (1979). It seems important, within this context, to review what might be usefully retrieved from within the psychoanalytical project for social work practice.

An important part of the background to any attempt to re-assess the contribution of psychoanalytic thinking must be the increasing concern within the profession that social work skills are gradually being eroded. In the late 1960s attempts were very properly made to redress the balance so that social work practice should not focus only on the individual and his or her problems, but should encompass the wider social and meterial influences upon the life of the individual. An unfortunate, but possibly inevitable dichotomy thereby arose between social action as against help for individual clients, the latter being seen as merely palliative and of no real avail. Attempts to combine social action strategies with an individually oriented therapeutic approach, as we have already indicated, have been very few and far between (cf. Holland & Holland, 1984; Banton *et al.*, 1985; Hoggett & Lousada, 1985). The more general emphasis has tended not to grapple with the undoubtedly difficult and important contradictions which will occur within such an enterprise, however, but rather to reflect the sweeping reversal of assumptions which had been most clearly in evidence in the 'radical' critique of social work of the 1970s – from the individual to the social; from the psychological to the material; from the 'personal' to the 'political' (cf. Pearson, 1975 & 1987). Indeed, it is important to recognise that this was not merely a fringe development, but also one which increasingly became part of the mainstream of social work thinking about what it was that clients most needed (cf. Mayer & Timms, 1970). Although, whatever gains were made in these changes, in terms of a more 'problem-focused' approach to work with clients, they undoubtedly formed part of the process which threatened to 'de-skill' social workers.

It is not a question of attempting to overturn these new directions in social work, which have in any case been in large part a consequence of the economic and political contexts with which social workers and their clients must contend. Social services departments, for example, must of necessity be concerned with monitoring and publicising the effects of severe social deprivation on the communities which they serve, and need to employ staff who are knowledgeable about clients' welfare rights and able to engage with community groups in combating different forms of deprivation within their areas. Although there are those who would prefer social workers not to engage with such matters of social and political controversy, it seems to us to be an inescapable and entirely legitimate sphere of concern. At the same time, however, social workers are daily coming into contact with individuals and families who are facing periods of painful transition in their lives, through illness, handicapping conditions or old age; both children and adults who are experiencing loss, either through bereavement or separation; and families who are suffering severe interpersonal conflict or disruption in family life.

It is precisely in these areas of difficulty that social workers need to draw upon the understanding which can be derived from psychoanalytic thinking; although it is important to stress once again that psychoanalysis has a wider sphere of application than merely that of therapeutic work or the treatment of neurotic disorders. It might be imagined, for example, that it would have been within psychiatric social work that psychoanalytical ideas made most impact during the 1950s and 1960s; and it would certainly be true that both in child guidance clinics and in their work with adult mental patients and their families, psychiatric social workers found a direct relevance in psychoanalytically informed debates on the use of relationships, the concept of transference and other psychotherapeutic considerations (cf. Sutherland, 1956; Irvine, 1952 & 1956; Goldberg, 1953; Hunter, 1969). Even so, this should not disguise the fact that it was in the field of child care where there was a less direct, but possibly even more far-reaching influence to be gained from the psychoanalytic understanding of the needs of children which had been made available through the work of John Bowlby, Anna Freud, Susan Isaacs and others. Anna Freud's account of the changing emotional needs of children and young people, for example, as it is expressed in her concept of 'developmental lines', is one that draws together a body of clinical experience with enormous relevance to the social worker who must often attempt to distinguish between normal and pathological aspects of a child's development. Indeed, it can be recognised at a quite fundamental level as corresponding to (whilst also adding to) our 'commonsense' understanding of children's needs as we know them, either in a professional capacity or through our own children and our families and friends (cf. Freud, 1965). Bowlby's work, equally, and that of James Robertson which used the immediacy of film studies of young children separated from their families in hospital or foster care, are essential resources for attempts to fashion good practice in a range of child care settings.

Other possible areas of application, some of them less well explored, are nevertheless indicative of the wide range of practical uses of psychoanalytic understanding. Questions of grief and bereavement, for example, which were touched upon by Freud himself and have been more recently studied in great detail by Colin Murray Parkes are repeatedly encountered by social workers, particularly in work with the elderly. These are experiences which, although entirely commonplace, are often utterly bewildering – involving complex shifts of emotion, a sense of unreality and the feeling that the deceased is still alive, hallucinatory states, and unaccountable feelings of anger towards the person who has died (cf. Freud, 1917b; Parkes, 1972). Sensitivity to the processes of bereavement and mourning also has relevance to other forms of loss, such as those brought about through illness or surgery, where a social worker's responses can either assist or inhibit the necessary 'grief work' which must be done as a part of the client's recovery and adaptation (cf. McCaughan, 1967; Caplan, 1969). Some aspects of the personal impact of unemployment can similarly be understood as experiences of mourning and loss (cf. Popay *et al.*, 1986; Pearson, 1988).

In attempting to understand how people respond to a variety of threatening experiences, another invaluable psychoanalytical concept is that of 'mechanisms of defence' (cf. Freud, 1937). In work with the families of handicapped children, for example, it will often be found that the child's parents will have erected various forms of defence mechanism – denial of the extent of the child's handicap, the projection of unwanted feelings such as anger, the displacement of these feelings into relations with other members of the family, or the development of over-protective attitudes through attempts at reparation of unconscious guilt – which hinder the family's capacity to respond meaningfully to the child's needs, or which make it impossible for the family to make an effective use of whatever services might be available.

In each of these spheres of activity, psychoanalytic understanding has a relevance to social work practice which should not be confused with therapy. Indeed, in areas of work such as these therapy might be quite irrelevant. Therapy can no more bring the dead back to life, than it can restore the loss of a limb, or heal a child suffering from cerebral palsy or Down's syndrome. Nevertheless, a social worker who has a sound understanding of the workings of defence mechanisms can avoid clumsy interventions which might only heighten the client's defensive anxiety, while also facilitating the exploration of areas of feeling which are not too threatening; thereby helping the client to respond more effectively to his or her actual circumstances, rather than being preoccupied with phantoms. Psychoanalysis has often been understood, quite appropriately in some circumstances, as an inward-looking retreat into the self. But psychoanalytic understanding can also facilitate an engagement with the outside world.

The question of 'effectiveness': the psychoanalytical and behavioural traditions

One more set of questions must be entered at this point, in terms of the 'effectiveness' of psychoanalytical therapy and social work approaches based upon it. This requires a shift of attention in our account of social work's relationship with psychoanalysis towards empirical research evidence, research which often carries with it either as an explicit or hidden agenda comparisons of psychotherapy as against other approaches such as behavioural therapies. We have already discussed the fundamental disagreements between be-haviourism and experimental psychology as against psychoanalysis in an earlier section. These controversies, as we described them, turned on debates within the philosophy of science as to what constitutes a 'scientific' approach to human enquiry and human self-understanding, with important implications for the epistemological status of not only psychoanalysis but also the human sciences in their entirety. If one way in which these controversies have been directed is concerned with whether or not psychoanalysis should be regarded as a 'science', however, then a more specific challenge to psychoanalytically derived therapies has been whether or not their claims to therapeutic effectiveness stand up against research evidence. Here the emphasis shifts from the status of psychoanalysis as a particular form of *understanding* towards psychodynamic therapy as a *practice* judged in terms of outcomes and effectiveness in bringing about change. The question then asked of analytic therapy, quite simply stated, is 'Does it work?'

Such a question is obviously of importance to social workers who are, after all, people charged with practical responsibilities and who are likely to be less concerned with the niceties of philosophical argument than with reducing pain and distress. Doing social work is a purposeful, professional activity intended to achieve beneficial change (or to prevent deterioration) for a wide range of individual and community problems. In part, this involves 'service delivery' – ensuring that the right kinds of resources reach the right people – but professional and public expectations go far beyond that. Social workers are expected to be able to help with a variety of individual and family difficulties: child abuse, delinquency, problems at school, marital conflict, anxiety and depression, homelessness, drink problems and other forms of drug misuse, the personal consequences of unemployment or impoverished old age are just some of the problems met with every day by social workers. These are problems, sometimes urgent ones, demanding actions and answers. Indeed, effectiveness is what some would place at the heart of the social work agenda.

The large part of research on therapeutic effectiveness has been directed towards behavioural approaches, and our account must therefore follow this emphasis – even though there are sometimes strong objections from within the psychoanalytical movement that the criteria of effectiveness assumed in this research tradition, together with the methodologies adopted in order to assess performance against these criteria, are inherently unsympathetic towards psychodynamic therapies. Nevertheless, on such criteria behavioural interventions undoubtedly do well, especially where they have a clear rationale, an explicit and agreed objective for what is to be changed, together with a systematic empirically based approach. Furthermore, they have been more rigorously evaluated than other approaches and are demonstrably effective with a wide range of problems (cf. Hudson & Macdonald, 1986). Where such research has been directed towards psychotherapy, on the other hand, it has often emerged in a less favourable light. To say this is not, however, to agree necessarily with what often appears as an orthodoxy within experimental psychology which argues that whereas behavioural approaches have a proven effectiveness, psychotherapeutic approaches are worthless. This orthodox argument has been recently restated by Eysenck, who delivers a characteristically disparaging judgement against psychoanalysis that the belief in its own efficacy is merely a form of superstition (cf. Eysenck 1986, pp. 66–91). Another view, however, is that these well-trodden lines of argument are being rapidly superceded by a range of evidence on different forms of therapeutic intervention which suggest the need for a more flexible response. One consideration is the need to recognise that more recent introductions of 'cognitive' approaches within the behavioural tradition imply a blurring and convergence between what were previously radically distinct therapeutic approaches. A further complication is that one way of interpreting the assembled research evidence is that it is calling into question the usefulness of overall comparisons between any one therapeutic approach as against any other. Rather, there is a need to attend to fine-grained differences between various therapeutic approaches in terms of their usefulness in relation to specific areas of human difficulty.

The key question here is: which approaches work best with which kinds of problem and which people? In addressing it, we should note first that there is very little work on social work effectiveness *per se*, and what research there is too limited to give definitive answers, although we can distil important pointers from the available research findings – with the necessary cautionary note that much of the evidence we have for the effectiveness of the counselling aspects of social work comes from clinical work in other disciplines, and for that reason these results cannot necessarily be assumed to hold good for social work practice (Rachman & Wilson, 1980). Much of this work again concerns the relative merits of behavioural and interpretative forms of therapy, and the cumulative results are far from clear. There is strong evidence, however, on two counts: the effectiveness of behaviour therapy with a number of conditions, and the advantage of focused interventions.

On the first count, behavioural interventions are demonstrably superior in the treatment of specific phobias, obsessive-compulsive disorders, sexual dysfunction and in the management of stress and anxiety, and self-control (Kazdin & Wilson, 1978). They are also effective with a wide range of childrens' difficulties such as disruptive behaviour, temper tantrums, sleeping difficulties, fears and phobias, hyperactivity, as well as deficits in language, learning and social skills where such methods have been widely used in the home environment, both by social workers as well as psychologists (Iwaniec *et al.*, 1985; Bunyan, 1987). This approach has also been employed with demonstrable success as the basis of various treatment milieux, such as assessment centres and special schools. Behavioural approaches are however less useful where target problems cannot be clearly isolated and defined, and there is no unambiguous evidence as to the general superiority of behavioural methods (Kolvin *et al.*, 1981).

On the second count, there is strong evidence supporting time-limited, focused interventions which seem to be generally more effective than long-term, open-ended, unspecific types of intervention. Brief, focused work is not of course incompatible with psychodynamic approaches and task-centred social work practice as described by Reid and Epstein (1977) includes analytically-based work although it perhaps lends itself more readily to a behavioural style.

There are also forms of brief therapy which have been developed specifically within the psychoanalytical tradition (cf. Balint *et al.*, 1972), and the 'crisis intervention' model also draws much of its inspiration from psychodynamic theory (cf. Parad, 1965; Caplan, 1969). While these approaches have not been subjected to rigorous research in terms of their effectiveness, they nevertheless indicate the process of cross-fertilisation between different styles of intervention which in some areas of work is breaking down the rigid barriers between 'interpretive' and 'behavioural' approaches. Recent research on the effectiveness of self-help groups for women suffering from compulsive eating problems, where once again psychodynamic concepts were brought together with different theoretical traditions, provides a further indication of this development which transcends the old divide and focuses on 'behavioural' criteria (for example, eating patterns or body weight) while using psychoanalytical concepts (cf. Parry-Cooke & Ryan, 1986).

In the treatment of depression another development which incorporates different theoretical assumptions is that offered by 'cognitive therapy' which derives both from behaviour therapy and traditional psychodynamic psychotherapy. Cognitive therapy is associated especially with the work of Beck (1979), Ellis and Grieger (1977) and Meichenbaum (1977). For the sake of simplicity, reference will only be made here to the first of these authors. Cognitive therapy in Beck's terms has similarities to behaviour therapy in that it focuses on here-and-now problems, and is highly structured: it is akin to conventional psychotherapy in that it emphasises the role of dysfunctional attitudes, beliefs and assumptions, together with the way in which an individual structures his or her world as the source of depression. Challenging and changing these cognitions, it is held, will lead to greater ability on the part of the individual to cope with and control depression, rather than being at its mercy. Unlike psychodynamic therapy, however, cognitive therapy makes no reference to unconscious factors or to the origins of (say) low self-esteem, dealing rather with its manifestations in the here and now. But although it is ahistorical, Beck would recognise the influence of early experience in the development of a negative self-concept – for example, excessive parental expectations which can never be realised. Equally he recognises a link between early loss and depression, though cognitive therapy would not explore this link. Cognitive therapies are 'known to work in some instances' and appear promising, though there are lacunae in the evidence as to outcome, particularly in the longer term.

The extension of behaviour therapy to include cognitive processes, representing an attempt to reconcile methods of traditional psychotherapy and behaviour therapy, is far from uncontroversial among behaviour therapists and is seen by some as a mistaken direction (Rachman, 1983). It is notable, however, that modification of the cognitions that mediate behaviour are given considerable emphasis in recent behavioural social work writing (Hudson & Macdonald, 1986). So that whereas in the case of 'brief therapies' we saw psychotherapeutic approaches accommodating themselves to closely focused styles of work that are more commonly associated with the behavioural tradition, the admission of cognitive elements into behavioural approaches signifies a movement in the other direction. It is perhaps above all the inclusion of the cognitive domain which has made the boundaries between behavioural and interpretative forms of therapy far more difficult to maintain. 'Slowly but surely over the years behaviour therapy has become more cognitive. Cognitions, re-labelled self-statements, are classed as behaviours' is how Ledwidge (12978) has described this process. Conceptually, then, it is possible that the distinction between behavioural and interpretative approaches cannot be sustained – or at least not in the excessively rigid way that had informed the orthodoxy of experimental psychology. This process of accommodation is probably inevitable. For one thing, the therapist is treating people, not behaviour or cognitions *per se*, though specific treatment interventions may focus on one or the other. There will always remain aspects of the total interaction, however, which cannot be classified or labelled. For another, complex human behaviour cannot be analysed in terms of behaviour alone: cognitive symbolic processes are essential to an adequate conception of the person (cf. Merleau-Ponty, 1965). Unlike the animal world, human beings have what Polanyi (1958, p. 20) refers to as 'tacit knowledge' – the power of understanding, of comprehending experience and making sense of it. The need to understand oneself and some part of the world in which one lives, to reflect upon experience and order it, is quintessentially human. Over and above the specific problems that cause pain and may be relieved or changed by behavioural methods, is a search for meaning, for comprehension of moral and intellectual struggle, which is of an altogether different order and which cannot be addressed within the categories of learning theory alone. The behavioural therapist could reply to this that there is no need for it to be, since therapeutic change takes place without it, and might also argue that existential and ontological questions are not part of the therapist's brief, except in so far as they determine goals for treatment. But once the practitioner is concerned with cognition, then questions of value, belief, purpose and intentionality must be addressed and the nature of therapy becomes very different. It does appear, in sum, that in so far as both behavioural and interpretative therapies involve cognitive processes, the conceptual distinctions between them are becoming blurred, though they do retain distinctive defining characteristics.

Further indications of these blurrings and cross-fertilisations is found in the field of family and marital therapy, where evidence of efficacy is however even less clear-cut. A huge literature now exists about processes and models of intervention, but very little relates these activities to outcome. In practice, moreover, a range of different approaches may once again be flexibly employed – for example, family work which incorporates a variety of therapeutic strategies (Dare, 1985). These may include elements of functional assessment, homework assignments, and the use of contracts. One study of conjoint marital therapy by Crowe (1978) compared three treatment approaches which were described as 'behavioural/ directive', 'group-analytic/interpretative', and a 'nonactive or supportive' approach for control purposes within the research design. Of these, the directive treatment produced significant change on all outcome measures, and showed significant superiority to the control (supportive) procedure in sexual and general adjustment and target problem measures. The interpretative treatment produced significant changes on marital and target problem measures only, but showed a significant superiority to the control procedure on two measures, marital adjustment and global assessment of improvement. Of greater interest to the present discussion, however, is the (incidental) finding that in *all three* treatment approaches there was a predominance of non specific statements; thus none of the approaches was used in a 'pure' form and there was some considerable overlap in the techniques employed. And this, moreover, was a research programme which set out to keep therapist styles as distinct as possible. It indicates once more how, in practice, different approaches may be far less clear-cut than the theoretical literature might suggest; the nonspecific interventions which practitioners use in common and which 'belong' to no particular model or orientation, may be as significant as specific techniques. This is in line with the strong research evidence for the salience of counsellor or therapist attributes such as nonpossessive warmth, empathy, and genuineness (Fischer, 1978; Wilson & Evans, 1977). Beneficial results have been found for a wide range of therapies, and there may even be specific therapeutic mechanisms that span otherwise different theoretical approaches (Rutter & Hersov, 1985).

The question of effectiveness is therefore by no means as straightforward as it has been sometimes portrayed in arguments between behavioural and psychotherapeutic approaches. Psychoanalysis and behaviourism, certainly, rest upon unalterably opposed conceptions of human conduct and human nature, just as they embrace radically divergent philosophies of what constitutes a scientific approach to human enquiry. However, in their applications in a variety of professional contexts each approach often seems to be adapted and modified to meet the specific circumstances and requirements of the helping process and the practice of welfare.

One way of attempting to understand these different blurrings and modifications of otherwise divergent theories is to employ a distinction between professional 'rhetorics' on the one hand as against professional 'practices' on the other: that is, between the accounts which people give of what they do as against what they actually do. Conflicts between 'rhetorics' and 'practices' have been found in any number of areas of professional activity. For example, research on the administration of justice has pointed to the lack of fit between what magistrates and lawyers say that they do (and the rules which they will say that they operate by) as opposed to the way in which they actually conduct themselves in the court (cf. Carlen, 1976; McBarnet, 1981). In the practice of medicine there are also significant areas of disjunction between the professional rhetoric of medicine as 'applied biological science' as opposed to how doctors actually behave in consultations with their patients and in managing the process of treatment (cf. Freidson, 1970). If professional rhetorics do not always correspond to professional practices in tightly rule-governed and scientifically-grounded professions such as law and medicine, there is clearly no reason why we should not expect to find similar disjunctions in more hazily defined professional activities such as psychotherapy, counselling and social work.

Faced with the kind of evidence outlined above which has identified significant areas of blurring between the actual practices of therapists of different theoretical persuasions, two possible lines of argument suggest themselves. The first we might think of as the 'convergence' thesis, proposing that in spite of rhetorical conflicts between different bodies of psychotherapeutic theory, what actually goes on between therapists and their clients does not differ nearly so much as the conflicting theories would suggest. The second argument, on the other hand, would suggest that in spite of blurrings which can be identified within actual therapeutic practices which tend towards eclecticism, these are nevertheless forms of eclectic practicality which ultimately rest upon quite separate lines of theoretical development, each with its own substantive tradition. According to the first argument, then, future progress would be seen to lie within attempts to cut across the theoretical and practical divides. Whereas, the second argument would see the prospects for further refinements and developments of both theory and practice resting with those who continue to orientate their activity within 'pure' and established assumptions as defined by tradition.

On the available evidence it is not really possible to choose between these two conflicting readings of the situation. However, what can be said with certainty in the context of social work is that even within the most 'protected' or 'clinical' settings (child guidance, for example) the responsibilities of social workers are such that they will never be able to work entirely within the 'pure' forms of either the psychoanalytical or behavioural traditions. Social workers in different settings might have preferred ways of working, but nevertheless the uses to which social workers put either psychoanalytical or behavioural understandings will invariably tend towards the eclectic. It would be no more appropriate for a social worker to employ only the strict observances of the psychoanalytical method in a case of suspected child abuse, for example, that it would be to enter a client's household armed with the full-blown technology of aversion-therapy. Even so, there would be no essential contradiction involved in a social worker assisting in the implementation of a learning theory programme of reinforcements designed to modify the disruptive behaviour of a mentally handicapped child, while also being engaged in counselling the child's parents on issues such as parental guilt and hostility through an approach informed by a psychodynamic understanding. One of the strengths of social work has been its openness to a variety of theoretical and practical approaches, where these are suited to the needs of its clientele. And this, in turn, points to the necessity of an effective education and training for social workers which can help them to understand and utilise different theories and practices in appropriate ways.

In summary, we can say that the debate on the effectiveness of differing styles of therapeutic intervention has begun to emerge from the old slanging-match between psychoanalysis and behaviourism into a situation where the possibilities of more fluid interchange can be glimpsed. This is not to say that there are not still some protagonists of behavioural orthodoxy who wish to continue with the debate in its old terms. Nor to dispute that there are also powerful arguments advanced from within the psychoanalytical tradition which reject any move towards a weakening of the distinctive Freudian legacy. Nevertheless, a careful reading of the effectiveness debate suggests that there is no reason for social workers to discard psychoanalytical understanding as an outmoded form of response to human difficulty. The psychoanalytical tradition has been a fundamental part of social work's mental landscape since the first stirrings of its professional ambitions in the early twentieth century. Subsequent developments, both in research and practice, mean that earlier forms of enthusiasm for psychoanalysis must be modified and that it can no longer be regarded as the only theoretical and practical resource which social workers draw upon – which is how it sometimes seemed in the immediate postwar period. Nevertheless, the Freudian legacy must still be counted as a major contribution to human self-understanding, and as such it remains as a vital dimension within an effective and humanly reckonable social work practice. Freud's own attitude towards the question of effectiveness was summed up in a characteristically sober judgement that although psychoanalysis could not solve all of life's problems, 'much will be gained if we succeed in transforming your hysterical misery into common unhappiness' (Breuer & Freud, 1895, p. 393). Perhaps the aim to alleviate the misery of clients and to help them to return to the common lot of 'ordinary human unhappiness' might even provide the best available description of what it is that social workers try to do.

About the book

Finally, we must say a few words about the contents of this book. It falls into two parts. Part I addresses a number of theoretical questions which indicate some of the growing points in psychoanalytic thinking. Part II, on the other hand, consist of chapters which explore the applications of psychodynamic theories in practice. Taken together these chapters deal with only a few of the fields of practice which might have been included, but it is hoped they are sufficiently representative to give some idea of how psychoanalytic ideas actually inform practice.

In the opening chapter, Robert Bocock develops a view of psychoanalysis as a social theory, examining in some detail the ways in which Freud's work has had a varying influence upon other bodies of social theory such as those of Talcott Parsons, the Frankfurt Institute, and more recently the French schools of structuralist and post-structuralist thought. An approach such as this, as he describes it, is one which 'avoids the narrowness of a purely individualistic approach' which characterised 'earlier uses of psychoanalysis in social work'.

Steven Wilson, on the other hand, suggests that the consulting room, and what goes on between the analyst and patient, provides the grounds upon which psychoanalytical knowledge is based. For him, as for so many other psychoanalytical theorists, the concept of 'transference' is central to our understanding of what psychoanalysis has to offer, and this is a theme which recurs throughout the book in different ways. Social workers are regularly in touch with clients who have urgent unmet needs and who are experiencing overwhelming feelings of fear, anger and anxiety as a result of these difficulties. It is only through an understanding of the counter-transference reactions of depression and helplessness that the social worker can be helped to feel free from powerful emotions and, as a consequence, be in a position to offer constructive help.

We have already indicated that the question of women's psychology and feminism is both one of the most powerful growing points within psychoanalysis, as well as one characterised by a vigorous and critical debate. In the third chapter of Part I, Janet Sayers reviews some of these controversies, with an emphasis both upon the contribution which psychoanalysis can make towards our general understanding of women's subordination, together with its more specific implications for women within social work – whether as workers or as clients.

A feminist perspective is also developed in Part II by Mira Dana and Marilyn Lawrence in their chapter on women's eating disorders, which addresses not only anorexia nervosa and compulsive eating, but more particularly the less frequently discussed problem of 'bulimia' – that is, eating to excess, followed by self-induced vomiting. As Dana and Lawrence describe it, bulimia is best understood as a 'metaphor' which symbolises other aspects of women's life situations. They also indicate the ways in which different eating disorders (anorexia, bulimia and compulsive eating) require quite different responses in terms of therapy and counselling interventions, their own work at the Women's Therapy Centre in London combining individual therapy, group sessions and also self-help initiatives.

Laurence Spurling's chapter, on the other hand, is concerned in a more single-minded way with individual therapy, based around a detailed study of work with a young woman who was experiencing multiple difficulties in her life. Individual therapy is, of course, the form of activity which has been most commonly associated with psychoanalytical thinking, and Spurling draws upon a number of sources for his approach, including the 'existential' tradition.

By contrast, group care is the focus for the chapter by John Simmonds, who examines the ways in which powerful feelings shared by group members are rarely explored and are instead subject to systematic repression, to the detriment of the group's effective functioning. He concludes by arguing that attempts to tighten up procedural guidelines in response to problems such as child abuse, although not unimportant, cannot in themselves dispel the possibilities of irrational decision-making where powerfully charged emotions are involved.

A similar theme is developed by Roger Bacon who looks at the possibilities of irrationality in the decision-making processes of case conferences concerned with child abuse. Through a detailed case study and analysis, he demonstrates how a group of concerned professionals can be drawn into a collusive alliance with the parents, through failing to understand their own feelings of identification with the child. The implication, again, is that bureaucratic procedures and regulations are in themselves quite inadequate as guides to effective action in such situations.

Whereas Bacon's chapter is based upon a Kleinian theoretical perspective, other chapters in this book are more eclectic in their orientation. Indeed, a variety of theoretical paradigms other than those derived from psychoanalysis are used by social workers. But even if they may be using a behavioural or contractual approach, an understanding of resistance towards change and ambivalence about it will help the worker when the client appears not to be cooperating with the agreed programme or to be sabotaging it in some subtle way. This is well illustrated by Catherine Crowther in her chapter on family therapy, where she shows how psychoanalytical concepts are still useful when working with a family systems model.

We have already seen, in the chapters by Simmonds and Bacon, how psychoanalytic concepts can throw light on the less rational aspects of group decision-making. Without the benefit of an understanding of such processes, social workers can be overwhelmed by the immensity of the problems which are brought to them, and this leads to a position of defensiveness, which is also vividly described by Celia Downes in her account of a social services area team. Psychoanalytic thinking can help us to see which feelings belong in the client and which in ourselves. It can increase our understanding about resistance to change and our appreciation of the struggle which any change involves. Without this help, social workers will continue to feel helpless against the tide of demands and unmet needs with which they are faced. But of course, if this help is to be available, there must be a recognition both in social work education and training, and in the sphere of practice and its organisation and management, that social workers need time and support to examine their own reactions to the clients with whom they are working. It is only with this kind of understanding that they can feel free to intervene constructively in people's lives with confidence in their own professional identity. Psychoanalysis might not be the only theoretical resource available to social workers, but it remains a vitally important one.

Note

1.   A further 'revisionist' approach to why Freud overthrew the 'sexual theory' of neurosis in favour of the 'seduction theory' is offered by Marianne Krüll in *Freud and His Father* (Hutchinson, 1986). Krüll's argument hinges on Freud's tangled relationship with his father, suggesting that Freud's change of mind was dictated by his hidden desire not to look too closely into his own past. Why it should be that so many 'revisionist' theories of this kind have surfaced independently in very recent years, each converging on the 'seduction theory', is one of the more intriguing aspects of the living tradition of Freud's psychoanalytical legacy.

Part I

Psychoanalysis and its Social Contexts

1 Psychoanalysis and Social Theory

Robert Bocock

Social workers have tended to see psychoanalysis as being both a way of conceptualising individual personality, and as a major clinical method lying behind modern psychotherapy. This view has been held both by those who use psychotherapeutic methods or insights in their practice of social work, and by those who are critical of such an approach. In this chapter I want to argue that psychoanalysis as it was first developed by Sigmund Freud, contained not only a theory about human personality and a therapeutic method for clinical work, but that it also contained an important social theory about major social institutions and culture. This wider social theory has an importance for social workers' own understanding and conceptions of what it is they are doing.

There is a view that Freud has been superceded in psychoanalysis and that his theory of personality is out of date in the light of more recent developments in clinical work and that the changes introduced into psychoanalytic theory as a consequence entail that Freud's theory is now outmoded (see N. Chodorow, 1978, for example). There are, I think, both epistemological reasons and reasons within the 'history of ideas' why Freud has to remain the starting point for a psychoanalytic theory about cultural and social institutions. This is in spite of later developments within psychoanalytic clinical literature. As Russell Jacoby argued it is not safe to assume that what comes later in time is necessarily better intellectually.

> The history of philosophy is the history of forgetting. . . . Problems and Ideas once examined fall out of sight and out of mind only to resurface later as novel and new . . . . Psychology is hardly exempt. What was known to Freud, half-remembered by the neo-Freudians, is unknown to their successors. The forgetfulness is driven by an unshakeable belief in progress: what comes later is necessarily better than what came before. Today, without romanticizing the past, one could almost state the reverse: what is new is worse than what is old (Jacoby, 1975, p. 1).

61

To appreciate the kind of position which Jacoby is maintaining, and that of other writers who see Freud as an essential reference point, such as Juliet Mitchell (1974) and Lacan (1977), it is essential to locate their positions within epistemology, otherwise they are read as though each was maintaining a dogma rather than an intellectual position which has to be taken seriously. It is important to be clear, or as clear as it is possible to be at any given point in time, what it is that constitutes 'a science' in this area, or if not 'a science' at least a serious area of rationally organised theory and research. This is a primary concern of modern epistemology because the development of natural science shook earlier ideas about what constitutes knowledge.

The main purpose here is to show how positions within epistemology have affected the development of the relations between psychoanalysis and social theory. There are three major issues: first, the issue about how far the natural sciences and the sciences concerned with social and human affairs are seen as similar or not; second, the relations between moral and political values and sciences, especially the social sciences; and thirdly, the role of theory and research in science. Each of these issues will be discussed briefly.

(1) Firstly, views about the similarities and differences between the natural and social sciences have affected the relations between psychoanalysis and social theory. Freud himself regarded the differences between the natural sciences and psychoanalysts as being insignificant. He claimed that eventually the propositions developed in psychoanalysis could become propositions within biochemistry and neuro-physiology. Freud had begun his professional career in the biological sciences concerned with human beings and this orientation never entirely left him. However, this viewpoint has produced problems in the eyes of later psychoanalysis and social theorists interested in psychoanalysis. Critical theorists, for example, have argued that there is a major logical difference between the sciences concerned with material objects and those concerned with human beings. This difference turns upon the presence of complex language among human beings and its absence among other natural objects.

The sciences of society and human action are concerned with the interpretation of meanings and with a critical appraisal of structures and cultural values on this view. This is not a matter of preference, as positivists assume, but a matter of logic – a social scientist cannot avoid interpreting the meanings of action and speech, and making appraisals, even, or especially, when claiming not to be doing so.

Interpretation and appraisal are contained in any attempt to describe what has been observed – there is no neutral language for reporting observations of human interaction. Attempting to solve this problem by moving into abstract languages, such as mathematical language, for example, does not overcome the problem but only confounds it, because it still requires decisions about the meaning of human action and language into other, non-verbal, categories. In this process of interpretation from one kind of coding to another, critical theorists argue that assumptions about meaning, which may or may not be reasonable or valid, have to be made. It is preferable to make these judgements explicit and open to public discussion, and not to hide behind the aura of 'science' when value judgements and political stances are inevitably involved as a matter of logic not personal failure on the part of the social scientist.

Structuralists, on the other hand, have maintained that there are no crucially important differences between the natural and the social sciences. Louis Althusser, for example, argued that any science must construct its own theoretical object for analysis using its own distinctive methods for creating knowledge, and that both Marx and Freud had created such theoretical objects and methods for researching them. Other social scientists, he argued, were producing ideology not science; that is they were working with concepts provided within existing thought patterns, rather than moving beyond what was already available. In this sense they worked within ideology rather than producing and working within a science with a distinctive theoretical object of investigation.

This distinction between science and ideology has proved to be very difficult, if not impossible, to define (see Hirst, 1979). One might be tempted to say that one person's science is someone else's ideology and vice versa. However, this would be unfair unless one were prepared to be committed to a completely relativistic position in which there would be no epistemologically viable category of 'science' in any case. On such a view even natural sciences appear as ideologies maintained by power and non-rational influences (see Feyerabend, 1975). The key issue then becomes whether or not it is possible to find a way of describing what goes on in any natural science which distinguishes it from an unscientific procedure, such as astrology for example, and, having done this to see if such a description fits any existing social science, or could potentially do so if it does not at a given moment. Even if Althusser has not succeeded in doing this to many people's satisfaction, the attempt to do it, or something like it, is intelligible and essential within the epistemology of both natural and social sciences. We shall return to this issue again after considering the second issue raised above, namely the relations between the social sciences and political and moral values.

(2) The major reason why there seems to be a special problem about the epistemological status of the social sciences is the inescapable link that they have with political positions. This is the problem, for example, with Althusser's solution to the definition of a science as distinct from ideology, for he seems to those who do not agree with his political position in Marxism to be merely dogmatic in his insistence upon counting a particular version of Marxism as science and not ideology. His view itself is seen by some as a dogmatic piece of ideology, not a statement within science.

The issue about the relation between the social sciences and political positions is not easily resolved. One might ask whether or not it really matters, for after all people are never going to agree about such things as political issues, so why should anyone expect that they will do so within the social sciences – economics, history, sociology, politics – or within applied areas such as social work, economic policy, health, or education? If one were to accept the implications of this position, however, it would entail that rational discussion will be of no avail in political matters, and that political differences will be settled outside of conscious human control, by one means or another, including violence.

Whilst it may be true that political disputes may continue to be settled in non-rational ways, this does not entail that we need to give up the hope that more rational means could be used in the future, given certain basic structural changes in the world economic and military systems. These structural factors are outside of conscious control, and the task for the social sciences is to make the mechanisms underlying these structures clear. There is a complex interaction between these structures, their theorisation in social science, and human groups aiming to be agents of change. To exclude human agency from our conceptions of societal change is to be unnecessarily restrictive. Such a perspective can have disastrous implications in terms of political violence for there is little to be done but to protest violently in some circumstances. This in turn provides the excuse needed for the forces of law and order to become more brutal and violent in return. It is surely romantic nonsense to imagine that out of such violent clashes human progress can emerge. This is because progress must include some notion of an increase in scientific, or rational, understanding and discussion about change which is not furthered in the aftermath of civil wars, or revolutions.

There is no alternative, therefore, to increasing violence as a means of settling political disputes within and between states, other than to develop the social sciences and to try to apply some of the insights gained from them in policy and in many forms of social action including 'social work'. The attack upon the social sciences comes in a number of forms, such as verbal criticisms and ill-founded innuendos about their intellectual standing from people whose own claims to philosophical rigour seem to be measured by the praise they receive from leading popular newspapers in Britain. The attack also assumes the form of financial cuts in resources to fund the necessary research and teaching, which is appalling when it comes from democratic politicians.

(3) Turning now to the third issue mentioned above, namely the role of theory and research in the social sciences; here the important point to bear in mind is that the injunction to test theories against 'the facts' is impossible in the social sciences, and some would argue in the natural sciences too. This is because there is no theory-neutral language in which to generate 'facts' or 'data' such that these can be used to adjudicate between competing theories. Any set of observations, or statistics, have to be organised and based upon some set of concepts held either explicitly or, more typically, implicitly. These concepts, in turn, will depend upon some view of the world, or some theory, derived from a science, or a religion, or a 'commonsense' view of the world which itself depends upon a point of view, a set of interests, held by some group or groups in a social formation. An explicit theory is, therefore, essential in social science if a piece of research is to be rationally evaluated. Facts do not speak for themselves. They only speak to those who share the same view of the world as that of those who generated them.

There have been three important groups of writers each of which has tried to develop systematic links between Freudian psychoanalysis and sociology and social theory more generally. These groups are, first, the Frankfurt School of critical theorists who worked in Germany before and after the Nazi period, and in the USA. The main members of the Frankfurt school included Fromm, Marcuse, Adorno, Horkheimer, and Habermas. This group used Freudian theory and a social theory derived from a modified version of Marxism and some themes from Weber. Second, the work of Talcott

Parsons in American sociology during the 1950s, 1960s and 1970s is important. Parsons tried to link, at the level of theory, a sociology derived from Weber, Durkheim and Pareto, but significantly not Marx, with a theory of socialisation derived from Freudian psychoanalysis. Third, the work of structuralists and post-structuralists in France and Britain during the 1960s and 1970s, has tried to use Freudian psychoanalysis. The main focus of this group has been upon language as a generator of meaning independently of subjective intentions. This has been done on the whole by writers working within a broadly Marxist perspective, albeit a modified, complex, version of Marxism.

It is proposed to examine each of these schools to show the way in which they have approached psychoanalysis and how they have tried to use it in their wider social theory. It will not be possible to discuss every author who has made a contribution, but only to select the significant themes in each of the groups of writers. The position of Parsons and American sociologists influenced by his works will be discussed first because the view of 'science' adopted by these authors is one which forms a base line from which the other two major approaches, namely critical theory and structuralism, may be seen to be radical departures.

Talcott Parsons and American sociology

Talcott Parsons developed links between his sociological concerns and psychoanalysis throughout the various phases of his work. His first major text, *The Structure of Social Action* (1937), did not discuss Freud, something which Parsons later said he would have rectified if he had been familiar with Freud when he wrote the book (see Rocher, 1974, p. 99). In this phase of his work Parsons was concerned with developing a voluntaristic theory of social action from his reading of the works of Weber, Durkheim, and Pareto, in particular. His concern was to establish the inadequacy of positivist and empiricist frameworks for the development of a theory of social action, because they ignored the normative orientations people have in a social interaction. Positivism, Parsons argued, assumed people face acting in the world with either valid or invalid scientific knowledge about their environments. No other kind of orientation is admitted or taken account of in such models of action, but Parsons made the case for including other features, which he called 'normative orientations', that is the values, beliefs, and feelings which affect interaction in his general theory of social action. He follows Weber in emphasising the subjective meanings attached to action as distinct from behaviour which lacks subjective meanings. Behaviourists in psychology and in biology were criticised by Parsons for their insistence upon working with the false assumption that human behaviour was identical to that of animals or social insects. Human action has subjective meanings attached to it, normative orientations as Parsons called this aspect, and this crucially distinguishes most, although not necessarily all, human performances from those of other species.

Parsons did distinguish his position from that of 'idealism'. He wrote: 'In an idealistic theory "action" becomes a process of emanation, or "self-expression" of ideal or normative factors.... Non-normative elements cannot "condition" action, they can only be more or less integrated with a meaningful system (Parsons, 1937, p. 82). Parsons, therefore, did also include in his own theory of action the non-normative features which condition action – the 'natural' features of the environment and of the human body.

There was a distinction between sociology and psychology as analytical sciences of action, and between the sciences of action and biology, and the other 'natural' sciences in Parsons' work at this time, a distinction he retained in a slightly modified form throughout his career. Psychology was to be concerned with 'subjective categories such as "end", "purpose", "knowledge", "feeling", "sentiment", etc.' (ibid.) p. 86). These concepts were not accepted by behaviourists and materialistic positivists, thus making such approaches reductionist and inadequate for the analysis of social interaction.

His approach to Freudian theory was made via his own conceptualisation of the functional prerequisites for what he came to call 'social systems' (Parsons, 1951). The key link concept he developed between the social system, the cultural system and the personality system was that of 'need disposition'. The term 'need' was intended to focus upon the internal personality and its requirements to maintain a sense of internal equilibrium; the word 'disposition' was to focus upon the propensity to act in some way. 'Need dispositions' were learned, not given by heredity or instincts (Rocher, 1974, p. 100). Parsons seemed to think that the drives, or instinctual wishes, in Freudian psychoanalysis were biologically based, and he missed the crucial point in Freud's own conceptualisation of instinctual desires as lying on the borderland between the psychological and the biological. Parsons treated instinctual desires as purely biological. The new Parsonian concept of need-disposition is, then, one of learned motivation to perform in conformity with the functional prerequisites of the social system (adaptation, goal attainment, integration, latency) and the values of the cultural system which have become internalised during the socialisation process (see Parsons, 1953; and Hamilton, 1983, p. 107).

Parsons assumed that conformity had to be explained theoretically, and he held that it should not be assumed to be either naturally given, or to arise spontaneously from members of a social system. Parsons made the Hobbesian problem of order – that is the problem of how order is maintained in a condition of a potential 'war of all against all' – his explicit starting point. He contrasted at one pole conformity which arose from the 'instrumental interests' of actors, and at the other pole the 'introjection' or internalisation of a standard, or value, so that conformity to it becomes a need-disposition in the actor's personality structure, relatively independently of any instrumental advantages of that conformity (see Parsons, 1951, p. 37).

From here it was an easy step for Parsons to integrate the Freudian concept of the superego, or the 'above-I' (Bettelheim, 1983), into his conceptualisation of the processes of socialisation and social control. The values of the culture become internalised in the personality of people while they are young. People are socialised to experience guilt if they contravene these internalised values as a consequence of learning that conformity wins the approval of others – the others being first of all the parents of the child and later other actors in a social system with whom the actor is interacting. Parsons also treated the concept of the ego (the 'I' according to Bettelheim, ibid. and the id (or 'it') as being produced by socialisation. The notion of reality and the procedures for reality testing which the ego performs according to Freud were seen by Parsons as being products of socialisation too. This has some plausibility in that standards of rationality and of what is to count as 'real' are culturally constructed. Parsons went on to argue that the feelings and desires of the id are also learned – there is no desire, or id-impulse, as such given outside of culture.

It is not only the superego which is internalized – that is, taken over by identification from cathected social objects – but that there are involved other important components which presumably must be included in the ego – namely, the system of cognitive categorizations of the object world and the system of expressive symbolism.... This may be felt to be a relatively radical conclusion – namely, that emotions, or affect on the normal human adult level, should be regarded as a symbolically generalized system, that is never 'id-impulse' as such (Parsons, 1952; & Bocock, 1977, p. 468).

This is indeed a radical conclusion, or perhaps 'conservative' might be a more applicable term than 'radical', because Parsons has here removed the major conceptualisation Freud developed of unconscious desire based upon the sexual and the death instincts. Such a move takes away the major point of using psychoanalytic concepts within social theory because it obscures, or removes entirely, the possibility of conflict between a person's feelings and the main cultural cognitive symbols and values. For example, the phenomenon of homosexual panic experienced by some men and women when they realise they are attracted to members of the same gender as themselves, in spite of having thought for much of their lives up to that point that they were like everyone else in their society. The dominant cognitive, cathectic and evaluative symbols in most western cultures will not prepare people for this type of feeling, but rather the culture socialises them into experiencing homosexuality as disgusting, or evil, or very peculiar and something which affects other people not themselves. It is difficult to see how Parsons could conceptualise this in any way other than as a lack of full, or adequate, socialisation into the dominant culture's symbols, for anyone who was fully socialised would not be able to feel attraction to others of their own gender because the only sexual desires they would experience would be those learned from the culture's dominant values and cathectic symbols.

A major criticism of the Parsonian position was advanced by Dennis Wrong (Wrong, 1961). This was that Parsons had developed 'an over-socialized conception of man' and lost the emphasis Freud had placed upon the body. As Wrong expressed it in a postscript to his original paper, published in 1976, 'in the beginning is the body' (Wrong, 1976). Wrong put his main argument in a succinct proposition: 'To Freud man is a social animal without being entirely a socialized animal' (ibid., p. 36). He went on to point out that there are two different ways in which the term socialisation is used, and that they should not be confused, although they often are, even in Parsons. On the one hand there is socialisation into the norms and values of a specific culture, and on the other there is socialisation into the general capacity to interact with others, and to use a language – in short the process of 'becoming human'.

There are still many problems about how the 'instincts' in Freudian theory should best be handled, but it is no solution to remove any connection between desires and the body in the way Parsons did. Freud had tried to develop a way of conceptualising the links between the body and emotions via the notion of unconscious desires. This is fundamental to any theory claiming to be based upon Freudian psychoanalysis. The point is that the concept of the unconscious, and the allied notion of unconscious desires of a sexual and destructive type, is the foundation of Freudian theory – the theory is about the unconscious and unconscious desires which are seen as rooted in the body in complex ways. Desires are affected by culture, language, symbols, but they do not originate in culture but in the human body in Freud's theory. It is this fundamental point which is lost in Parsons' use of Freud despite some otherwise useful ideas about socialisation which Parsons developed, in particular his stress upon the values, beliefs, and cathectic symbols concerned with emotions in culture and in socialisation.

Critical theory

The group of writers known as the critical theorists included Adorno, Horkheimer, Fromm, Marcuse, and Habermas, and they were among the most important in the forging of links between a revised Marxist theory and Freudian psychoanalysis. The early work was carried out at the Frankfurt Institute which was established as an independent social research centre in 1923. It functioned in Germany until Hitler came to power in 1933. From then until 1950 the critical theorists worked in the USA, from where some returned to work in West Germany. Marcuse and Fromm remained in the New World and wrote in English, and hence they became among the best known of the critical theorists in the USA and Britain. During the first few years in the 1930s Erich Fromm had joined the Institute and had begun to formulate ways of linking Freudian ideas with the interests of the other members, such as Horkheimer, the Institute's director from 1930. Fromm came to diverge increasingly from the others once in the USA, and he severed his connections with the Institute in 1938, six years after it had moved to New York (Bottomore, 1984, p. 14).

Initially Fromm had developed the position that Freudian psychoanalysis and Marxism were both materialist theories in that they sought to explain ideology by tracing the material interests which lay behind ideologies. Marxism, however, was not able to explain all ideologies by showing the economic interests which lay behind some ideologies such as Nazism and nationalism, for sometimes there were no clear economic interests involved. The basis of the appeal of some ideologies was emotional, non-rational, and non-economic. Freudian theory could show that there were material interests of a different type involved here – unconscious, libidinal, instinctual desires. These were produced within the family in specific class situations in a given society. In Germany the role of father in many lower-middle-class families, for example, was such as to produce people seeking a strong leader to follow, an authoritarian movement and political system, not a libertarian, freedom-enhancing, set of policies. (Fromm, 1932). During the early stages of his career, up to 1939, Fromm accepted and used the Freudian theory of unconscious sexual desires, although he never used the death instinct theory as Freud was developing it in the works he published after *Beyond the Pleasure Principle* (1920). After his break with the Institute, Fromm pursued his own path moving away from Freudian theory, arguing that it overstressed sexuality, and he became more accomodating to religious beliefs and sentiments, as in *The Art of Loving* (1957), than Freud had been.

The other major critical theorist who both, like Fromm, stayed on in the United States after 1950, and who wrote explicitly about Freudian theory, was Herbert Marcuse. Marcuse was highly critical of Fromm, seeing him as a 'revisionist' within psychoanalysis. This implied, for Marcuse, that Fromm had removed the critical theoretical edge from psychoanalysis, and that he had pursued individualistic goals within private therapeutic work settings, forgetting his own earlier understanding of Freudian theory as having an important social and critical dimension which was applicable to dominant political, cultural and economic institutions (Marcuse, 1955; Bocock, 1976).

Marcuse developed his own critique of advanced capitalism, using a particular reading of Freud, in *Eros and Civilisation* (1955). In this text Marcuse used both the concept of the sexual instincts and the death instincts in ways which both Parsons and Fromm had failed to do.

The main argument Marcuse developed in *Eros and Civilisation* was that American society of the 1950s was enforcing more repression of sexuality than was needed to maintain the economic system. This Marcuse called 'surplus repression'. There was more repression of polymorphously perverse libidinal desires than was needed to maintain modern production. Indeed Marcuse went on to argue that consumption, which was being fostered by modern capitalism through new and complex forms of advertising, required some loosening of the instinctual repression – a process Marcuse termed 'repressive desublimation'. It was repressive because the desublimation which was being developed did not allow or encourage the actual satisfaction of desires, but offered substitute gratification of libidinal wishes through purchasing the goods being advertised. People had to keep working for money in order to buy the new consumer goods and experiences, such as television sets, cars, and trips, and so found no fundamental satisfaction of their desires because surplus repression was needed to remain in employment. A vicious circle was established in which pseudo-gratification was offered in return for repression and sublimation of instinctual wishes, or desires, of a libidinal kind. All this was taking place in a situation in which the weapons of nuclear warfare were being developed, and in which people were being prepared for the possibility of nuclear war between the superpowers. Marcuse wrote:

> The difference between war and peace, between civilian and military populations, between truth and propaganda, is blotted out. There is regression to historical stages that had been passed long ago, and this regression reactivates the sado-masochistic phase on a national and international scale . . . . It is with a new ease that terror is assimilated with normality, and destructiveness with construction (ibid., p. 90).

These ideas of Marcuse were a development of critical theory, and they have been regarded as unscientific both by positivists and by structuralists. They are seen as untestable and therefore as meaningless, or closer to poetry than to science by positivists, and as too evolutionary, historicist and even economistic by some structuralists such as Juliet Mitchell (see Mitchell, 1974, p. 410). Juliet Mitchell argues that Marcuse's theory contains an idea of evolutionary progress in that modern technology is seen as having reached a stage

of overcoming scarcity of material things, and thus modern capitalism does not need as much repression as it still enforces to provide
the goods. This argument traps the unconscious processes within an
economistic and historicist framework, even when it appears not to
be doing so, Mitchell argues. Structuralists try to maintain a
separation of the scientific theory of the unconscious from the
science of modes of production based upon Marxism. Critical
theorists are seen to mix the two in an incoherent way, such that the
specificity of the unconscious is lost even in the work of someone
generally sympathetic to Freudian theory such as Marcuse.

It is worthwhile to look at the work of two other critical theorists
briefly before passing to the structuralists and post-structuralists.
Two other critical theorists of some importance in the debates about
the social theory in psychoanalysis are Theodor Adorno and Jurgen
Habermas.

Adorno's work has only recently become partly available in
English translations. He held that he had to write in German in order
to be able to express his thought properly. His main work in English
was carried out using empiricist methods whilst he was in New York.
He and his co-authors had to obtain research funds and the only way
they could do so was to devise questionnaires and interviews even
though they were intellectually critical of positivist methods of this
kind. The issues for the study were derived from their experience of
the rise of Nazism in Germany. The research work in which Adorno
was involved concerned the authoritarian personality (Adorno *et al.*,
1950). This particular study formed part of a larger set of studies,
Studies in Prejudice (see Jay, 1973, pp. 234–52), in which others were
involved. Adorno used ideas from Freud on the Oedipus complex to
explain the origins of the 'authoritarian syndrome', that is the desire
for a strong leader to replace the inadequate father in the home and
the hostility to out-groups such as the Jews, or the blacks. Where the
Oedipal conflicts were poorly resolved in childhood, Adorno argued,
aggression against the father was transformed into masochistic
obedience towards a leader, and displaced sadistic hostility towards
other groups (see Jay, 1973, p. 246). This work was individualistic in
orientation, although Adorno and Horkheimer did try to provide
more social and economic analyses of the rise of Nazism and of anti-
semitism in other writings, arguing that 'bourgeois anti-semitism has
a specific economic reason; the concealment of domination in
production' (Bottomore, 1984, p. 21). Bottomore was critical of the
way anti-semitism was seen as the core of Nazism by Adorno and

Horkheimer, and of the over-concentration on cultural and personality issues to the exclusion of the economic in the writings of these critical theorists.

Jürgen Habermas belongs to the postwar generation, and his interest in critical theory and psychoanalysis reflects West Germany of the 1960s and 1970s rather than of the 1930s and 1940s. This means that Nazism is not of central concern to Habermas; the situation of postwar West European and North American capitalism is his main concern. Here in this context it is the interest which Habermas has shown in the role of psychoanalysis in social theory is of importance.

Rather than being primarily interested in the substantive theory of psychoanalysis Habermas has concentrated instead upon the significance of the therapeutic method of 'self-reflection' for the wider social goal of emancipation. In psychoanalytic encounters the analyst 'instructs the patient in reading his own texts, which he himself has mutilated and distorted, and in translating symbols from a mode of expression deformed as a private language into the mode of expression of public communication' (Habermas, 1972, p. 228). The problem for Habermas then becomes one of finding an equivalent process to that of psychoanalytic therapy of the individual at the level of social institutions. For the assumption which Habermas makes is that ideologies are distorted forms of communication and that they are in need of being interpreted rather like the dreams or symptoms of an individual.

What is not clear in Habermas is how this psychoanalytic process in deciphering the distorted forms of communication in ideologies is to take place. For an important feature of the individual's neurotic problems is that they are private and distorted forms of communication, capable of being made meaningful in the medium term with the aid of the transference in the psychoanalytic situation. It is difficult, if not impossible, to envisage an equivalent of this process for a public form of communication such as an ideology. Who is to say that an ideology is or is not a distorted form of communication? What criteria could be used to decide which ideological social practices need interpretation and which do not? Who, in other words, are to be the psychoanalysts of culture? We seem to be back to Comte's sociological priests, or Plato's philosopher kings.

The core difficulty of critical theory in both Marcuse and Habermas has turned on this problem, that in the name of democracy a small elite must educate the rest because this elite knows what the rest of us need for our own good. It is this intellectual and moral elitism in critical theory which has led many to reject it as a basis for a social theory which remains materialist and equalitarian in tone, (see Held, 1980).

Structuralism and post-structuralism

The different types of social theory, including those which use or address psychoanalysis, have arisen on the basis of different epistemological conceptions of the relation between political, moral values and social science. The positivists and neo-positivists, including Parsons, assumed that the two can be logically separated so that social theory is seen as part of science, and political theory as a branch of philosophy and ethics. Critical theorists hold that no such distinction can be maintained as a matter of logic. They hold that any proposition about social, economic, cultural and political issues is inherently caught up in language which conveys the values of those who use it. On this view it is, therefore, more honest, more objective, to reason about the values involved in a social theoretical perspective than to try to claim that a politically neutral, value free, theory can be produced. Such claims always prove to be invalid. This is not because the authors fail to live up to their own standards, and so let a value judgement slip through as it were. It is because it is logically impossible to do otherwise. Language contains such values in its roots. This cannot be avoided by a spurious move into statistics or into a mathematical language, as in some types of economic theory, because this has to be translated back into ordinary language if it is to form the basis of a policy, and so it becomes embroiled in value judgements again.

Structuralism did for a while seem to offer a way out of the impasse which social science seemed to be in. The impasse was produced by the difficulty of creating social science in a way which avoided the naive belief that one could become free of value judgements simply by asserting that one aimed to be, for this ignored the implicit and hidden nature of values in language. On the other hand it was difficult to produce works which had to be taken seriously as science using critical theory. Critical theory was often ignored in university departments because it appeared to be too partisan – on the radical side – in the eyes of many American and British social scientists. It was too easy for these groups to dismiss it as unscientific.

The structuralism of Louis Althusser, the French philosopher, was also partisan in the sense that it was Marxist. Althusser argued, however, that there were only two properly constituted social sciences, namely historical materialism, based upon his own reading and interpretation of Marx, and psychoanalysis, based upon the French psychoanalyst Jacques Lacan's reading and understanding of the work of Sigmund Freud (see Althusser, 1971). A science, in order to count as science and not ideology, has to have a theoretically constituted object as its area of study if it is to avoid studying areas set by non-scientific institutions such as dpartments of the state. In the case of Marx the object is 'mode of production', and in the case of Freudian-Lacanian psychoanalysis the object is the 'unconscious'. These objects are theoretically constituted as are the objects of the physical sciences such as 'gravity' or 'protons'. This theoretical constitution of the object is not seen as a reason to ignore these sciences, as in Anglo-Saxon ideology, on the grounds that they are unverifiable or unfalsifiable, but as their major strength.

Structuralism, then, offered a way of establishing a firm basis for two social sciences (historical materialism and psychoanlysis) as theoretically constituted areas of study which avoided the naivety of positivism on the one hand and the collapse into ideology, as distinct from science, of critical theory on the other hand. What went wrong?

Two major types of criticism emerged of Althusserian structuralism. First, at the level of epistemology, it has been difficult to find rigourous and sustainable ways of distinguishing science from ideology. One person's science is another person's ideology, it has been argued. Second, at the level of politics and psychoanalytic work more substantive criticisms have been made of Althusser and Lacan respectively.

To deal with the first point very briefly, for it is too complex to be discussed here in detail, either it is the case that everything is ideology in the area of social affairs and no sciences are possible, or some criteria do exist for distinguishing 'science' from 'ideology' when social matters are being discussed. If the first proposition is accepted, then only force can settle which kind of social, religious, political and economic system exists in any given territory, for rational discussion cannot be of any avail if all is ideology and ideologies are defined as discourses which are outside of any rational criteria for determining sense and correctness. If it is thought that some rational criteria can be arrived at for deciding between different ideologies, then it becomes possible to rate ideologies in terms of their internal consistency, and their commitment to rationality itself. If this is done then it is possible to assert that some ideologies are more rational than others. One could then agree to define as 'sciences' those rationally organised ideologies which are committed to rationality being increased in a society, with all that that commitment entails in terms of social institutions such as universities, and freedom of publication. This criterion is one which Althusser would not accept as he would see it as being too Hegelian and 'idealist' in its stress upon 'reason'.

However, it is possible to see reason at work in concrete social institutions in some societies and not in others. Reasoning is not, therefore, an inherently idealist notion, having no material basis. The absence of the value of reason, or science, is all too materialist in its consequences in those societies which torture writers and free thinkers. The commitment to reason is not idealist in the sense that it is vacuous at the level of concrete social institutions.

Whilst it may be the case that Althusser never adequately stated the difference between his notions of science and ideology, it is not the case in my view that such a distinction cannot be made. If it is made, as above, a way could be found to bring critical theory back in from the cold, for it too has created some rationally organised theory which can count as contributions to science, to both historical materialism and to psychoanalytic social theory.

Structuralists have had an understanding of the importance of the role of theory as constituting a scientific area, unlike positivists who have stressed 'scientific method', which is difficult if not impossible to define. The emphasis upon the theoretical constitution of sciences made by structuralists is a valuable contribution, and a point acceptable to critical theorists such as Habermas.

The second set of points about structuralism are more substantive. Here those points made in criticism of structuralist psychoanalysis will be mentioned after the major points contributed by Lacan have been outlined. However, these are almost impossible to specify, precisely because Lacan wanted to avoid being popularised in secondary sources such as this chapter in this book. He wrote, therefore, in a style which is very difficult to read and impossible to summarise. This was because many of the writings were produced for a series of seminars which were originally designed for training psychoanalysts, and as part of psychoanalytic praxis as Lacan saw it (see Lacan, 1977, p. 61). Lacan defined psychoanalysis as the science whose object is the 'unconscious' (ibid., p. 8). The unconscious is defined in a new way by Freud, Lacan claims. It is not the 'unconscious as instinct', as in Wilhelm Reich. Lacan says 'The unconscious is the sum of the effects of speech on a subject, at the level at which the subject constitutes himself out of the effects of the signifier' (ibid., p. 126). The subject is not some substance, a personality system, nor an ego, an I, as in American psychoanalysis which Lacan saw as a departure from Freud's radical discovery of the unconscious. The subject appears as an effect of language and as an ideological construct, as Althusser was to express the point, not as given outside of language, culture, or society, as in religious notions of the soul and their secular derivatives in modern American ideology and ego psychology.

The Lacanian understanding of psychoanalysis as a science of the unconscious, this being seen as structured like a language, is a major shift away from individualistic conceptions and practices in psychotherapy and in some forms of social work practice. The Lacanian conception of the unconscious in Freudian theory and therapy emphasises splits, alienation, the lack of autonomous control for anyone in modern societies, gaps in our self-understanding, and above all, the flows of desire outside, underneath, and on top of the conventions and social institutions which seek to contain them. The Lacanian and Althusserian emphasis is, therefore, upon a deeper conceptualisation of the point made in much sociology, whether structuralist, Marxist or Durkheimian, that modern individualism is a social, cultural product and not given by human biology. In other words, the notions of individuality, 'doing your own thing', personal growth and achievement, and conceptions of individual responsibility, which pervade modern middle-class ideologies and popularisations of psychotherapy, are seen as ideological maskings of the underlying structural components of modern life.

Lacan's approach has had considerable influence in France (see Turkle, 1978) and in Britain (see Mitchell, 1974; MacCabe, 1981). This influence has been not so much upon professional psychoanalysts, who accused Lacan of intellectualisation (see Lacan, 1977, p. 133), even though a Lacanian school of analysts developed in France, as upon researchers on the mass media and upon some feminists. The reasons for the Lacanian approach taking off are partly intellectual ones, as discussed briefly above, and partly political. The events of May 1968 in Paris were of major significance in this context. The external failure of the workers' and students' revolt against the Gaullist state and its educational institutions led to a reassessment of the best areas in which to work for change if the major political and economic framework was to remain. This entailed work on the means of cultural production and their role in maintaining ideological versions of social affairs, which included the mass media and the schools and colleges, and therapeutic work upon the unconscious. Many turned to Lacanian psychoanalysis to further their interest in this area. Some found paid employment in psychiatric hospitals and clinics in France, which was seen as an important area of operations by many after the events of 1968, partly because such work did not entail too much distortion of oneself to fit the capitalist system which other kinds of paid work would do, and partly because the patients were seen as victims of the system in need of care, if not as potential rebels.

Later critics of Lacan emerged, primarily in France. These critics built upon Lacan's work whilst being critical of it in certain key respects. The most important of these critics have been the philosopher Gilles Deleuze and the anti-psychiatrist Félix Guattarri. Their book *Anti-Oedipus* was first published in French in 1972, and in English translation in 1977. They have in turn influenced Guy Hocquenghem in his book *Homosexual Desire* (1978).

These authors are critical of Lacan for maintaining the centrality of oedipus within psychoanalysis. They want to treat oedipisation, that is the process whereby a person is 'constructed' to work, to consume and to reproduce within the nuclear family, as a process that is not essential nor universal. They read Lacan as maintaining, like Freud, that oedipisation is a necessary and universal event – the entry of the subject into the symbolic, or culture, whose central component is what Lacan termed 'the Law of the Father'. Schizophrenics are one group who resist this process of oedipisation; but there is a schizoid part of everyone which has tried to refuse full oedipisation on this view. For Deleuze and Guattari it is the task of what they term 'schizo-analysis' to reveal this and help people to function in modern conditions.

Theoretically, Deleuze and Guattari insist on linking two economies: the economy of material production analysed by Marx, and the economy of libidinal desires analysed by Freud. This returns them to many themes to be found in the work of Wilhelm Reich – especially in the links they try to make between historical materialism and Freudian psychoanalysis. Structuralism insisted initially upon the separation of the sciences with distinct objects – historical materialism for the analysis of modes of production, and psychoanalysis for the analysis of the unconscious. The work of Deleuze and Guattari breaks with this methodology and epistemology by insisting upon fusions. For example, man and nature are to be fused and not separated as in the work of the structuralist anthropologist Claude Lévi-Strauss, as the production of desires and of goods are fused. They wrote for instance: 'There is no such thing as either man or nature now, only a process that produces the one within the other and couples machines together. Producing-machines, desiring-machines everywhere, schizophrenic machines, all of species life: the self and the non-self, outside and inside, no longer have any meaning whatsoever' (Deleuze and Guattari, 1977), p. 2).

Hocquenghem (1978) develops the main theme of *Anti-Oedipus* with specific reference to homosexuality, particularly male homosexuality and its eroticism of the anus as well as of the male body in general. Patriarchal societies of the capitalist West, and of the communist East, find homosexuality a threat to the preparation for war, and to the family. Homosexual desire is not a problem for anti-oedipal schizo-analysis, as it has been for most forms of psychoanalysis, for it is just one channel desire may flow into. But patriarchal cultures require oedipisation and, therefore, a taboo upon homosexuality, especially male homosexuality. This is because males are involved in warfare and preparations for warfare. Males who erotically relate to other males are seen as a threat to discipline in the armed forces and as poor fighters. 'The problem is not so much homosexual desire as the fear of homosexuality: why does the mere mention of the word trigger off reactions of recoil and hate?' (Hocquenghem, 1977, p. 35).

Post-structuralists have left behind the intellectual rigour of earlier forms of structuralism and have moved into new territory. One could say that the attempts to overcome patriarchy in the gay men's movement and in the women's movement are the new areas for the attempt to link theory and praxis, and that post-structuralism finds its relevance in these new social movements.

What are the implications of this kind of psychoanalytic social theory for social workers? There are two main ones. First, the awareness of the links which have been made in the last six decades between psychoanalysis and social theory should help to change perceptions social workers may have had of psychoanalysis. An important dimension of this changed perception is that of the social implications of psychoanalysis – that it is not only a therapeutic perspective upon individual personality, but that it also contains a perspective with application to authority relations in various social situations, to gender and sexuality, and to problems between ethnic groups, for instance.

A second major implication of psychoanalytic social theory for social workers lies in the area of professional authority issues. In the English-speaking world, largely as a result of the dominance of empiricism in the culture, the issues about the professional authority of social workers are seen in terms of a dichotomy: 'science or religion' (see Halmos, 1965). In other words social workers and counsellors are seen as not being applied scientists, which is something some have tried to claim they are, but as being 'secular priests' (North, 1972). Their authority and social licence to practice stems from their connection with Christianity and its values of care and love for the poor, sick, old, and delinquent. On this view social workers are secularised versions of clergy and nuns and perform similar kinds of good works.

An alternative view of professional authority is, however, possible. On this view there is a realm of philosophy and social theory which can give a grounding to claims to authority and a licence to practice for social workers. This kind of theoretical knowledge is neither 'science' in the way natural sciences are, nor does it follow that it must therefore be religious. The alternative is to claim that philosophically-grounded social theory, of the kind considered in this chapter, can provide a valid claim to professional authority for social workers, and one which avoids the narrowness of a purely individualistic approach which earlier uses of psychoanalysis in social work had.

2 Psychoanalysis: The Third Culture?[1]

Stephen Wilson

In his 1959 Rede lecture, C. P. Snow suggested that a division existed in intellectual society between two cultures. He pointed to a surprisingly wide and deep gulf in attitudes, standards, patterns of behaviour, common approaches and assumptions that had grown between scientists and those educated in the arts; with literary intellectuals at one pole and physical scientists at the other. He described how highly intelligent people, standing on either side of this gulf were unable to communicate because they had little understanding of each other's discipline. Each group was isolated in its own world with its own language. Snow felt that this division unnecessarily impoverished our lives; he felt that science and art could be mutually enriching if they were brought together and 'assimilated along with, and as part and parcel of, the whole of our mental experience' (Snow, 1959, p. 16).

Psychoanalysis is not and never has been easy to define. It comprises both a clinical method and a way of looking at the mind – a technique, perhaps an art and a body of systematic observations, perhaps a science. It exists in the world of ideas and is kept alive as a growing and developing entity by those who study and practice it. Though it remains rooted in the work of Freud, it can now no longer be solely identified with his writing, nor are its practitioners limited to the membership of psychoanalytic institutes (Rycroft, 1985). It belongs to humanity for the benefit of mankind, not to any establishment or professional guild; and it follows that what it has to offer should be available to stimulate the imagination and inform the thinking and practice of contemporary social workers. It represents perhaps a 'third culture'.

But what does psychoanalysis have to offer? Clearly it is concerned with human mentality and behaviour, but it is not this concern which distinguishes psychoanalysis from other branches of enquiry. As Gilbert Ryle long ago pointed out in his book *The Concept of Mind*, historians, philologists, literary critics, dramatists, novelists and many others have for thousands of years been studying the deeds, words, opinions, thoughts, feelings, habits, weaknesses and strengths of men and women; which alone deserve the title 'mental phenomena'. In modern times, too, scientific psychologists, underpinning their work with a positivistic empiricist philosophy, have made determined efforts to apply the experimental method to the study of mental events.

Psychoanalysis, however, is none of these things; and if we wish to understand the special contribution that it has to make we must look not to its subject matter, but to its method and its conceptual framework. The web of psychoanalytic knowledge hangs delicately by a thread from its central concept 'transference', while the psychoanalytical method is designed to create optimal conditions for the development of the relationship which this concept denotes. Its epistemology consists in the study of precisely what inferences can be drawn from the experiences occurring in the consulting room.

The psychoanalytical method

The roots of the psychoanalytical method, as it is practised now, reach back to the turn of the century and can be seen most clearly in Freud's 'Fragment of an Analysis of a Case of Hysteria' familiarly known as 'Dora'. This case is as compelling to study today as it plainly was to Freud in 1901: and it is evident from the following exultant passage that he felt it had led him to a major discovery:

> When I set myself the task of bringing to light what human beings keep hidden within them, not by the compelling power of hypnosis, but by observing what they say and what they show, I thought the task was a harder one than it really is. He that has eyes to see and ears to hear may convince himself that no mortal can keep a secret. If his lips are silent, he chatters with his finger-tips; betrayal oozes out of him at every pore. And thus the task of making conscious the most hidden recesses of the mind is one which it is quite possible to accomplish (*Standard Edition* vol. 7, pp. 77–8).

What was it that Freud had discovered? On the face of it as he pointed out the case seemed a medical commonplace, hardly worth presenting: an 18-year-old girl with a long history of nervous cough, shortness of breath, loss of voice and possible migraines in childhood had become withdrawn and depressed. She had consulted many doctors over the years, all of whom had been unable to cure her symptoms; and she had as a consequence developed a lofty contempt for medical efforts. Nevertheless, when she left a suicidal note in a place where her parents would find it, and subsequently after an altercation with her father appeared to have some kind of convulsive fit, they insisted she came to Freud for treatment.

Dora's father was convinced that her symptoms were linked with an episode alleged to have occurred when she was 16 and spending the summer holiday with old family friends, the Ks by a lake in the Alps. Dora had told her parents that Herr K made a sexual advance towards her, causing her to cut short the vacation and return home: but when confronted with this, Herr K totally denied it, insisting that the episode was a figment of the girl's imagination. Dora herself recounted to Freud an even earlier episode in which, when she was 14, Herr K had invited her to his office, ostensibly to watch a Church fete. He had engineered a situation whereby they would be alone together and taken advantage of it to suddenly steal a passionate kiss on the lips. According to Dora, at this point she felt an intense feeling of disgust, tore herself free and rushed out into the street. Nevertheless they continued to meet on social occasions without any mention of the secret happenings. The situation was further complicated by Dora's conviction that her father suffered from venereal disease and was having an affair with Frau K.

Freud concluded that Dora's own sexuality had been aroused by these events, and that the symptoms represented a symbolic transformation of her desires. At one point in the treatment it became clear that Dora was worried she had inherited her father's venereal disease, which was the cause of her persistent longstanding white vaginal discharge. When Freud suggested that this leucorrhoea was more likely to be due to masturbation, she denied any knowledge of such a practice. Notwithstanding this a few days later she came to an analytical session wearing for the first time a small reticule round her waist. As she lay on Freud's sofa talking, he noticed that she kept playing with it, opening it, putting her finger into it, shutting it again, and so on. He was left in no doubt as to the meaning of this 'symptomatic act' which clearly could be taken to represent mastur-bation thus confirming his earlier suspicions.

What a person said and did during their consultations began to take on a new light for Freud; he saw that a patient's communications should be taken not only at their face value, but also as symbolic representations carrying hidden messages. More than this, he began to see that people not only gave expression to their desires in this way, but that they were driven inexorably to do so. As the philosopher Susan Langer put it:

> The great contribution of Freud to the philosophy of mind has been the realisation that human behaviour is not only a food-getting strategy, but is also a language; that every move is a gesture. Symbolization is both an end and an instrument . . . . The fact is I believe that it did not originate purely in the service of other activities. It is a primary interest, and may require a sacrifice of other ends, just as the imperative demand for food or sex-life may necessitate sacrifices under different conditions (1942, p. 51).

It was but a short step from this realisation for the idea to suggest itself to Freud that he himself had been used by Dora for purposes of symbolic representation. Thus, it dawned on him that not only had he replaced her father in her imagination at the beginning of the analysis but that her sudden termination of the treatment represented a re-enactment of her flight from Herr K's house; an action Freud had previously interpreted as a wish to escape from the expression of her own feelings of sexual attraction towards Herr K. It was borne in on Freud that the psychoanalytical setting presented an ideal theatre for the symbolic re-enactment of hidden conflicts of this sort.

Here then was a methodological tool of immense importance for it now seemed that the old 'archaeological' model of analysis, rooting around in the patients recollections for 'traumatic events', could be superceded by a new and far more powerful source of information. As Freud put it in his seminal essay on 'Remembering, Repeating and Working-Through' (1914, p. 150):

> we may say that the patient does not *remember* anything of what he has forgotten and repressed, but acts it out. He reproduces it not as a memory but as an action; he *repeats* it, without, of course, knowing that he is repeating it. For instance, the patient does not say that he remembers that he used to be defiant and critical towards his parent's authority; instead, he behaves in that way to the doctor. He does not remember how he came to a helpless and hopeless deadlock in his infantile sexual researches; but he produces a mass of confused dreams and associations; complains that he cannot succeed in anything and asserts that he is fated never

to carry through what he undertakes. He does not remember having been intensely ashamed of certain sexual activities and afraid of them being found out; but he makes it clear that he is ashamed of the treatment on which he is now embarked and tries to keep it secret from everybody.

With this kind of data to be plumbed, the aims of the psychoanalytical method became clearer: namely, to provide a kind of playground in which the compulsion to repeat earlier experiences could be given expression and then thought about. Thomas Szasz (1963) put it succinctly when he said: 'Just as the pre-Freudian physician was ineffective partly because he remained a fully 'real' person, so the psychoanalyst may be ineffective if he remains a fully 'symbolic' object. The analytic situation requires the therapist to function as both. Without these conditions 'analysis' cannot take place.'

A setting that allowed the creation of an intermediate world somewhere between pure phantasy and real life was required, and the techniques for achieving this had to be developed. These quite simply depended on the analyst's stability, reliability, tolerance, restraint, and friendly non-judgemental attitude combined with an uncompromising determination to search for the truth.

No special skill in reasoning is needed to see immediately a formidable logical objection to this psychoanalytical method. What if Freud were wrong? How can we be sure that when Dora played with her reticule, Freud was correct in imputing the meaning of masturbation or that when she suddenly broke off her treatment with him she was re-enacting her flight from Herr K's house? Freud himself raises the question when he says: 'Transference is the one thing the presence of which has to be detected almost without assistance and with only the slightest clues to go upon, while at the same time the risk of making arbitary inferences has to be avoided' (1905b, p. 116).

To put it another way, what principles can establish whether a particular interpretation of the meaning of a given symbol is correct? An interesting paradigm for this problem is created when a dictionary definition of a word is challenged in the courts. If for example a dictionary asserts that the meaning of the word 'Hoover' is a 'vacuum cleaner' and the Hoover manufacturing company contest this interpretation on the grounds that the word refers only to those cleaning machines manufactured by themselves, the publishers of the dictionary will be required to prove that their definition is correct. In order to do so they must turn to 'usage', for there is no final arbiter, no other source that can authoritatively adjudicate the meaning of a symbol. Nor can this meaning be fixed, since usage changes with the elapse of time. They will have to search for citations in current newspapers and books that demonstrate beyond doubt from their context that the word can be and is being used in a particular way.

Freud follows a similar procedure, adducing evidence from usage: fairy-tales, literature, jokes, slang, other languages, roots of words, slips of the tongue, and contextual settings. All are brought into play in order to add weight to his interpretations. It is certainly not difficult on this basis to demonstrate that a reticule can mean the female genital. Indeed, Freud produces an amusing and convincing account of another of his patients bringing out a small ivory box during a consultation ostensibly to refresh herself with a sweet. Finding the box difficult to open, in a state of agitation, she eventually handed it to Freud; it must mean something very special, he said, since it was the first time he had seen it although she had been coming for more than a year. She immediately replied, 'I always have this box about me; I take it with me wherever I go.' Freud comments: 'She did not calm down until I pointed out to her with a laugh how well her words were adapted to quite another meaning. The box like the reticule and the Jewel Case, was once again only a substitute for the shell of Venus, for the female genital' (1905b).

But a symbol can be used in an idiosyncratic way; how can we be sure that in any particular case we have arrived at a correct understanding of its meaning? The answer, I think, is that we cannot be sure, nor can we ever prove or disprove a meaning; for meanings are no more susceptible to the methods of Newtonian physics than billiard balls are to an understanding of dinner-table conversation! To quote Langer once again:

> If we follow the methods of natural science our psychology tends to run into physiology, histology and genetics; we move further and further away from those problems which we ought to be approaching. That signifies that the generative idea which gave rise to physics and chemistry and all their progeny, technology, medicine, biology does not contain any vivifying concepts for the humanistic sciences. The physicists' scheme so faithfully emulated

by generations of psychologists, epistemologists and aestheticians is probably blocking their progress, defeating possible insights by its prejudicial force. The scheme is not false, it is perfectly reasonable, but it is bootless for the study of mental phenomena. It does not engender leading questions and excite a constructive imagination, as it does in physical researches. Instead of a method, it inspires a militant methodology (p. 24).

However, although it may be beside the point to attempt to prove or disprove the correctness of a given interpretation, it does not follow that all interpretations are of equal value. We may continue to ask whether our interpretation adequately covers the data at hand, whether it enriches or impoverishes the symbolic universe, whether it fits into a consistent pattern and articulates with other meanings; and though we can never prove it, still it may or may not be true and has to be taken account of in our deliberations.

Psychoanalytical concepts

Most of us are exquisitely sensitive to any failure in the environment to recognise our qualities or to take account of our needs. This is not surprising as we all start life with a multitude of needs, a minimal ability to communicate them and a total dependence on others for their satisfaction. It seems obvious therefore that early frustration must be an inevitable part of the human condition. Just how this is experienced by any particular baby would remain forever unknowable and a matter for speculation unless it were true that the examination of transference in the psychoanalytical situation really tells us something about the past.

It is idle to ruminate on this problem however, since there is no way it can be resolved. What seems more useful is to recognise that transference is a descriptive term, allowing us to outline the regressive phenomena that obtrude so forcefully on attention during the heat of the psychoanalytical moment. Transference is a special experience, an event in the here and now. We say that transference love is infantile, and mean that it seems to us to have the qualities we would not be surprised to find in an infant's emotional life, if only we had direct access to it.

If *transference* is the name given to the process whereby the analyst comes to be used as a living symbol for the reanimation of unconscious infantile conflicts, a careful study of this process should be able to tell us something about the way in which symbols are formed. Fortunately, the analyst is able to make use of his own subjective responses in order to carry out this investigation. This activity is essentially introspective and is set in motion and nurtured during the course of his experience as a patient. It is this self-analytic capacity that enables him to examine his *counter-transference* and use it as a tool for discovery (Heinmann, 1960; Racker, 1968).

The dramaturgical analogy I alluded to earlier helps us to a better understanding of this. It is as if there exists in the mind of the patient a play of which he himself is unaware yet which he inadvertently directs. The cast consists of a wide range of people and objects in his life, but gradually, as he becomes involved in the analytical process, a new performance is produced within the confines of the consulting room. The psychoanalyst is required to take many roles in this play, and by listening to the instructions of the unconscious director and above all recognising his own emotional responses, he slowly comes to unravel both the script of the play and the character of the director. He is then in a position to report back to his patient what he has noticed and discuss the intricacies of the plot. Needless to say he must refrain from actually taking part in the drama!

This, then, is what a modern psychoanalyst is able to reconstruct: not so much a veridical version of the past but a fiction that makes the present intelligible and adds coherence to a person's picture of himself. He is a kind of poet rather than a kind of archeologist (Spence, 1982; Kermode, 1985).

While with adult patients the arcane drama of transference often requires laborious effort to demonstrate, since if offends against 'common sense' (Money-Kyrle, 1956), in material derived from child psychoanalysis we can see the process displayed with graphic clarity. Consider the following short example from the analysis of a very troubled 6-year-old girl treated by Melanie Klein (1932).

> Erna began her play by taking a small carriage which stood on the little table among the other toys and letting it run towards me. She declared that she had come to fetch me. But she put a toy woman in the carriage instead and added a toy man. The two loved and kissed one another and drove up and down all the time. Next a toy man in another carriage collided with them, ran over them and killed them, and then roasted and ate them up. Another time the fight had a different ending and the attacking toy man was thrown

down; but the woman helped him and comforted him. She got a divorce from her first husband and married the new one. This third person was given the most various parts to play in Erna's games. For instance, the original man and his wife were in a house which they were defending against a burglar; the third person was the burglar and slipped in. The house burnt down, the man and woman burnt and the third person was the only one left. Then again the third person was a brother who came on a visit; but while embracing the woman he bit her nose off.

From this and other material, Mrs Klein was able to infer that the little man, the third person, was none other than Erna herself, while of course the woman in the carriage, said by Erna to be Mrs Klein, clearly also represented Erna's mother. Erna had expressed her destructive wishes towards the parents' intercourse, as well as her primitive wish to eat them. At the same time she had also shown the intricate and paradoxical organisation of her conflict; for while she clearly wished to oust her father and marry her mother (*negative oedipus complex*), who was portrayed as helpful and comforting in one scenario, she attacked her unmercifully in another. Later still, she demonstrated her wish to be rid of mother altogether and to win father (*direct oedipus complex*). Thus she made a toy teacher throw down his book and dance with his girl pupil, kissing and embracing her. Then she suddenly asked Mrs Klein if she would allow a marriage between teacher and pupil.

During the course of the analysis (Klein, 1929) Erna often required Mrs Klein to play the part of a child, while she took the role of mother and teacher. At those times the child had to undergo fantastic tortures and humiliations. She was constantly spied on, and her parents ganged up against her, while she herself spied upon and tormented others. At other times Erna herself played the part of the child, and the game generally ended in her escaping persecution, becoming rich and powerful, being made a queen and taking cruel revenge. But this consistently led to a reaction, in the form of deep depression, anxiety, and bodily exhaustion.

With the advent of Melanie Klein's play technique of child analysis, we can see that a vast world of unconscious child phantasy was laid patent, a noumenal world in which all of us live, every bit as real as the phenomenal world of external reality. Careful observation then enabled Mrs Klein to make use of this rich source in formulating some new and far-reaching ideas. The process of symbol construction, in its most primitive form began to be comprehended in terms of the infant's need to cope with overwhelming anxiety (Klein 1930). Where the world was unacceptably threatening, it seemed that from childhood onwards we altered it by the simple expedient of omnipotent phantasy.

Of course analysts had long been familiar with the concept of infantile omnipotence and hallucinatory wish-fulfillment – Freud's *pleasure principle* (1911b) – for the way we make reality tolerable, the distortions we impose upon reality are leitmotifs in psychoanalytical thinking. But this had previously always been conceptualised as a unitary process concerning the magical experience of dealing with frustration through hallucination of a good and gratifying object.

What impressed Klein again and again was the spontaneous creation, as in Erna's case of two groups of symbols, representing both extremely good *and* extremely bad characteristics: the complicated mixtures of qualities inherent in real people appeared to be reorganised into much simpler schematic structures. Children, it seemed created their own gods and devils without the help of organised religion! It is easy to see why there should be a need for powerful gods that can comfort us and temper anxiety arising from helplessness, but it is more difficult to understand the necessity for devils. What Mrs Klein saw was the unavoidable duality of the phenomenon, that for every idealised object generated a reciprocal diabolic object was of necessity brought into being, the existence of which had perforce to be denied. 'Splitting' was intimately linked with *idealisation* and *introjection* of the good and its correlative, *denial* and *projection* of the bad. More than this, our adult characters were seen to be rooted in these fundamental processes, and to depend for development on their successful accomplishment (Klein, 1946).

The formation of mind was thus placed in a familiar age old pattern of creative myth. Just as the book of Genesis describes the creation of a firmament as the first step in giving form to chaos and void, so Klein in her psychoanalytical poem saw differentiation in the *paranoid-schizoid position* as the foundation of psychological growth. Failure to make a clear distinction between love and hate, led to further difficulties in distinguishing between self and object, inside and outside – a state of confusion; while an excessively profound split inhibited later integration and carried the danger of a complete divorce from external reality. Adequate splitting however modulated anxiety and allowed progress to occur towards a greater tolerance of imperfect things. The *idealised object* could then give way to a mere *good object* or in other words an object whose mixed qualities were recognised and acknowledged but whose 'badness' had been forgiven. This process was accompanied by a profound change in values. Meltzer (1973) saw it in the following way:

> Where this primary splitting and idealisation of infant self and objects has satisfactorily taken place, where the parental services are reasonably adequate, where neither jealousy, envy nor intolerance to mental pain are excessive, a miraculous and beautiful thing tends to take place, known in flat scientific jargon as 'the phenomenology of the depressive position'. In the language of life, tender concern for the welfare of the beloved object tends to supercede selfish concern for the comfort and safety of the self. The capacity for sacrifice emerges – babies wait for their feeds instead of screaming, leave off sucking when more is still available in breast or bottle, try to control their sphincters to spare the mother, bear separation despite worry. Out of obedience, goodness emerges; out of competitiveness, the capacity to work; out of toleration of deprivation, pride in development.

The description of these developmental processes had important consequences for the programme of psychoanalysis. Clearly what analysts were able to 'see' being re-enacted in the transference depended to a large extent on how they viewed the original infantile course of events. Where Freud had focused on the vicissitudes of biologically determined instinctual phases and the negotiation of the oedipus triangle leading to 'genital' character formation, a process driven by *castration anxiety*, Klein shifted the emphasis on to the subtle interplay of projective and introjective processes in earliest infancy, leading to the *depressive position* – a state of mind characterised by the capacity to bear remorseful feelings and the willing acceptance of the wish to make reparation.

The aims of psychoanalysis

The therapeutic aims of psychoanalysis have been reformulated over the years in the light of clinical experience, and in order to keep pace with changes in the model of the mind being used. In the early days, Freud was able to state its aim quite simply – to make what was unconscious conscious. This was in keeping with the relatively simple topographical model he had put forward (Freud, 1915a) dividing the mind into two regions – unconscious and conscious – between which was located a censor whose job it was to prevent unacceptable wishes moving from one place to the other. It also squared with the early clinical experiences described in *Studies on Hysteria*. Anna O, Breuer's hysterical young patient, suffered among other things from horrifying hallucinations of death's heads and skeletons during the day, but she was able to cure herself by inducing a state of auto-hypnotism at night which she called 'clouds', in which she narrated in detail her daytime troubles so that she woke up calm and cheerful. It seemed consistent to hypothesise that the hypnotic state had allowed consciousness access to some of the contents of the unconscious and in doing so had somehow disarmed them.

This model of the mind, however, was inadequate to cover the burgeoning clinical data Freud was accumulating. In particular resistance to free association, masochism, and melancholia presented problems for the topographical model. According to the model, the 'unconscious' was conflict-free, unaware of contradications, and interested only in seeking pleasure; censorious and repressing forces, however were supposed to be located only in the sphere of the 'conscious'. But Freud was regularly encountering blocks to his clinical investigations of which his patients were quite unaware, and punishment seeking behaviour which forced him to postulate an 'unconscious sense of guilt'.

Eventually he lost interest in the distinction conscious/unconscious (somewhat surprisingly warning us to emancipate ourselves from the importance of the 'symptom' of consciousness), and reformulated his model in terms of the relationship between three mental agencies or structures known to the English speaking world as the ego, the id, and the superego (1923). It is true that he continued to speak of the id being unconscious and the superego dipping down into the unconscious, but the primary concern was now clearly the nature of the relationship between them. In this model, the ego was portrayed as a servant required to work for three masters and constantly torn between their demands: the demands of the id for instinctual gratification, the demands of the superego for obedience and renunciation, and the limitations imposed by external reality.

Symptoms were now seen as arising from an imbalance between the three mental structures – for example, an excessively punitive superego, or an excessively weak ego; and Freud, in a famous

passage, was able to liken the work of psychoanalysis in strengthen-
ing the ego to that of land reclamation:

> Its intention is, indeed, to strengthen the ego, to make it more
> independent of the superego, to widen its field of perception and
> enlarge its organisation, so that it can appropriate fresh portions of
> the id. Where id was, there ego shall be. It is a work of culture –
> not unlike the draining of the Zuider Zee (1933a).

But how was this to be accomplished? How, for instance to render
the ego more independent of the superego, well known to be
extremely severe in small children even when their parents are mild
and benign?

Using Klein's conceptualisation of the superego as an archaic
internal object, essentially influenced by the child's own aggression,
amplified in a vicious circle of projection and re-introjection,
Strachey (1934) was able to come up with an answer. The analyst's
role was to act as an auxiliary superego that could help to break the
vicious circle by making 'mutative interpretations':

> If all goes well the patient's ego will become aware of the
> contrast between the aggressive character of his feelings and the
> real nature of the analyst, who does not behave like the patients
> 'good' and 'bad' archaic objects. The patient, that is to say, will
> become aware of a distinction between his archaic object and the
> real external object. The interpretation has now become a
> mutative one since it has produced a breach in the neurotic vicious
> circle. For the patient, having become aware of the lack of
> aggressiveness in the real external object, will be able to diminish
> his own aggressiveness; the new object he introjects will be less
> aggressive, and consequently the aggressiveness of his superego
> will be diminished.

Note that in this formulation the analyst's role is essentially a
negative one, he facilitates change by *not* behaving in accord with
expectations derived from the patient's unconscious phantasies. The
disjunction thus created stimulates mental work on the part of the
patient to accommodate the 'reality' he is confronted with. He has to
'adjust' his phantasies. But this model also only goes part of the way
towards a satisfactory description of the psychoanalytical relationship. It was left to Wilfred Bion (1973, 1977) to provide a fuller
account.

Perhaps as a result of his work with psychotic patients (who were not prepared to adjust their phantasies so easily), Bion was led to a more positive conception both of the role of the mother in the development of infant mentation and of course of the analyst in the transference relationship. In this view, when mental pain arises it can either be dealt with by being converted into thoughts and symbols (what Bion called alpha function), which can then be subject to further modification by the process of 'thinking'; or it can be evacuated in its raw non-symbolic form (beta elements), and transferred into another object. What this means in terms of infant care is that where the child lacks the ability to transform pain into thoughts, the mother can do this work for him and thus actively help the development of mind. In order to accomplish this, of course, she has to tolerate a great deal of pain herself. She has to 'contain' and 'metabolise' the infant's projections.

This is how Bion imagines the situation of a baby who is very upset and perhaps afraid of some impending disaster, which it expresses by crying:

> Suppose the mother picks up the baby and comforts it, is not at all disorganised or distressed, but makes some soothing response. The distressed infant can feel that by its screams or yells, it has expelled those feelings of impending disaster into the mother. The mother's response can be felt to detoxicate the evacuation of the infant; the sense of impending disaster is modified by the mother's reaction and can then be taken back into itself by the baby. Having got rid of a sense of impending disaster, the infant gets back something which is far more tolerable. Susan Isaacs has described a situation in which the baby could be heard saying something like 'oo el, oo el', which the mother recognised as an imitation of herself saying 'well, well'. In that way the infant was able to feel comforted by a good mother inside and could make reassuring, comforting noises to itself exactly as if the mother was there all the time (1973).

But the mother is only able to do this by virtue of her own capacity for 'alpha function'. If this is impaired she will react irritably and anxiously towards her child; forcing the infant to take back into itself the sense of impending disaster, which only worsens the original situation and sets up a vicious circle. Once again we can extrapolate to the analytical situation, seeing the function of the analyst as analagous to that of the mother. He must break the vicious circle but this time actively, using his own capacity for giving symbolic expression to inchoate pain and thus bringing it within the domain of thought.

When Melanie Klein transformed Freud's structural agencies into 'internal objects' located in an interior world of phantasy she had clearly taken a step that profoundly altered the nature of psycho-analysis both as theory and therapy (Meltzer, 1984; Wisdom, 1984). She had thrust psychoanalysis from its closed system of scientific energetics into the open system of an imaginative, artistic discipline, and in doing so laid the foundation for contemporary object-relational psychology. It remained for Wilfred Bion and others to develop this open system of imagination and hone it into a clinical tool capable of helping people give form to their most ineffable anxieties and thus to suffer them.

Note

1.   I should like to thank Dr Kate Wilson and Ms Connie Wilsack for their editorial help during the preparation of this chapter. Many thanks are also due to Mrs Pat Finlay for patient secretarial assistance.

3 Feminism, Social Work, and Psychoanalysis[1]

Janet Sayers

Women social workers and their women clients share a common oppression in so far as they are both treated less well than men because of their sex. Women are concentrated in the lowest and least well-paid ranks of social work and have much less power than those in higher levels of the profession to determine either their own conditions of work or the overall character of the service provided to clients by social workers. Similarly, in non-professional jobs, women are concentrated in poorly paid, 'un-skilled' work, often with few of the fringe benefits – training, paid holidays, sick leave, and pensions associated with 'skilled' employment. And because women are less well paid than men both in middle- and working-class occupations they often find themselves economically dependent on men, or on the state where they have no one else financially to support them. Women's lack of economic independence also results from the fact that even when they take on potentially well-paid jobs, either say as social workers or as factory operatives, their domestic commitments prevent them working on a full-time basis in these jobs, or doing the shift work or overtime that might secure them the same wages as men. And this reflects another inequality between the sexes, namely the fact that domestic work and the care of dependent members of society involved in that work – care of children, the sick, handicapped, and aged – falls primarily to women.

The inequalities between the sexes suffered by women both at home and at work are a major cause of the resurgence of feminism in our times. The place of psychoanalysis within this resurgence has been ambiguous. On the one hand feminists, like social workers, are wary of psychoanalysis. It all too often seeks to adjust people to the social inequalities that oppress them rather than help them to question and change the social conditions producing these inequalities whether they be those of sex, race, or class. On the other hand some feminists and social workers also see in psychoanalysis a means of understanding and undoing people's acquiescence in their oppres-

97

sion so that they might better deal with the conditions causing it.

This latter attitude to psychoanalysis has a long and worthy tradition in radical welfare practice. Thus, for example, Wilhelm Reich (1932) in the 1930s used psychoanalysis both to explain the acquiescence of the German working class in Hitler's rise to power, and to expose the illusion perpetrated by Hitler that this class's economic problems might be solved through fascism. Not only did he contribute to the provision of counselling services in Berlin for this class. He also joined forces with the socialists of his day in their struggle to bring about social changes to meet the needs of the working class in reality, rather than in the merely illusory fashion afforded by fascist ideology. Similarly in the 1960s the French psychoanalyst Frantz Fanon (1967) used psychoanalysis to explain the internalisation by Blacks of the negative images of Blackness spawned by colonialism. And, like Freud who early argued that the neurotic's sexual needs can only be met by being freed from fixation to the illusions and phantoms of the past, Fanon argued that the needs of Blacks would only fully be met given the undoing of the constraining images of Blackness produced in the unconscious by the past history of colonialism and racism. Today some feminists likewise look to psychoanalysis as a means both to explain and undo women's psychological acquiescence in, and unconscious internalisation of our society's negative images of femininity, images that both reflect and reinforce their social subordination.

It is with this last, feminist use of psychoanalysis that I shall be concerned here. I shall start by briefly outlining four different ways that feminists have used post-Freudian theory to explain women's psychological acquiescence in their social subordination. I shall argue that although these theories explain this acquiescence they fail to explain women's simultaneous resistance to their subordination. By contrast, as I shall then go on to explain, Freudian – as opposed to post-Freudian – theory does provide a means of understanding this contradiction in women's psychology. Furthermore, as I shall also indicate, psychoanalysis offers a means of undoing the untoward psychological effects of this contradiction whereby, instead of dealing actually and in fact with the social conditions that give rise to it, women all too often deal with these conditions in the illusory fashion afforded by neurotic, depressive, and paranoid symptoms. I shall conclude by briefly indicating the ways social workers and feminists go beyond psychoanalysis in so far as they seek to bring about social as well as individual change, not only psychological change but also the material changes necessary for women's needs to be met adequately and equally with those of men.

I. Feminism and post-Freudian theory

i. *Karen Horney*

The feminist poet Adrienne Rich (1976) uses the work of Karen Horney, one of the earliest explicitly feminist psychoanalysis, to explain the psychology of women's social subordination. Horney argued that men's psychological attitude of dominance toward women results from their envy of women's powers in reproduction, in bearing and rearing children. Men, she claimed, have sought to compensate themselves for their inability to create life by creating the state and its social and cultural institutions. But, she said, since these creations fail adequately to compensate men for their 'womb envy' they also seek to allay this envy by excluding women from the domains created by them. At the same time they disparage women's creativity as mothers. The resulting dominance of men in society, wrote Horney, has had the effect that women have come to share the negative images of maternity and femininity whereby men have sought to justify their dominance over women.

Adopting this perspective Rich argues that women will only become liberated by rejecting our society's negative images of femininity. She urges women to celebrate their bodies, psychology, and maternity. But this is a bit like being told to pull oneself up by one's own bootstraps! It is no good simply pressing women to value themselves for themselves unless this is also backed up by the material rewards by which value is measured in our society, that is by securing better pay, working conditions, and support services for women in the jobs they do both outside and inside the home. But Adrienne Rich like Karen Horney fails to address these, the material as opposed to psychological aspects of woman's social being. As a result, while she goes some way toward explaining the psychological roots of women's acquiescence in their social subordination, she fails adequately to explain their simultaneous resistance to it, their struggle to change the social and material conditions currently maintaining their subordinate social status.

ii. Melanie Klein

Dorothy Dinnerstein (1978), an American psychologist, draws on the work of another early analyst, Melanie Klein, to explain the psychological acquiescence of men as of women in patriarchy. On the basis of her pioneering psychoanalytic work with young children, Klein argued that from the beginning of life babies both love and hate the mother. To the extent that it loves the mother, Klein says, the baby experiences her as a good external object which, in phantasy, it also experiences as incorporated within itself as a good internal object. So precarious is the baby's ego, writes Klein, that it fears lest it might be destroyed by its hatred. It therefore disowns these feelings and instead projects them out of itself into the mother. It now experiences her as hating it. Like all defences this one has an untoward effect. It gives rise to 'persecutory anxiety' in the baby lest it be attacked by the mother on account of her supposed hatred of it. Babies, says Klein, deal with this anxiety by denying their negative experience of the mother as frightening. Instead they idealise her. But this leads the baby to envy and attack the mother for seemingly withholding the now idealised contents of her body from the baby. In turn this produces fear in the baby lest its mother retaliate by attacking it as it enviously seeks to attack her.

With time, claims Klein, the child's ego becomes increasingly integrated. As a result it no longer feels the same need to disown and split off the feelings of love and hate that cause it initially and unrealistically to fear, idealise, and envy the mother. The baby thereby comes to experience both itself and the mother more realistically as whole, independent people, as both loving and hating, loved and hated. But this brings with it 'depressive anxiety' lest in attacking the mother it might thereby have destroyed and lost the loved and idealised mother whom it now recognises to be one and the same as the hated, envied, and attacked mother. However, argues Klein, as the baby's ego becomes still more integrated it begins to feel confident that it has enough inner resources to make 'reparation' to the mother for its attacks on her. As a result the baby begins to be able to acknowledge its hatred as well as love of the mother. For it now feels confident that it can make good any damage done her by its hatred and anger. It thereby experiences both itself and her yet more realistically as whole and independent, as capable of both gratification and frustration, of both love and hate.

Klein was not noted for being sympathetic to feminism. What then is the bearing on feminism of her work? According to Dinnerstein its relevance lies in the fact that in our presently sexually unequal society we can permanently avoid working through the persecutory and depressive anxieties Klein claimed to be necessary to our becoming whole, integrated, and independent beings. Instead of dealing with these anxieties and realising our independence, says Dinnerstein, we become dependent on men who, because they are relatively uninvolved in childcare, are not imbued with the primitive phantasies of love and hate that makes dependence on women so fearful and abhorrent to us. The effect, says Dinnerstein, is 'our current sexual malaise' whereby, as Erich Fromm (1942) earlier wrote, we fear freedom and abrogate the autonomy and independence that would otherwise be ours by instead seeking to be ruled by men. The solution, says Dinnerstein, is for men equally to share childcare with women. Children would then no longer be able to avoid working through the persecutory and depressive anxieties necessary to their becoming whole, independent, self-governing individuals. Dinnerstein however fails to explain how shared parenting is to be brought about. If, as she claims, girls and boys now grow up happily acquiescing in men's rule over them why is it that women are even now seeking to overthrow this rule and bring about the shared childcare Dinnerstein advocates?

iii. Object relations theory

Klein herself argued that whether or not the child becomes a whole and independent being is determined at base not by the behaviour let alone by the sex of the person who first looks after it. Instead she argued that this development is basically determined by the balance between the instincts of love and hate with which she supposed the child to be endowed at birth.

Object relations theorists like Donald Winnicott reject Klein's instinct theory. But they retain her view that the psyche is constituted by internalisation of its relations with others. They argue that whole and independent ego development depends on social not instinctual factors. In particular they claim this development is conditional on the mother initially subordinating her needs to those of her baby. By psychically identifying and merging with the baby, writes Winnicott, the 'good enough mother' anticipates its needs before they emerge to break up and interrupt its 'continuity of being'. It is this continuity, says Winnicott, that constitutes the foundation of the baby's secure and independent ego development. Where the mother fails to identify with her baby's needs, he argues, the baby finds itself having to react to the 'impingements' of internal and external need. As a result its ego does not develop on an integrated and whole basis but becomes split between a 'true' self and a 'false' reactive and compliant self.

Winnicott's account of child development hardly seems a likely candidate for incorporation into feminist theory. For it attributes all failures of ego development basically to women not being good enough mothers. An American sociologist, Nancy Chodorow, (1978) has nevertheless sought to turn this theory to feminist effect. She argues that girls retain the sense of mergence with the mother which Winnicott claims to be the corollary in the baby of the good enough mother's psychical mergence with it. On the other hand, she claims, boys deny this initial sense of mergence and identification with the mother. She maintains that, in becoming individuated from the mother and forging a sense of his separate, personal, and masculine identity, the boy negates his first, female-based identification with the mother. Instead he identifies with men. But, she says, since work takes men out of the home this identification is perforce formed on an 'abstract' and 'positional' rather than 'personal' basis. As a result, claims Chodorow, boys are well prepared psychologically for the impersonal demands of occupational work but not for the more personal demands of childcare – a task for which she states girls are better prepared because their gender development does not cause them to deny their earliest sense of mergence with the mother, a sense that, like Winnicott, she implies to be necessary to childare, to ensuring the child's secure and independent ego development.

In sum, Chodorow claims that the current sexual division of our society whereby women mother while men go out to work reproduces in women and men the psychological attributes called for by this division. The solution to the resulting social inequalities between the sexes, she argues, is for men equally to share childcare with women. Both sexes, she suggests, would then grow up equally possessing the psychological attributes functional to the occupational and caring work of public and private life in our society. Like Dinnerstein, however, Chodorow fails to explain the struggles of feminism to bring about the shared parenting she recommends. If, as Chodorow says, women grow up with the need and desire for mergence in personal relations that is supposedly fulfilled by childcare why are they not content with this, their assigned social role? Why do they also want to work?

iv. Jacques Lacan

Chodorow assumes that the child negates or affirms its sense of mergence with the mother depending on whether it is the same or opposite in sex from her. Feminists who adopt a Lacanian rather than object relations version of psychoanalysis point out that this negation or affirmation by the baby of its initial hallucinated sense of mergence with the mother in the process of self-individuation depends on its recognising sexual difference. They argue that this recognition – at least in the sense in which it bears on gender identity – does not occur in the pre-Oedipal stage when the child has the 'imaginary' sense of itself as one with the mother. Instead, they claim, this recognition only comes about later with the Oedipus and castration complexes when the child then comes to understand sexual difference in terms of the antithesis of having or not having a penis and to interpret this difference as entailing the paternal prohibition of union with the mother. This antithesis, says Lacan, constitutes the meaning of the phallus which in turn symbolises patriarchy, the fact that in our society women are treated as the objects of social and sexual exchange. Only through the castration complex, write Lacanian feminists, does the child begin to recognise this, the social elaboration of sexual difference that constitutes the core of gender or 'sexed subjectivity' in male-dominated society. As a result of this complex, they argue, the child begins to situate itself either as passive object or as active agent of social exchange and interaction. Repressed into the unconscious, this complex acts as a powerful force to perpetuate men's position as agent, women's as subject of social relations. This situation, write Juliet Mitchell (1974) and others, will only change given the overthrow of patriarchy. But Lacanian theory fails to explain from whence women gain the sense of agency in social interaction that presently empowers and motivates their struggle to alter the current dominance of society by men in the ways recommended by Lacanian feminists.

II.　Freud and psychoanalytic therapy

i. Freud on sexual sameness and difference

The above theories all usefully address the fact of women's psychological acquiescence in their social subordination. They variously focus on the way women are brought up to adopt our society's derogatory attitudes toward them, to avoid becoming independent, to remain merged in personal relations, and to take on the position of passive object of men's agency. But these theories fail to address the fact that women, like men, also grow up to be self-respecting, independent, unmerged and individuated agents of their own destiny. It is for this reason that they fail to explain the psychology of women's resistance to their current social subordination. For this resistance results from the fact that women are brought up to be both self-respecting and self-loathing, independent and dependent, individuated and merged, agents as well as subjects of social interaction. The post-Freudian theories outlined above fail adequately to spell out these contradictory forces shaping women's psychology, forces that are the source of their simultaneous resistance to and acquiescence in being treated as passive and dependent beings. Freud, by contrast, did deal with this contradition as I shall now explain. First I shall outline his account of the way girls and boys are equally brought up to be both active and passive in social interaction. I shall then outline his account of the fate in women of their active aims when they recognise the sexual inequalities of our society whereby these aims are more often gratified in men than in women.

On the basis of his clinical work with neurotic patients, consideration of the sexual 'perversions', and observation of children, Freud maintained that children derive sexual pleasure from their very first social interactions with others. Why else, he asked, do they seek to repeat these interactions? He described various ways children attempt to recapitulate their pleasurable interchanges with others both autoerotically (e.g. in thumb-sucking) and socially. Socially this takes the form in both boys and girls of seeking to go on being the passive object of another's agency and care, and of seeking to take on the active part of the mother as the child experiences being cared for by her. Orally it involves the baby not only trying to go on passively being fed by the mother even when sated, but also actively trying to feed the mother or its dolls, say. Freud likewise gives examples of the way the child seeks to repeat the pleasure it derives from being cared for in having its toilet supervised and watched over by its parents. Passively this takes the exhibitionistic form of getting others, its parents and playmates, repeatedly to watch while it urinates and defecates. Actively it takes a voyeuristic form. The child contrives to watch others at their toilet as it experienced being watched over by its parents when they taught it to control its bladder and bowel functions. Freud goes on to point out that the child also clearly derives pleasure from its mother's accidental touching of its genitals in the process of cleaning and dressing it. It seems, says Freud, to experience itself in this interaction as though it were the passive object of the mother's seduction. And he points out that children regularly try to persuade the mother to repeat the action – the cleaning or dressing – that gives them this passive pleasure. On the other hand the child also seeks to take on the active, seductive role of the mother as it experiences her part in this interaction. This is the wish expressed in masturbation, says Freud. He goes on to say that when the child is punished or disapproved of for masturbating it also seeks to recover the pleasure of this interaction. Passively this takes the form of imagining or actually getting others to punish it so that it is once again the passive, masochistic object of disapproval by others. Actively it takes the sadistic form of attacking others whether in imagination or reality as it experienced being chastised by its parents for masturbating.

Freud claimed that social disapproval of childhood masturbation has another crucial effect. Until this stage in development, he argues, boys and girls equally indulge the passive and active aims (exhibitionistic and voyeuristic, masochistic and sadistic, etc.) brought into being in them by their interaction with those who first look after them. So far, writes Freud, the child does not recognise sexual difference in the sense of appreciating that while boys have a penis girls do not. Although the child might already have seen the genitals of the opposite sex, reports Freud, it does not initially accept what it sees. Instead it denies the evidence of its senses. Seeing the girl's genitals the child at first concludes that she has a penis which is small but will grow bigger as she grows up. Only when it is disapproved of on account of its masturbation, writes Freud, does the child recognise what it has until then denied, namely that girls do not have a penis. It interprets this fact in the light of its parents' disapproval of its masturbation. It concludes that it is the effect of punishment for masturbation and of the incestuous impulses therein expressed.

What happens to the girl's previously consciously expressed belief that she has a penis once she recognises that she does not in fact have one? This does not result, says Freud, in the girl altogether abandoning her previously voiced belief that she has a penis. Instead this belief is repressed into the unconscious. From here it continues to gain expression either in the disguised form afforced by dreams and neurotic symptoms, or in the undisguised form afforded by psychosis when the unrealistic and hallucinatory beliefs of the unconscious once more gain conscious expression.

Normally woman's belief that she has a penis is repressed into the unconscious on account of its contradiction with biological reality. But there is no reason on this biological score why women should also disown the traits socially associated with having a penis, with being male. In our male-dominated society these traits include all those associated with social dominance, with governing and controlling others rather than with being governed or controlled by them, with being an active agent rather than passive subject of social interaction. Freud, I have argued, shows these traits equally to be elicited in girls as in boys by the social experiences of their infancy. And these traits continue to be elicited in girls as in boys by the myriad ways in which our society encourages its members, regardless of their sex, to believe themselves to be free and independent agents of their own destiny. And, of course, women like men regularly seek to realise the active aims thereby brought into being in them both in private and public life, both individually and collectively as in the struggles of feminists to change the social conditions that presently obstruct women's freedom of action. On the other hand women all too often succumb to the fact that, although they are promised the same freedom as men, they are also discouraged from exercising this freedom. And this is not only because of the social obstacles currently standing in the way of women realising their freedom. It also results from women being told that it is callous selfishness for them to be free and independent. They are constantly urged by psychoanalysts like Winnicott, by social workers, and by countless others to put the needs of others, particularly those of their dependents, before their own.

The obstacles and sanctions against women realising the independent and active aims socially produced in them as in men by their upbringing cause women often to disown these aims in themselves. And this process is reinforced by the fact that, because realisation of these aims is socially equated in our male-dominated society with being a man, it contradicts women's sense of themelves as female – a sense that Freud claimed first comes about with the castration complex, with the recognition of sexual difference, and with the narcissistic investment in the self as female or male therein involved. The French historian of ideas, Michel Foucault (1976), has also shown that investment in our sexual identity has become increasingly important as historical factors, including the development of psychoanalysis, have increasingly produced sexuality and, with it, sexual identity as central to our sense of self and self-respect.

What happens to women's so-called 'masculine' aims when these aims are disowned on account of their contradiction with women's psychological, narcissistic, and egoistic investment in their femininity? What happens to these aims given the social obstacles to their realisation in male-dominated society? Freud held that just as woman's belief that she has a penis continues to be expressed even when that belief is disowned and repressed into the unconscious, so too are those aims disowned on account of their association with having a penis, with being male. But, in so far as these aims are therefore disowned by consciousness, they can then only be expressed in unconscious, unreal, and illusory form. In explaining this point I shall show how psychoanalysis seeks, through therapy, to expose the illusory character of the gratification seemingly afforded patients by their symptoms. It thereby seeks to restore to consciousness the disowned aims bound up and expressed in symptoms so that patients might realise these aims actually and in fact rather than in the merely illusory fashion afforded by repressing these aims as in neurosis, turning them against the self as in depression, or mislocating them in others as in paranoia.

ii. Repression and neurosis

Faced with the social equation of agency with masculinity, says Freud, women often repress their active aims. A contemporary example are the eating disorders – both bingeing and starving – that so regularly afflict women in society today. So anxiety-laden is active sexual desire for women given its association with men's dominance over them that women often disown and repress this desire in themselves. It can then only gain expression in disguised form such is the then opposition of consciousness to its undisguised and actual gratification. In anorexia and compulsive eating repressed sexual desire is displaced on to an obsession with food – an obsession that many women find easier consciously to express given the feeding role assigned women in our society than they do consciously to express their active sexual aims and needs so often properly believed to be absent in women. On the other hand neurotic disorder in both women and men gives them the illusion that their needs are met. By fasting and controlling her food intake the anorexic has the illusion that her wish to control herself and her sexual being is met. Bingeing likewise gives women the illusion that their needs are gratified. By stuffing themselves they seemingly leave no room for ungratified need. On the other hand these disorders do not actually gratify the active sexual aims and needs they express. In Freud's terms they only afford the sufferer 'primary gain', hallucinatory gratification of her sexual needs. It is because neurotic symptoms do not actually gratify the needs they express that they are compulsive or addictive. The anorexic and compulsive eater both remorselessly persist in starving or stuffing themselves because neither activity actually gratifies, staunches, or brings to an end the repressed aims it expresses.

Neurotic symptoms do however afford their sufferers real 'secondary gain' in so far as others physically look after them on account of their illness. Like many others both before and since Freud pointed out that women's social situation is such that they often have no other option but illness whereby to secure physical care and attention from others. He insisted however that it is no good colluding with the secondary gains afforded women by neurotic illness, by hospitalising them or giving them a vacation or break from the social situation that brought their symptoms into being in the first place. If neurotics are to gain actual gratification of the sexual as well as physical needs their symptoms express, he said, these symptoms must be analysed in the context that caused the needs their symptoms express to be repressed. And this, he argued, includes not only getting the patient to 'free associate' to the origins of her (or his) symptoms. It also involves making conscious the aims expressed in her (or his) symptoms as these aims are manifest, albeit again only in disguised form, in the 'transference' relation the patient unconsciously seeks to establish with the therapist.

Lastly Freud pointed out that neurotics seem to cling to their symptoms as much for the pain as for the pleasure they afford them. In dealing with this, the 'negative therapeutic reaction', he argued, the therapist not only has to make conscious the illusory character of the pleasurable gains afforded the patient by her (or his) symptoms. The therapist also has to undo the defence of the ego, specifically of the super ego, that he claimed to be responsible for the pain and punishment neurotics inflict on themselves through their symptoms. In particular, Freud argued, it is necessary to make conscious and to review with the patient the construction of sexual difference that he held to constitute the childhood origin of the super ego's punishment of the self. The super ego, he maintained, originates in the child's internalisation of its parents' disapproval of its masturbation. It is instituted by the ego to punish and thereby prevent the sexual aims of the id actually being gratified so threatening does this gratification seem to the ego given the child's interpretation of it as involving being a woman (i.e. being castrated) in the case of the boy, as being a man (i.e. having a penis) in the case of the girl. Analysis of this defence or resistance of the ego to cure, to realising rather than repressing the sexual aims of the id, poses a major obstacle however to therapy with women. For in our male-dominated society there is all too much basis in social if not in biological reality for the belief that sustains the repression by women of their sexual needs, namely the belief that gratification of these needs is tantamount to being a man. I shall return to this point in my conclusion.

iii. Introjection and depression

A second way in which women (and men) express their disowned aims, again in illusory form, is by turning these aims against themselves. Freud described how this occurs in depression. Instead of acting on the anger they feel at the disappointments and frustrations of their lives by seeking actually to change the social conditions responsible for these frustrations, people respond in depression as though the ones they hold responsible for their disappointments were internalised as frustrating objects within the self. It is the criticism of these internal objects, wrote Freud, that constitutes the stuff of the lamentations and unhappiness of the depressed.

Such shadow-boxing, however, confined as it is to dealing with phantoms and internal objects, hardly serves actually to deal with the all too real frustrations of women's (and men's) lives. If these frustrations are actually and effectively to be dealt with and overcome then people have to act on the anger these frustrations elicit in them rather than turning this anger self-destructively against themselves so that neither their physical nor the sexual and psychological needs are met.

Psychoanalytically-oriented therapists seek to enable their patients to act on, rather than depressively 'introject' their anger. They seek to do this by making conscious the anxiety they believe holds people back from acting on their anger actually and constructively to change their social lot. According to Klein (see p. 100 above), the unconscious anxiety sustaining depression is the fear lest were one to act on one's anger one might thereby harm and lose those one loves and on whom one depends. And, as feminists have pointed out, women are particularly liable to be fearful on this score given that they are often economically as well as emotionally dependent on those they love. It is therefore little surprise that women are much more at risk than men of suffering from depression – a sex difference that is also attributable to the fact that, because of their social subordination, women are more readily allowed to bewail than to protest their social lot, to bemoan it than forcibly to express the anger it produces in them.

Kleinian and object relations therapists, including those working at the London Women's Therapy Centre, seek to enable patients constructively to act on such feelings of anger by making conscious the anxiety about object loss which they claim sustains depression. They seek to do this by making conscious this anxiety as it manifests itself in the transference, in the patient's expressed fear for instance that by unloading on to the therapist the anger she feels about her situation she might thereby wear out the therapist thus destroying the therapist's capacity to help her. By making conscious this anxiety object relations therapists hope to enable their patients to recognise that the helpful aspects of their relations to the therapist are not rendered nought by the patients' angry outbursts about their lot both inside and outside therapy. The patient is thereby hopefully enabled to appreciate and hence to internalise the good aspects of her relation to the therapist. This in turn, it is anticipated, will help the depressed woman feel better about herself and hence more able to act on her anger with confidence that she has the wherewithal within herself to make reparation to those she loves and may harm in the process of doing so.

Other therapists take this approach to the treatment of depression one step further – like Sue Holland who works with depressed women in the White City in London. Holland reviews in individual therapy with these women the factors in their personal biographies that cause them to turn their anger against themselves – factors that, in the case of the West Indian women with whom she works, are associated with wider social factors such as Britain's restrictive immigration policy and the racism it expresses. She also encourages them collectively to use the anger made available to consciousness through therapy so as to struggle to change and improve the resources of their community and neighbourhood. Such action in turn seems to protect women from depression. This was evident, for example, in women's accounts of the beneficial effect on them of being involved in the 1984–5 miners' strike, and from sociological evidence documenting the way employment protects women (and men) against depression.

iv. Projection and paranoia

A third way in which women (and men) all too often disown their capacity to act to change the world is by projecting this capacity into others, only recognising it in them, not in themselves. In our sexually unequal society, where agency is more readily accorded to men than to women, women regularly disown their agency in this way. This occurs, for example, in agoraphobia – a condition that affects many more women than men. Agoraphobics often find it very easy to recognise the independence and autonomy of others, say of their husbands. They find it much harder to acknowledge their own freedom and independence. Their agoraphobia is often constituted by fear of the independence and agency of others. While agoraphobia in men seems to be related to fear of the damage they might do themselves, it is more often related in women to fear of the damage that others might do them were they to go out.

Agoraphobia nicely parodies women's housebound social lot. However it hardly serves to challenge the social subordination of women expressed in the equation of femininity with domesticity. A like problem arises for those battered women who, while recognising the aggression and brutality of men, fail to acknowledge the feelings of anger this elicits in them. This buys women the illusion of innocence at the cost of divesting them of the anger that might otherwise fuel their capacity to deal with the all too real violence perpetrated against them.

Just as Kleinian and object relations therapists seek to enable depressed women (and men) to act on their anger by making conscious the anxiety about object loss that causes them to turn their anger against themselves, so they also seek to help women (and men) to act on the anger that in paranoia they otherwise project into others by making conscious the anxiety that sustains this defence. At root, argued Klein, this anxiety involves the fear lest in being angry one might destroy oneself (see p. 100 above). And feminists have pointed out that this fear is liable to be particularly acute in women in so far as they feel more helpless and vulnerable than men in male-dominated society. Kleinian treatment of the projection of anger resulting from feelings of vulnerability and anxiety for the self involves interpreting this anxiety as it is manifested in the transfer-ence. It also involves making conscious the way the patient projects her (or his) anger into the therapist, experiencing not herself (or himself) but the therapist as angry and hostile. This, however, incurs the risk that the patient will have yet more reason to experience the analyst as hostile in so far as the patient construes the therapist's interpretations as persecuting. Furthermore such interpretations may confirm the patient in the feeling that her (or his) hatred is indeed destructive of the self. Why else, patients might ask themselves, are their therapists so keen to disown this feeling in themselves by interpreting it as the result of the patient's projection? Some Kleinians accordingly suggest that it might be more helpful to the patient for the therapist temporarily to identify with and 'contain' the patient's projected feelings. The therapist may thereby convey to the patient that these feelings can be borne without destroying the self, the therapist. The patient may then be more able to recognise her (or his) own hatred and anger as bearable, as feelings that can be acted upon without destroying the self.

III.   Conclusion: Psychoanalysis, feminism and social work

In this chapter I have outlined various ways in which feminists have used psychoanalytic theory to explain women's psychological ac-quiescence in their social subordination. Freudian theory, I argued, also provides a means of explaining the psychology of women's resistance to their subordination. Finally I briefly sketched out various ways psychoanalytically-oriented therapists seek to undo the defences whereby, instead of realistically dealing with the conflicts of their lives including those arising from the sexual inequalities of our society, women (and men) all too often deal with these conflicts in the illusory fashion afforded by neurosis, depression, and paranoia.

Freud once wrote that his aim in therapy was to transform 'hysterical misery into common unhappiness. With a mental life that has been restored to health,' he argued, the hysteric 'will be better armed against that unhappiness' (Freud & Breuer, 1895). Feminists and radical social workers go beyond this stated aim of psychoanalysis. They argue that the better arming of women (and of men) to deal with the unhappiness caused them by the frustrations of everyday life depends on social as well as psychological change, on collective as well as individual action. If women (and men) are to realise all their aims and desires – active as well as passive, masculine as well as feminine, sexual as well as physical – then not only must they become aware of these aims rather than disown them in themselves. It is also necessary to change the social conditions currently preventing them realising these aims and desires. Without the social changes sought by feminism and radical social work taking place the psychological changes sought by psychoanalytic therapy and counselling can only be short-lived. Otherwise the conditions that cause people to disown their aims and needs will continue to cause them to disown these wants even though therapy might temporarily render them conscious. Feminists are accordingly joining with radical social workers in campaigning for an extension of the social services so that women's and men's needs as carers and as cared for might be met actually and in fact rather than in the merely illusory fashion described above and which is so cynically and ruthlessly exploited by those who presently seek to dismantle the welfare state in the name of individual freedom which their doctrines meet more in phantasy than in reality.

Note

1. This chapter is based on my book *Sexual Contradictions: Psychology, Psychoanalysis, and Feminism* (1986), in which will be found a more detailed exposition and further references to the feminist and psychoanalytic theories and therapies briefly summarised here. My thanks to Brenda Smith and others involved in the Social Work course at the University of New South Wales, Sydney, for their comments on this chapter.

Part II

Varieties of Practice

4   A Psychodynamic Approach to the Work of an Area Team

Celia Downes

Social work within area teams of Social Services Departments offers great potential for varied and interesting work and, with it, a high level of stress. Workers frequently talk of feeling deskilled and of their fear of becoming emotionally blunted. There is a sense that if the work could be organised differently, it would be more creative and a better service would be offered, yet there is often considerable resistance to change.

The focus of this chapter is on the social worker within the context of a particular immediate working environment. It explores the way psychodynamic theory might help workers understand the inter-meshing between the organisation and their own inner worlds or inner psychic reality. Underlying this is the premise explored by Jaques (1970): 'it is in a just environment that creativeness and the capacity for work find their optimum conditions for expression'.

The developing association and integration of psychoanalytic theory and systems theory provides a perspective from which to explore the ways worker and organisation continually act upon each other to manage anxiety at work and evade or avoid being overwhelmed by it. This perspective starts from a number of premises: that a certain level of anxiety enhances coping capacity; that all organisations function defensively; and that it is possible for the work group or organisation to support its members in the task of dealing creatively with anxiety at work. Conversely, when primitive anxiety, which may be manifested in a sense of unspeakable impending disaster, is engendered in workers by the nature of their work, their agency is liable, over time, to develop and establish ways of functioning which may indirectly increase the anxiety of its members still further. These particular forms of agency functioning may prevent an effective service being offered. Some of these ideas are also explored in the chapter by John Simmonds, who applies them to social work practice in day and residential settings.

117

This chapter explores the theme of the worker operating from within area teams which are functioning in ways which hinder rather than support creative work. It looks, firstly, at the way particular policies and practices designed to provide an enabling structure for efficient work may unintentionally come to have the opposite effect. Secondly, it explores some of the implications when an area team develops a mode of operation which fails to encompass the range of strong feeling engendered in the interaction between workers and clients. Thirdly, it suggests ways in which the area team in organising its work to focus on certain needs in the community may inadvertently ignore or avoid other needs.

Area teams have developed as the basic organisational unit responsible for local authority social services provision in a particular geographical area. They usually include a team leader, social workers, increasingly these are all qualified, clerical staff and often ancilliary workers. In the study undertaken by Stevenson *et al.* (1978) the number of people in a team ranged roughly between 6 and 12.

The work is mainly with vulnerable people in the community: families at risk, with their children or adolescent members living at home or in care; physically and mentally disabled people and their families; and the frail elderly and those who care for them. Area teams, even if they specialise, are likely to be involved in some form of statutory work. Workers are experienced as powerful and they feel uneasy about this. The responsibility for making decisions which have far reaching effects on people's lives demands complex judgements, and sometimes these decisions have to be made when there is little time for reflection. In some authorities, assessments of need and eligibility for resources such as residential or domiciliary care seem almost meaningless, because of the relative scarcity of the available service. The burden of worry and risk continue to fall on frontline workers and carers, and statutory social workers may quite irrationally feel blamed, as though they were responsible for withholding a service they had the power to offer.

Public awareness of the activities of social service departments and the harsh exposure of their social workers by the media adds to the pressure of unrealistic expectations and the sense of stigma for the workers. Stereotypes abound: clients of social service departments are depicted variously as scroungers, monsters or deserving victims of bureaucracy. Area team social workers are depicted as naive, incompetent, inexperienced or officiously bureaucratic. In practice, the recurring struggle to identify, confront and be released from the impact of these stereotypes can seem like working one's way out of a thorny thicket when, having disentangled an arm, a leg is held fast. Genuine encounters are hard won, both by area team workers and those referred to them.

Against these stereotypes, Stevenson's overview of area team social work offers a much more moderated picture of the actual state of affairs as her research team found it in the mid seventies. It is a picture of 'commitment and hard work, of concern and sympathy for clients, and of valiant efforts by many individuals to cope with the pressures and strains'. However, she sees this picture undermined by a lack of clarity about objectives and roles, a lack of imagination and creativity, and by restraints and cutbacks. An underlying theme identified in the responses of the area team social workers who were interviewed, was one of fear. Anxiety, she comments, is not a strong enough term to convey the intensity of feeling engendered by the job.

Policies and practices which hinder or enable creative work

Menzies (1960) in her exposition of the development of defensive social systems points to the primitive anxiety aroused for nurses offering intimate care to patients who were likely to be fearful, possibly hostile, and highly dependent. As in nursing, work in an area team brings workers in daily contact with people who may be engaged in a struggle for survival, it may be the struggle of an elderly person to survive independently in the community, or the struggle of a child to survive in a family where destructive impulses are felt to be out of control. The worker also has to bear the impact of chronic unmet emotional need, and of chronic disability. There is the additional contagious anxiety from working in a team, often in an open plan room, as well as the anxiety that reaches the team via referrers and workers in other agencies. None of this is peculiar to area team social work, of course, but their wide-ranging brief, the enormous variety of the work, and their statutory responsibilities all combine to give workers a sense of having work and anxieties dumped on them, and of being part of a 'dustbin agency'.

Menzies argues that when the objective work situation resembles the workers' primitive unconscious aggressive and libidinal fantasies, the worker in turn projects these back into the current work situation. By consciously and painfully re-experiencing feelings which are actually appropriate not only to the work, but to their unconscious fantasies, they master anxiety. Up to this point anxiety can be creative and constructive, since the workers are in touch with their clients' emotional pain as well as with their (the social workers) own powers for coping. Beyond a certain level of anxiety, however, primitive anxieties cannot be reassimilated and anxiety is in danger of becoming overwhelming. To avoid this, workers collude so that techniques and procedures are built into the structure and functioning of the agency which have the effect of distancing worker and client, fragmenting the work, so that it becomes task-centred rather than person-centred and depersonalising those seeking help. This does not happen all at once. Most of the time workers find themselves crossing and recrossing a threshold between policies and practices providing an enabling framework to a defensive use of the same procedures.

This experience has been vividly illustrated by Mattinson and Sinclair (1979) from their action research in a London social services department on clients' marital problems. Here I shall confine examples to procedures and policies which have evolved to facilitate good work, but whose usage becomes subtly altered as they become more deeply embedded in the defensive agency structure. As Parton and Thomas (1983) have commented in their discussion of cases where child abuse is suspected, 'procedures seem to take on a life of their own so that it can be difficult for the social worker to control or even influence the final outcome.'

For example, in social service departments, much thought and energy has gone into ways of determining which clients should be given priority. This inevitably involves categorisation. A widow, applying for financial assistance with her telephone rental, is listed as 'telephone rental assessment'. Following one fact-finding visit, probably from an ancillary worker, her eligibility is determined. But she persists in ringing the area team daily to ask about the outcome and with a number of anxious queries. This nagging is experienced as one more minor irritation in the life of a busy team which has assessed that there is nothing further they can 'do' for her. Their fear is that to acknowledge her loneliness, with the possibility of unresolved grief, would open the floodgates and result in unlimited long-term work, and 'dependency'. Fantasies of vast unmet needs which must be kept at bay, for 'we only do statutory work', build up. Then the creative possibilities of risking a real encounter which may involve 'being' without doing, and which may acknowledge together that perhaps some needs cannot be met, is lost.

The spectre of the danger of aimless visiting engendering passive dependency is used to further strategies which limit 'involvement' but may actually engender the very dependency they seek to avoid. A team is known to favour a brief contractual approach, focusing on a practical task to be accomplished, after which the case is closed unless statutory 'monitoring' is called for. A young, rather isolated mother repeatedly re-refers herself, presenting practical problems of increasing severity. Each time she returns she finds herself encountering an unfamiliar worker. This is eventually rationalised to a student on placement as 'she has difficulty trusting people, so it's good to give her practice with different workers'. In both these examples the team is tending to polarise the choices that they perceive as being open to them. On the one hand it must be limited to focusing on a practical task to be accomplished, rather than on a person presenting themselves and their needs in a particular form. The alternative is perceived as opening the floodgates on emotional need, which it is feared will necessitate endless work while the team bears the burden of the client's passive dependency. What cannot be considered is the possibility that for many people the experience of having emotional need and anxiety heard and acknowledged in a sensitive way, even in the course of one conversation around what using the phone means to them, may do much to mobilise them towards their own creative solutions. For a minority, the painful work of 'looking at the gaps' may need to take place more slowly, with someone who proves reliable and available over time. This may well be difficult work for all concerned but it also has within it the potential springs for change and growth.

One of the implications if organisational defensiveness is to be minimised is that team leaders are in a key role to challenge and modify it, but at the same time this puts them in a particularly vulnerable position. Stevenson *et al.* (1978) found in the DHSS research study that it was difficult to exaggerate the influence of the area team leader, and that team leaders were often idealised by members of their team. It was as though their goodness was preserved by projecting bad feelings upwards through the hierarchy, blaming senior management, or outwards resulting in a sense of bombardment against a hostile community. In supervision the team leader must be able to hold the tension between his management and enabling role. If he either errs too far into an exclusively management role or avoids it, he will not enable workers to confront the anxiety involved in holding on to both their caring and controlling functions, which frees them to use their judgement and discretion in complex decisions.

A small action research project (Jones, 1978) explored social workers' experience of their interaction with their supervisors on reporting a case where child abuse was suspected. The pattern was for the team leader at this point to shift suddenly from enabler to a role experienced as 'policing'. The focus was no longer on what was actually happening in the family concerned, but on 'interrogating' the worker to ensure that procedural guidelines had been followed and the department was covered. We know enough of the dynamics of the 'reflection process' (Mattinson, 1975) to expect that when this happens the worker is likely to take up a similar stance with his client.

Secondly, the team leader needs to focus on ways the agency operates on its boundary with the community it serves. The skills involved in effectively responding to new referrals and in initial assessments are among the most sophisticated in social work – and require specialisation, possibly in the form of specialist intake workers or teams (Addison 1982). Some of the implications of leaving unsupported clerical staff doing initial front line work are explored in the section which follows.

Modes of operation within the area team system

In this longer example, themes of consensus and conflict within an area team operating in a particular mode; attention to what happens at the boundary where client and team meet; and implications for the role of the team leader are explored further in an account of a near day-long episode in the life of one area team.

Neil, a newly-qualified social worker had been a member of the team for four months. The team specialised in long-term work, mainly with families with young children at risk. Since joining the team Neil had been working with Janice, a 16-year-old girl who had been in care since she was 7, and Janice's 9-month-old baby. Janice had had a turbulent pregnancy, spending most of it 'missing' from the community home where she was living, but always keeping her ante-natal appointments. After Gary's birth, the work Neil had engaged in with her had also been turbulent and when Janice fraudulently claimed that her social security giro book was missing and attempted to enlist Neil as advocate in getting a new one he was not slow to confront her with evidence that she was lying, but he supported her as she reinstated herself on a legal footing with the local DHSS office. Janice's mothering was uncertain, but she remained highly motivated to learn, that is until her new boyfriend was arrested and received a custodial sentence some miles away, when she became increasingly preoccupied with visiting him, leaving Gary short of food. Neil observed that Gary was not looking so well cared for, and took note of minor bumps and bruises. He had more than once provided small sums of money to Janice to buy food for Gary at the weekend when her funds had run out. Neil was clear that his overall strategy with Janice was to work with her as an adult, concerned, if inexperienced mother, and he encouraged Janice to adopt a 'problem-solving approach'. He had recently posed her with the question, 'Are you going to see your boyfriend or look after Gary?' Despite the vicissitudes of their relationship, Neil was not despondent about the overall progress of the work he and Janice were engaged in.

Simmonds (1984) explores the way a case may take on an added significance within a team when worker and client are struggling with similar issues, though in completely different psychological contexts. He explores this, using the particular example of the newly qualified worker making the psychosocial transition from student learner, even allowing for previous maturity and experience, to qualified worker. He suggests that this transition involves the new worker in letting go, perhaps mourning the loss of his protected student status and finding new and appropriate ways of exercising personal and professional authority. While this is happening, work with a client undergoing a similar psychosocial transition may take on added significance and arouse considerable anxiety in the worker. In the example cited by Simmonds, the case became the focus of discussion, week after week in supervision. Simmonds suggests that although the parallels may not be immediately obvious, a new young mother crossing the boundary from her protected status as a teenager concerned mainly with her own needs and wishes, to the 'leadership' role of managing the boundary between her own needs and those of her baby, may be engaging in some respects in a similar transition to that of the newly-qualified worker.

Neil might also be considered as a worker joining an agency already operating a well-established defensive system. He had been aware of some of the processes involved in his own transition into the team and had tried to share with his colleagues some aspects of what it was like for him finding his feet as a newly qualified worker. Neil identified his own approach and style of work as one of high commitment and open involvement which he combined with problem solving strategies aimed at enabling people to take responsibility progressively for themselves. He felt his colleagues disapproved of his approach. He was told he was being unrealistic, that such was the deprivation of this particular client group, they could not be expected to keep regular appointments. Furthermore, he was advised that the most appropriate style of work was that of long term nurturing and support. When Neil's style resulted in stormy confrontations with clients on office premises, he was made to feel that he was no more than a raw teenager himself.

The team's mode of operation might be described in the terms used by Bion (1968) as predominantly that of basic assumption dependency. By formulating their role as good and giving parents, the team avoided confronting their clients' hostility and aggression, and themselves seemed to be operating without much constructive use of their own assertiveness or aggression. In challenging this, Neil became involved in a split within the team, in which he was cast by 'responsible parents' in the role of 'irresponsible child', and blamed for all the mess and turbulence he was seen to have introduced. Neil could see this happening, but the best he could think of doing in relation to his work with Janice was to discuss his planned strategy with her at a team meeting, which included the clerical staff who doubled as receptionists, and seek their cooperation.

Janice arrived at the area team office in the middle of one Friday morning; it was not one of her regular appointment times, and the team were all engaged together in informal interviews to fill a vacant post. The receptionist phoned through that Janice wished to borrow £2 to visit her boyfriend. Neil asked that a message be given that he was not prepared to agree to finance this, but would see her at 2 pm if she wished to return then. Janice did not leave, and an hour later the receptionist phoned into the meeting urgently. Janice was very worried by Gary's cough, she needed money to buy medicine and the receptionist did not like the sound of Gary's cough either. Neil reiterated his message but sensed his colleagues' embarrassment and disapproval. Nothing was said, however, with 'outsiders' present. Janice stayed on.

By the time Neil saw Janice, before 2 pm, she was furious and declared, 'anyone can get £10 from a social worker'. When he asked her to leave she fought with him in the reception area, shouting 'I hate you, you bastard' and attempting to bite him; Janice demanded to see the team leader, 'everyone knows that none of you can get jobs anywhere else'.

Neil felt thoroughly isolated by now. He was blamed by the clerical staff for having irresponsibly provoked Janice, and they considered him too inexperienced to know a bad cough when he heard one: 'You haven't had children of your own.' When Janice succeeded in waylaying the team leader and demanding that Neil be sacked, he felt the team leader would have been only to glad to comply. The team leader asked Janice to leave, but she stayed on in the reception area with Gary, who seemed relatively unperturbed. The next phone call from the receptionist was to say that Janice had swallowed 30 pills. Neil returned to the reception area to find Janice being comforted by the motherly receptionist who had her arms round her. Janice was unable to specify anything about the pills. No one made any move to call an ambulance. Neil now felt he was held responsible by his colleagues not only for Gary's cough but for Janice's 'suicide' attempt. A few minutes later Janice left the office, 'abandoning' Gary with the receptionist, and thus adding to Neil's crimes. To Neil's immense relief, Janice returned, just before office closing time to collect Gary, and she looked more composed. Neil said he had only been able to recount this episode because after the weekend Janice had come in at her regular appointment time and repaid all the money she had previously been loaned.

It would be fair to say that, as the drama unfolds, nobody is behaving very well, apart from Gary who restricts himself to a minor cough. This episode can be considered as another form of defensive functioning within the agency system encompassing Janice and the team, and in which all members take part. In the morning the team appear to have withdrawn into an inner sanctum, leaving the receptionist alone to deal with the pressures of the real world. It is as though the barricades are up, allowing the team to function as a basic assumption group where defences against anxiety are at the same time defences against reality. Bion makes the point that when a work group is functioning as a basic assumption group, the operational leader and the leader of the basic assumption group may not necessarily be the same person. The latter is likely to be 'an individual whose personality renders him peculiarly susceptible to the obliteration of individuality by the basic assumption group's leadership requirements' (Bion, 1968). In the narrative, the receptionist remains nameless, she might have been set up as the mouthpiece of the team to play the role of the idealised, all-giving mother to Janice's turbulent deprived adolescent at risk of abusing her baby.

Neil seems trapped. Probably he overreacts in his demands and expectations that Janice behave in an adult, responsible way while he is refusing her demands in a series of phone messages. He is holding on by the skin of his teeth to his new-found professional authority, without support from his colleagues, and his judgement may be clouded by his reaction to their disapproval as he digs his heels in. There are inevitable comparisons to be made between this episode and that described by Mattinson and Sinclair (1979) which they call 'Suckers and Bastards'. In this, two experienced workers spend an afternoon resisting the ambivalent demands of Mrs Yates that they take her children into care after a fire extinguisher falls off the wall close to one of them in the team reception area. 'How easy it would have been for Mrs Yates to split the workers, one made into the bastard – the withholder – one into the sucker the giver and giver in. It is unlikely that one worker on his own, and without comparable seniority could have resisted this demand, particularly as there were young children involved.'

Neil resists Janice's demands, but he cannot on his own resist the split between himself, the withholding bastard and the rescuing all-giving receptionist, because it is a split already being built into the team. And there is nobody free of this dynamic who is in a position to come to their rescue. We see some of the powerful processes at work, as the group seeks to assimilate a new member into its existing mode of operation, and which may lead to deskilling. Stevenson noted a high degree of consensus in the area teams visited by the DHSS research team, with a tendency to idealise the team leader. In this instance the team leader of this well established team appears to have been well and truly sucked into the group dynamics. He is no longer able to hold his leadership position on the boundary of the agency system, from where he might encompass and contain the defensive splits between Neil and the receptionist, or indeed between Neil and the rest of the team.

This raises the question of the team leader's own support system. Could he be enabled to regain his leadership position on the boundary of the area team system through supervision or consultation from within his own department? Would anybody from a position within the organisation manage to stay outside the dynamics of blame, and support the team leader in operating in such a way that he could find himself leading a less compliant team, which showed more signs of healthy criticism of each other, and quite probably of their team leader? Or is such support likely to be offered more effectively either to the team leader or to the team as a whole from a position of consultancy external to the agency?

Social systems encompassing area team and local community

With moves towards community social work and the possibilities and potential for new forms of collaboration between area teams and members of the local community, it is important to understand the defensive functioning of social systems encompassing both team and local community. Failure to be aware of this may result in a defensive split between work for and by members of the local community, on behalf of its well-functioning members, the response to the majority of 'minor' referrals, and specialist services offered by 'experts' to a hard-core minority, the 20 per cent of 'difficult' cases.

Miller and Gwynne's (1972) slightly different perspective on the defensive operation of social systems offers models developed out of their action research in residential institutions for the physically disabled and young chronic sick. They view such institutions as open systems, encompassing three subsystems, each with its own distinctive task.

First they identify the organisation for dependence in the residential institution. This concentrates on good nursing care, but if it is over-emphasised results in a 'warehousing' model of care in which inmates are treated as more disabled and incapable of running their own lives than they actually are. In contrast to this, they describe an organisation for independence which focuses on the inmates need to develop unfulfilled capacities as independent individuals, to take control of their lives and the way the institution is run for their benefit. In its extreme form it runs the risk of an over-emphasis on achievement or anti-dependence; they call this the 'horticultural' model of care. Both systems, they argue, will be used in unhelpfully defensive ways if not kept in balance, as both may encourage residents and staff to avoid confronting their conflicting needs and wishes for care and for running their own lives. Both the 'warehousing' receptionist and the 'horticultural' Neil were in danger of such defensive polarisation with Janice, who needed help to stay in touch with her ambivalence and find some resolution that enabled her to care for Gary without losing sight of her own needs.

Much of the recent debate around the relative merits of community social work and traditional models of social service delivery appears to centre around ideas similar to Miller and Gwynne's organisations for independence and dependence, or in their extreme forms the horticultural versus the warehousing model.

Cooper (1983), describing the development in Normanton from neighbourhood work through patchwork, reaches a third stage where 'it is recognized that aspects of specialist work at one extreme, and preventive and development work at the other cannot be met within the existing structure of resources.' He envisages the area team becoming the point of tension at the critical interface between 'the need for new community-controlled resources and the need for special intervention in very difficult cases'.

The third system which Miller and Gwynne identify is the organisation for support. This needs to be positioned to enable members of the institution to negotiate their roles between the systems for dependence and independence. In Cooper's model the area team takes on the leadership role of maintaining the boundaries between these two systems, and negotiating between them. This, he implies, will involve the need for much clearer communication about the needs of the local community on the one hand and what the specialist 'experts' might offer, on the other. For example, it could involve finding ways of enabling a local community to hold on to a troublesome adolescent or family rather than enlisting the specialist services to take the problem off the hands of an apparently well-functioning community. Hopefully the area team in turn might enlist resources from the local community to provide a critique on their defensive functioning which will enable them to modify this.

A psychodynamic approach which focuses on the interrelationship between the worker's capacity to work, and the functioning of his or her work environment, has the explanatory value of pointing to some of the reasons, extending beyond the work itself, why social work within area teams is experienced by the workers as so stressful, and yet seems so resistant to change. It illuminates some of the enabling tasks of the team leader and suggests there may sometimes be a need for a supervisor or consultant positioned outside the team, or possibly encompassing the team and members of the community it serves.

5 A Psychoanalytic Perspective on Family Therapy

Catherine Crowther

The families I work with are young. They are families in the making, with children still at home, tackling the ordinary but awesome responsibilities of procreation, nurture, socialisation, and the launching of offspring into adult life. They learn about dependence and individuation, sharing and fighting, continuity and change. These opposite poles represent the human ambivalence towards change with which psychoanalysis has always been so intimately concerned. It is a central theme also in family therapy. Minuchin and Fishman (1981) write of 'the family's essential tasks of supporting individuation while providing a sense of belonging', which echoes Gordon (1973), a Jungian analyst, who speaks of 'the two most fundamental and basic archetypal themes . . . our need for union on the one hand, and our need for differentiation and separateness on the other.' It is the difficulties encountered in this human condition which are the bread and butter of both family therapy and psychoanalysis.

I work with families in which a child presents with a problem, the seriousness or persistence of which is less significant than that the family feel themselves unable to resolve or contain it by their own unaided resources. Often it is some social agency (Education, Social Services) which worries or complains about the problem more than the family, and sends them – to some extent against their will – to the hospital child psychiatry department where I work.

The work I undertake with them is whole family therapy, usually on a problem-solving model, usually lasting three to six months, rarely longer than a year.

On the face of it, family therapy and psychoanalysis have little in common as clinical activities. The mainstream family therapy literature tends to assert the differences in theoretical viewpoint (Watzlawick *et al.*, 1974; Haley, 1973, 1976). Some writers however (Stierlin, 1977; Boszormenyi-Nagy & Spark, 1973; Bowen, 1978;

Dare, 1979, 1981; Cooklin, 1979; Box *et al.*, 1981) acknowledge the profound influence of psychoanalytic thinking on their practice. The hostility to psychoanalysis of some family therapists seems to be based on an outdated assumption that psychoanalysis is still concerned primarily with instinct and drive theory (Freud's topographical model) whereas object relations theory (Fairbairn, 1952), which studies the individual in interaction with others, is now the dominant model.

The psychoanalytic literature hardly acknowledges any doubt to the new insights of family therapy, although analytic curiosity is growing about common values and parallel concepts. Indeed, Freud's treatment of 'Little Hans' (Freud, 1909), in which he affected change in the 5-year-old boy's phobia by working solely through his father, is cited sometimes as the first family therapy. It is unfortunate that mutual misunderstanding has delayed what could be a fruitful exchange between the two perspectives, both equally committed to understanding the place of the individual within his developmental context.

Unlike many family therapists who describe themselves as having left behind the restrictions of their psychoanalytic upbringing for the broader horizons of family therapy, I have found myself, as a social worker and family therapist, moving somewhat against the stream, increasingly drawn to psychoanalytic ideas. I find not only does psychoanalysis shed a particularly illuminating light on family dynamics and family-professional dynamics, but it gives an edge and clarity to my interventions in family work, and, perhaps most importantly, helps to anchor me as a therapist more confidently in my own feelings and bodily perceptions, better able to make use of my own reactions to the immediate impact of being with each particular family: in psychoanalytic terms, that is, taking account of the counter-transference.

This does not mean that the actual techniques I employ are recognisably psychoanalytic. The models of family therapy I follow are largely strategic (Haley, 1976), systemic (Palazzoli *et al.*, 1978), and structural (Minuchin, 1974), and influenced by a constant awareness as a social worker of the social context of my clients. In contrast, Box *et al.*, (1981) have described their work as a conscious attempt to transfer both the concepts and techniques of psychoanalysis to whole family treatments. Their use of transference interpretations, containment of psychic pain, and working through past conflicts in the present, mirrors the activity of the analyst with an individual patient. However, there are problems, as Box admits, in the direct transfer to another treatment setting of a method developed for long-term individual work with motivated clients. In my experience, few of the families referred to social workers or child guidance can be engaged in such insight-promoting and personal growth therapy, or feel its relevance to their pressing problems or crises. Such families have often been badly knocked around by life, but its members are extremely dissociated from the feelings and behaviour evoked in the present by events in their distant past. They may tend to think more concretely than the therapist and to press him or her for action and solutions to their immediate distress. It was with pragmatic expediency that family therapy developed techniques to undertake short-term treatments, with the presenting problem as focus, because such families were dropping out of traditional psychoanalytically derived therapies. I believe that short-term, problem-solving, pragmatic family therapy is nonetheless indebted to psychoanalysis.

Clearly, the therapeutic activities of the analyst and the family therapist are different. The analyst is occupied with the mental activity and intra-psychic processes of an individual patient. He attempts, by attention to the patient's fantasy and dream material, and through the transference and countertransference in sessions, and to a lesser extent by a historical reconstruction of the patient's infancy, to uncover the unconscious roots of current behaviour and symptoms. He aims to help his patient towards lasting self-understanding and personal individuation.

In analysis, the vehicle for change is the analytic relationship. In family therapy, on the other hand, it is 'real life'. The family therapist is predominantly interested in the 'here and now' patterns of interaction between family members, and in understanding their part in currently maintaining symptoms in one or more members. He does not aim to promote insight (although this may often follow), so much as lasting alterations in family interaction patterns. The belief is that such changes in behaviour will 'reframe' a family's habitual view of reality, and give its members such a new or unexpected way of experiencing each other, that relationships will necessarily change also, making symptoms less necessary, and giving both the family as a whole, and the individuals within it, the opportunity for growth. If psychoanalysis is interested in the influence of the family on an individual's personality development, family therapy's primary object of study is the family itself. However, very importantly, the family therapist owes an enormous debt to the psychoanalytic attitude of seeking to understand the processes underlying the phenomena that the family present him with.

Object relations and internalised rules

Object relations theory (Fairbairn, 1952), with its account of the slow development of structural relationships between the parts of the individual's psyche, has many parallels with family therapy's thinking about the development of interpersonal structures of relationships within families (see Dare, 1979, 1981; Cooklin, 1979). Both the analyst and the family therapist are interested in the nature and qualities of the formative relationships within families. They share a belief that internalised experiences within one's family of origin are crucial in determining the nature of the adult personality. Object relations theory holds that the individual's sense of 'self' and 'other' is established from the infant's earliest interactions with and perceptions of his mother. Unconsciously these experiences colour all future expectations of himself, of the world, and of relationships. The analyst experiences the patient's transference on to himself of internalised unconscious expectations, needs and longings, which do not derive from the actuality of the present, but from the patient's infant and childhood experience. The work of analysis is to use the immediacy of the transference relationship to modify the lingering power which the original (unsatisfactory) relationships still have to distort and disturb present relationships.

It is the actual nature of relationships in the original situation which the family therapist seeks to modify. Stierlin (1977), an analyst and family therapist, writes:

> Transferences originate within families. It is family transactions which give rise to those relational patterns which later, inappropriately and repetitively, are transferred to non-family contexts . . . . Children are recipients of their parents' transferences, of those expectations, unfulfilled longings, needs for nourishment, wishes for revenge, etc., which derived from their own child-parent interaction.

The re-evocation of strong feelings from infancy throughout our adult lives is by no means always inappropriate, but is an inevitable process, whether we are conscious of it or not. Freud called this the 'repetition compulsion'. Commonly, for example, a marriage is invested by both partners with a need for it to make up for or reproduce some longed-for aspect of the lost parent-child relationship. Such a 'shared fantasy' (Dicks, 1967) can be either an enrichment of the marriage or doomed to disappointment, depending on the 'fit' of the partners' mutual demands. Or, the extent to which a new father tolerates the arrival of a first baby will depend on how much his old oedipal jealousy is re-evoked by the need to share his exclusive marital relationship with a third person.

Pincus and Dare (1978) and Boszormenyi-Nagy and Spark (1973) stress the lasting presence of these 'ghosts', activated not only throughout the individual's own life relationships, but also transmitted down the generations in the form of shared family 'myths'. The family therapist seeks to make these myths conscious in order to free the family from its blind obedience to them, just as the analyst seeks to free the individual from the unconscious influence of his internalised past.

Whereas the analyst is alert to notice the patient's transferences to himself, the family therapist is alert to the repetitive patterns of interaction and communication between family members, so that he can build up a picture of the largely unconscious 'rules' whereby the family habitually conduct their daily transactions. These rules are elaborated into a hypothetical map of the structure of the family, analogous to the analyst's hypothetical map of the intrapsychic structure of the mind. Cooklin (1979) and Dare (1979, 1981) both equate the internalisation of these transactional patterns and rules with the formation of object relations. For example, if a family therapist notices a repeating sequence in which a mother and her two daughters are usually contradicted or overridden by the father and son's opinions, but do not seem to notice or object to the process, he can hypothesise that a tacit family 'rule' exists that males are expected or allowed to dominate. It is as if an agreement has been reached between all parties. The family rule is 'learned' through the repeated transactional patterns and thus becomes an internalised aspect of the children's psychic self-representation. It will unconsciously affect their choice of spouses, their attitude to male or female employers and workmates, and their expectations of their own male and female children. Boszormenyi-Nagy and Spark (1973) have called such patterns 'relationship needs templates'.

When I assess a family, I make use of object relations theory in noticing ways in which the children are in the process of internalising the family's rules, at the same time as trying to reconstruct the internal objects which the parents hold from their past families, and assessing whether these are benign ego-building influences or entrapping ghosts. Like many family therapists I often draw up a geneogram or family tree in a session, to make more conscious and public the rules and myths embedded in their history, in obedience to which families are often compelled to conduct themselves. For example:

A 10-year-old, angry, rebellious boy, Martin, treated his divorced mother as if he were her abusive, violent husband. She could see little good in him. Through the geneogram, she showed him that he was preceded by three generations of alcoholic violent husbands, whose wives had been self-reliant, but bitter and lonely. It also became clear that the women in Martin's life, his mother, grandmother and sister, were quite indignantly excited by the 'liveliness' of their menfolk, and challenged by the wish to save them. It was at the point of sharing this information through the geneogram that Martin was able to say to his mother, 'I'm not like them', and she, recognising that, was then able to start the difficult work of consciously preventing her expectations of him from becoming a self-fulfilling prophecy.

When families can see where a child's 'life-script' derives from, the present can be freed from the past, and the child's choices of path can expand.

Transferences are made to an institution, as much as to an individual. Commonly, the presumed expertise of professionals is coloured by family members' fantasies about parenting. The family's ostensible request for help from an agency may have a hidden agenda of proving wrong some invisible, critical parent, or placating a reproachful parent, or cajoling and wooing a witholding, disappointing parent. Britton (1981) writes about the risk that professionals unconsciously respond to these hidden expectations and act out the very role prescribed for them. I believe an analytic background helps me become more easily aware of countertransference responses both in myself and in other professionals. The unconscious processes surrounding a family may emerge during the referral process, even before the family are first interviewed, and show as professional 'symptoms' – for example, 'inappropriate unconcern; surprising ignorance; undue complacency; uncharacteristic insensitivity or professional inertia' (Britton, 1981). I often work with a family system which includes the network of professionals surrounding it. Often a 'treatment alliance' has to be established between the helpers as much as with the client family, if the family work is not to be unconsciously sabotaged. Psychoanalysis has shed light also on the unconscious 'rescuer fantasies' of many of us in the helping professions, which we need to guard against.

The family life cycle

Families are by their nature continuously evolving. One of family therapy's anchoring concepts is the family life cycle, which owes a considerable debt to the psychoanalytic model of normal development. Each phase of human life is characterised by essential tasks which must be performed if entry to the next phase is to go well. The analytic literature concentrates predominantly on the individual's maturational tasks in infancy, and considers environmental influences mainly in so far as they encourage or inhibit the infant's development. Family therapy has much common ground with analytic authors like Jung (1953) and Erikson (1950, 1959) who emphasise the continuing task of individuation in later years and in relation to social groups. Family therapy further broadens the notion of developmental tasks to look at the simultaneous effects on all family members not only of each person's inner drive towards maturation, but also the expectations from and towards each other, and from and towards the wider environment, that fulfilment of the tasks requires or imposes.

Often what determines the point at which a family reaches a crisis and seeks professional help is the stress caused by several members of a family simultaneously being in critical transitions in their lives. My assessment of a family takes account of their flexibility and resources around the nodal points in their life cycle (e.g. birth of first child, school entry, children leaving home, retirement).

An example of stress in the family life cycle was John, age 11, referred suffering from vomiting and fear of school two months after transfer to secondary school. The anxiety he provoked in the family was extreme. Mrs M. sat with him all night; Mr M. lost money by taking days off work to sit and talk over John's worries with him; and his sister, age 15, protected him in the school playground. Enquiry revealed that Mr M.'s father had died the previous year and he had taken over the financially shaky family business. Mrs M.'s mother's increasing disability meant that their roles had recently been reversed, with Mrs M. now caring physically for her mother. John's sister, Kay, had just started dating her first serious boyfriend and was on the brink of entering the adult world of employment. Thus, John's own developmental hurdle (school entry) coincided with significant developmental changes for each member of his family, and his regressive symptoms could be seen as expressing for the whole family the fear and stress of transition. It allowed them all to regress with him to provide care and protection more appropriate to a little boy, and to get 'care' for the parents from professionals. The therapy subsequently concentrated on the whole family's life cycle crisis, not just John's.

In psychoanalytic terms, such stress can cause developmental arrest, or regression to a fixation point. In family therapy terms, it is also conceptualised as a regression, but is described more in terms of a family's regression to the inappropriate use of outdated or redundant ways of relating to one another, unable to expand their repertoire to make adjustments and compromises necessary for moving on. The capacity for 'leaving home' (psychologically and literally) is a common benchmark of health in family therapy. If one sees, for example, a young adult anorexic daughter enmeshed still with her parents in a damaging, hostile, dependence, one recognises that the very early stage of symbiotic fusion (Mahler, 1968) has been re-evoked by the threat of separation implicit in her age, and still has valency in the present. Individuation towards the age-appropriate next stage is blocked by habitual behaviour suitable to the earlier stage: e.g. parental overprotectiveness; parents speaking for the daughter; the daughter demanding nurture rather than independence, throwing tantrums instead of leaving home to lead her own life.

Circular interaction and causality

Much psychoanalytic writing concentrates on the intrapsychic rather than interpersonal factors in the developmental phases of life. Family therapy and social work have found more in common with psychoanalytic writers like Mahler (1968), Winnicott (1965) and Spitz (1965), who emphasise those aspects of environmental provision and the real (not just the internalised) figures surrounding the child, who facilitate or hinder the child's maturation. Winnicott's facilitating environment' and Mahler's concept of a symbiotic relationship between mother and infant strike a chord with the family therapy concept of circular interactions and continuous mutual influences within a family system, so that no one person can be said to 'cause' behaviour, but only to be a participant in a habitual pattern or 'dance' of interdependent circular causes and effects, inevitably involving all members of the system and balancing out their needs. As a family therapist, I am drawn to the psychoanalytic infant observation literature which sees baby and mother having mutual needs of and effects on each other, such that the baby is not merely the passive recipient of its mother's ministrations, but even at a few days old takes an active part in 'coaching' its mother. Similarly, I find useful Winnicott's persistent emphasis that alterations in the child's actual environment make a difference to his internalised objects and past objects. His aphorism: 'There is no such thing as an infant', meaning 'whenever one finds an infant one finds maternal care' is echoed by the family therapist, Whitaker (1983), who declares he does not believe in persons, only in bits of families.

Intergenerational boundaries

Another family therapy concept which seems to me to express familiar analytic ideas in a different framework, is that of 'boundaries'. Minuchin (1974) describes lucidly how the family therapist, by close attention to the family's repetitive patterns of interaction, can draw a hypothetical map of the structure of the family, dividing the family system into sub-groups. In particular Minuchin emphasises the importance for healthy family functioning of maintaining appropriate hierarchies and boundaries between the generations, neither so rigid that children are cut off from their parents' care, nor so diffuse that the children are looking after their parents. Like Holmes (1983) I believe family therapy's emphasis on intergenerational boundaries parallels the pre-eminence in analytic thinking of the oedipal situation. Oedipal over-involvement of, say, a father and daughter can be conceptualised in structural terms as a dangerous crossing of the generational boundary, and a weakening of the boundary around the marital pair.

Much of my structural family work consists of concrete – almost simplistic – indirect work on oedipal situations. For instance, I might encourage the sibling group to do more activities together and with friends, aiming to reclaim the oedipally over-involved daughter into her proper subsystem. The parents might be asked to spend more time in each other's company, not as parents, but as spouses (e.g. having a night out at the pictures on their own). Often I ask parents to show each other affection, or to have good, resolved arguments together, 'to teach the children how', or 'to prepare them for adult life', stressing the generational hierarchy.

The degree of difficulty with which these tasks are performed (the father may interfere with the sibling subsystem's prescribed activities), or their non/compliance with the 'task' (the parents resist going out together), give valuable concrete material for us to explore together their oedipal confusion of boundaries. Their resistance, as in psychoanalysis, reveals the nature of the conflict, and is the starting point for therapy.

Rarely would I offer the family any such interpretation of their family structure. Some families, once they have made alterations in their overt behaviour, and if symptoms have diminished, become reflective and curious to understand the relationships which underlay the problem behaviour. Therapy may then move into a different, insight-promoting phase. But for the majority of families seen in child psychiatry settings, who leave treatment quickly once the symptoms have abated, interpretations are singularly ineffective, and it is behaviour change itself which promotes insight.

Symptoms as symbolic and adaptive

From psychoanalysis I have drawn an attitude which I find abidingly and centrally useful. That is, to understand the symptom as a symbolic expression, and to see it as having positive, adaptive and progressive functions, signalling an opportunity for growth. I have found Bion's (1962) comments useful. He describes the infant's inevitable experience of frustration as he matures. The critical decision for development is whether frustration is evaded or the attempt is made to modify it. Thus the developmental crisis can become an opportunity or a threat. I see this crisis recurring throughout the family's (and individual's) life cycle. Sometimes the effect of the symptom in a family is to bring unresolved conflicts into focus, so that they can be worked over and modified, giving the family an opportunity to heal each other's wounds. At other times, the symptom is 'needed' by the family system to preserve old ways of relating in the face of imminent threats from maturational demands. This is Bion's evasion of frustration. It is, on the whole, such families who come for professional help.

Freud's (1923) structural theory sees ego, id and superego negotiating conflicting demands both between each other and from the external world. Sandler, Dare and Holder (1973) write: 'In order to resolve these often conflicting demands, the ego has at times to create the most complicated compromises, and in the last resort these compromises may result in the symptoms which, although painful and distressing to the individual who experiences them, represent the best possible adaptation that he can, in the particular circumstances, bring about.' This important idea is adapted in family therapy theory into an awareness of how the symptom 'organises' a compromise between different family members' needs and demands so that the system's homeostasis is maintained, and allows no change to occur too great for the family's fundamental stability and continuity. Sometimes, the system's compromises are so extreme that it is hard to see any positive adaptational benefit. Sometimes the symptom bearer is sacrificed or scapegoated, the only apparent arrangement whereby the family group can remain intact. But, significantly, the family is preserved, as much for the rejected member as for the rest.

I find Klein's concept of projective identification useful here. It is a truly interactional process. Not only do parents project anxiety-provoking aspects of themselves onto their children, the children collude and behave in a way that fulfills their parents' fears (Martin, above). The parents are able through their children to experience vicarious gratification of their projected impulses (without guilt or anxiety) and can punish the children for expressing them. The children's unconscious self-sacrifice to the needs of the system earns them paradoxically the important sense of belonging, and of predictability.

It is essential for the therapist to respect the positive attempts at adaptation that even the most destructive symptoms represent. Psychoanalysis and family therapy share a belief in understanding a symptom as a communication – both an expression of and an attempted solution to the problem. A family therapist tries to make a systemic assessment of the symptom's function in preserving impor- tant relationships, and defending the family group from some greater imagined danger. This brings him close to the analytic idea of 'secondary gain'. The whole family colludes to preserve the 'sick role' for one member because its hidden advantages, for the time being, outweigh the evident disadvantages of having a 'problem' in the family.

Alice, 16 years old, was referred to the Child Psychiatry Department because she had become depressed, stopped eating because of stomach pains for which no physical cause was evident, and had suffered severe weight loss. Her father had also been losing weight because of a recently-diagnosed terminal stomach cancer. The rest of the family were coping with the terrible situation by pinning all hope on father being a fighter. Because they were unable to express their anger with father for letting them down, they instead turned furiously on Alice for not 'helping herself', and for 'enjoying' the doctors' attention.

Alice's symptom was a graphic expression of the family problem. She, unlike father, could openly weep and express her suffering about her bodily pain and wasting, and about feeling near death. Mother, unable to care for father, had to nurse Alice. Her symptom converted the family mood from courageous denial to angry suffering. Alice's attempted 'solution' can be seen as allowing mother to reassure father that parenting would continue despite death, and also as deflecting the family's (unfair and attacking) anger towards father on to herself, thus allowing its expression.

Another aspect of the way a symptom functions to 'solve' a problem is that, especially in families with children, a symptom often mobilises help, from family, friends or professionals. Children are often seen as 'bringing' their families for treatment, and as having the positive and helpful capacity for expressing the family's pathology. Similarly Winnicott (1956) writes of the 'antisocial tendency' which is 'characterised by an element in it which compels the environment to be important. The patient through unconscious drives compels someone to attend to management. . . . The antisocial tendency implies hope.'

The 'Milan method' of family therapy, developed by Palazzoli *et al.*, (1978) has many concepts congruent with psychoanalysis. It sees chronic symptoms in families as desperate attempts to preserve the status quo under pressure from some threat of change, usually provoked by the requirements of maturation. The Milan method is interesting for psychoanalysis because, unlike many schools of family therapy, it offers families an interpretation. The interpretation is designed to be both systemic and 'binding' – that is, to describe the bind or dilemma that a family finds itself in, so that each member of the system (including the therapist and other social agencies) can see themselves as playing an essential part in maintaining the problem complained of. The wish to move on and the wish to regress are brought into vivid focus, are acknowledged as equally valuable, but the conflict is emphasised. The symptomatic behaviour is 'positively connoted' (Palazzoli *et al.*, 1978) as being in the service of preserving existing patterns of family relationships from the dangers of too rapid development or change within the family system. This reflects psychoanalytic respect for defences as necessary constructs of the ego in the face of more demands on the psychic structure than can be managed. There is a large psychoanalytic literature on resistance, and family therapy has been much influenced by analytic awareness that change and growth are both wished for and feared. The paradox, familiar to family therapists, of patients seeking help for solving problems, but wanting a solution which costs little in terms of change or pain, has long been the business of 'working through' in analysis. Often a transference interpretation is made, for example, respecting the family's earnest search for 'expert' advice from the therapy team, but noting that to give such advice undermines the family's confidence in their own problem solving abilities. The Milan interpretation derives its power from the insertion into the collective 'family mind' of a new, more expansive world-view, a paradoxical reframing of their reality in a way that will make their old perspective on life inoperable, and thus free them for change. An example of such an interpretation is taken from midway through the treatment of a couple in their late thirties, who were unable to decide whether to have children or to separate:

> We've been struck by the way the two of you are united by a great sense of disappointment in relationships. On the basis of this disappointment, you have built a hope that things will be better.
> If your sense of hope is the strongest bond between you, you may choose to separate and look elsewhere for a better relationship with another person. If, however, your sense of disappointment is the strongest bond between you, then you may choose to stay together and accept that you may never satisfy each other in the way you would have wished'.

The hope that this seed will germinate in each partner's unconscious parallels analytic technique.

Counter-transference and affiliation

A major way in which psychoanalysis influences me is in the use of my counter-transference. Whilst ostensibly paying attention to the manifest content of people's discourse, the family therapist, like the analyst, is also looking to understand 'process', in the belief that latent unconscious content is being enacted in the relationships in the room. From psychoanalysis, family therapy has learned the value of the 'frame', the formal, artificial structure of the therapy session, in which relationships become distilled and intensified.

Every family therapist knows what a powerful experience it is to interact with a family, and much has been written about the dangers of the therapist being sucked in or 'affiliated' to the family's habitual rules, so he loses both objectivity and therapeutic leverage. But it is also acknowledged that, to a degree, a family therapist needs to become part of the family system, needs to empathise with and experience the pressures and realities of relationships within the family, as part of his assessment. The ability to get in and get out again is one of the first and most difficult techniques a family therapist has to learn. The use of a one-way screen, and an observing therapy team is invaluable, and, in my own experience, also a personal analysis.

I use my counter-transference, for example, when a polite, anxious family lets me know – by the same subtle, non-verbal means which they use to communicate with each other – that certain subjects which may lead to argument cannot be noticed, let alone discussed. The discomfort I feel may lead me unconsciously to avoid that area of potential conflict, if I unwittingly obey the family's rules. However, if I can raise my awareness of discomfort to consciousness, and notice the covert process whereby I have been silenced in the service of homeostasis, then I am in possession of a valuable new piece of psychological information, which aids my assessment of where the family's conflicts lie. With other families, I may find myself feeling irritable, rescuing, punitive or helpless, and recognise that these feelings are evoked in me by the family's power to affiliate individuals to their 'dance'.

This affiliation is a pitfall if it remains unconscious, but also is a rich source of therapeutic knowledge. This is exactly parallel to the analytic literature on counter-transference feelings, which were first regarded by Freud as an impediment, and later as a major therapeutic tool.

Techniques

The techniques of psychoanalysis and family therapy are dissimilar. Family therapy, as a short-term therapy, cannot rely on the development of a dependent, trusting treatment alliance to overcome resistance, and therefore has developed techniques to engage the family, and keep their attention. The techniques I use are active and directive, usually demanding interaction between family members in the session, often intensifying or prolonging it, or blocking their traditional, redundant patterns, in order to have the family experience the immediate impact of different ways of communicating with each other.

Sometimes family therapy technique is caricatured as manipulative, or as only interested in the 'here-and-now' and therefore inimical to psychoanalysis. I believe this overlooks many parallels. It is clear from what has been said earlier that many family therapists are as much interested in what the family brings of its history into the present, as in their visible interactions in the therapy room. Analysts too are interested in the past largely insofar as it helps to understand the present. The layman's view of analysis is that it provides the patient with intellectual understanding of his problems. In fact, analysis, like family therapy, is essentially experiential, and derives its power from the here-and-now immediacy of the patient-analyst relationship. Thus, Strachey (1934) identified the here-and-now interpretation as 'mutative'.

Some of family therapy's most characteristic techniques are experiential and playful. The use of metaphor, role-playing, task-setting, story-telling, pretend games, rituals, are all designed to shake families, often unwittingly, out of their habitual patterns. Sometimes it is possible to achieve change by persuading them to play a game of pretending to act differently. The experience can be revelatory and moving. The ability to play is recognised in the analytic literature (see Winnicott, 1971b) as necessary for emotional growth and healing, as much in adults as in children. Jung (1954) writing about the value of fantasy and play, says, 'My aim is to bring about a psychic state in which my patient begins to experiment with his own nature – a state of fluidity, change and growth where nothing is eternally fixed and hopelessly petrified.' This sentiment is echoed by family therapy's abhorrence of a 'stuck' system where the family dances forever to the same tune.

Playful, strategic techniques which encourage the family to interact differently can also be powerful promoters of insight.

For example, a single mother and her two sons, aged 5 and 9, had used family therapy very well to control the boys' aggression and anxiety following the parents' divorce. But the therapy lingered on inexplicably because of periodic (mild) crises in the boys' behaviour. The mother (whose relationship with them was usually warm) always reacted by blaming and punishing them. The therapy team understood this both as the boys' testing of their mother's ability to cope with them single-handed, and as mother's wish to preserve a relationship with the therapist.

In an attempt to end the therapy at the same time as bolstering mother's confidence in her undoubted parenting ability, the therapist made the following intervention:

We're surprised that the boys can be alternately so well and so badly behaved, and that no one can predict which they will be at any moment. We have a rather crazy idea, which is that they may feel unconsciously they have to keep up the bad behaviour in order to make sure you [mother] keep getting the help and support from us which you have valued and used so well.

We would like to test our hunch, for an experimental period of two weeks, by asking you [mother] to pretend that they are behaving well and that things in general are getting better. You [boys] shouldn't change your behaviour at all. Be both good and naughty as usual, but try to guess when your mother really means it, and when she's only pretending that things are so much better.

The result two weeks later was mother's new insight that her own attitude to the boys was a major determinant of their behaviour, since they had behaved well; and also her recognition that her lack of a husband, and wish for one, had been inappropriately transferred into the therapy situation. The remaining two sessions before closure centred on mother's efforts to start a new social life.

Conclusion

As a social worker, I have felt sometimes torn between the principle of client self-determination on the one hand and the expectation on the other that social workers should find solutions and 'do something' about clients problems. Analysis and family therapy share a belief, which I have found increasingly central to my work, that people wish to take responsibility for themselves, and their wellbeing depends on a sense of self-reliance. Obviously there are some families who cannot master their own circumstances, and the statutory role of the social worker, and the direct provision of services must come into play. But I believe social workers sometimes attribute incompetence too readily, and by talking over a problem and 'solving' it, demote the client both in fact and in the client's own self-perception. Both the family therapist and the analyst believe that the aim of therapy is to reveal expanded options, freeing the client to take them up. Family therapy may set its sights lower than psychoanalysis, but is no less committed to securing enduring change. Analysis has furthered my development as a social worker in understanding when 'being helpful' is not helpful. I have unlearned many of my old social work ways through the experience of trying new and challenging methods. It is just such an experience I seek to give the families with whom I work.

6 Understanding Bulimia: A Feminist Psychoanalytic Account of Women's Eating Problems[1]

Mira Dana and Marilyn Lawrence

The approach to eating disorders which is presented here was developed by the authors at the Women's Therapy Centre in London. The Women's Therapy Centre is a small voluntary organisation which receives funding from the District Health Authority, the London Boroughs and the DHSS as well as a range of charitable trusts. The Centre provides long and short-term group and individual therapy for women with a variety of problems. In addition, there is a very popular workshop programme which allows many women to explore and focus on specific issues which are relevant to them.

Since its foundation, ten years ago, the Womens Therapy Centre has taken a pioneering approach to women's eating problems. Women with problems of compulsive eating have been offered individual and group therapy, as well as self-help groups set up from the Centre. There have always been requests for help from anorexics, who are usually referred for individual therapy. In recent years, the Centre has received an enormous number of enquiries from women suffering from the eating disorder we here call bulimia – women who compulsively overeat and then make themselves sick. We have therefore been concerned to formulate an understanding and a range of treatment responses to this problem. The authors are also closely involved in the educational programme at the Women's Therapy Centre and are therefore aware of the amount of interest in this problem from mental health professionals. We are closely involved with social workers, community psychiatric nurses, psychologists and doctors who are working both within the health service and in community settings with a group of women who create a good deal of concern and anxiety in their helpers.

The understanding we have developed at the Women's Therapy Centre can be used in a range of different helping strategies in a variety of settings. Social workers have had considerable success in using these ideas to run groups and workshops in hospital outpatient departments as well as GP practices and community based organisations such as the Family Welfare Association. In this chapter we set out to offer an understanding, a way of approaching, women's eating disorders and in particular bulimia nervosa.

A great deal has been written about eating disorders, especially within the last decade. The most valuable approaches from our viewpoint are those which are concerned with the meanings these symptoms have in women's lives, which tend to be derived even if only loosely from psychoanalytic understandings. The work of Hilde Bruch (1974, 1978) is especially important in this respect, based on a psychodynamic understanding of developmental issues, which is interesting to compare with that of Thomä (1967) who had earlier developed a psychoanalytic approach. Mara Selvini-Palazzoli (1974), on the other hand, uses an object-relations analysis which she later came to feel was superceded by her family transactional approach, and the family therapy tradition is continued by Minuchin, Rosman and Baker (1978) in their study of psychosomatic families. A number of writers opt for an emphasis on the management of eating problems rather than the meanings of them (cf. Palmer, 1980; Dally & Gomez, 1979), while Crisp (1980) is interested in both understanding eating problems and managing them within a traditional psychiatric in-patient setting. More recently, a few books have appeared which attempt to understand eating disorders within the context of women's lives and experience, and which could be described as a feminist contribution (cf. Lawrence, 1984, 1987; MacLeod, 1981; White & White, 1983; Orbach, 1986).

The distinctive feature of the approach of the Women's Therapy Centre to women's problems is its emphasis on both the inner psychological world of the woman as well as the social situation within which women exist. Our approach is to understand all eating disorders as significant and meaningful expressions of women's difficulties. We shall therefore spend some time looking at anorexia and compulsive eating, but our main emphasis will be on bulimia – eating followed by self-induced vomiting.

Many of the women who have this symptom and the professionals who treat them, find their particular patterns of eating behaviour bizarre and impossible to understand. There seems to be no point to it; it does not seem to achieve anything. Our contention here is that like other forms of disordered eating, bulimia contains a message that goes far beyond the limits of the behaviour itself. It is with this meaning that we will be concerned and with its implications for the kind of therapy we offer.

Eating, taking nourishment, is a fundamental human concern. It is not, like breathing, a reflex action, but it is an activity in which we must all engage if we are to survive. As babies we are entirely dependent on being fed by others. As adults, a wide range of social, cultural and symbolic meanings are attached to the activity of eating. By observing people's eating habits, we can learn a good deal about their attitudes towards themselves and others, their social world and their status within it. Eating is never a mere physical function: it contains and carries much more than is evident on the surface. This is why any disturbance in the eating function is bound to fascinate and appall us. The almost obsessive interest of the media, of literature and of the medical and helping professionals can also be attributed to the fact that these symptoms are powerfully symbolic metaphors.

When we talk about a metaphor, we have in mind a situation, an incident or a piece of behaviour which represents or correlates directly to another situation which has the same meaning. If we look at one, we can learn and understand something about the other. To relate this more specifically to eating disorders – bulimia, for example – we can look at the actual eating behaviour and attempt to see from it what is happening in the woman's inner world. To be of any use in formulating a therapeutic response, our understanding must be based on more than mere hypothesis or theory. In fact it is derived from work over a number of years with women who suffer from these difficulties and who have discussed the connections with us.

The literature on women's eating problems has two distinct areas of focus: one is the *results* of the disordered eating pattern; the other is the nature of the disordered eating itself. The first focus would describe anorexia in terms of a wish to avoid weight gain, perhaps a way of avoiding physical maturation. Compulsive eating, on the other hand, can be understood in terms of the woman's need to stay fat in order to protect herself from certain conflicts. In the case of bulimia this kind of approach does not take us very far. The bulimic woman is usually fairly 'normal' in appearance, looking neither particularly fat nor especially thin. In our more recent work with bulimic women, we have become convinced that we need to focus on the second area, the disordered eating, if we are to understand the problem. If we ignore the meaning of the eating pattern, we miss the essential symbolism of the problem.

Eating and its meanings

We can generalise by saying that a woman's eating pattern symbolises that woman's capacity for self-nurturance, her capacity to take nurturing in and her ability to nurture other people. The woman who eats compulsively feels under pressure to take in everything; she cannot discriminate. She is aware that she needs something, that something is lacking, but instead of finding out what these needs are and attempting to meet them, she swamps herself with all sorts of things that she doesn't really need at all. She tries to limit herself, to ration herself, but she always ends up greedily gobbling up everything she can find. A woman who eats in a compulsive way is actually very bad at asking for appropriate things for herself. She may experience herself as demanding, greedy and insatiable, but she usually ends up doing the nurturing rather than receiving it.

An anorexic woman on the other hand, feels that she has to deny that she has any needs at all. Nothing can be taken in and there is little to give out. Or at least that is what is being proclaimed by the symptom. Relationships are experienced as intrusive and dangerous. The only hope lies in self-sufficiency – a denial of any possibility of dependency or nurturance by self or others.

The woman who is bulimic, who eats quite large quantities of food and then makes herself sick, is using her symptom to say something rather different. Symbolically, she is able to take things in, unlike the anorexic. However, unlike the woman who eats compulsively, she is not able to hold on to it. What bulimic women can take in varies. Sometimes it is everything, without discrimination, sometimes it is more measured amounts. But whatever the quantity, once it has been taken in, it is no use. It is not experienced as nourishing but rather as poisonous. It is not satisfaction but danger that the bulimic woman associates with her food. This is indicative of her inability to hold onto anything good, and not only at the level of food. Bulimic women often find it extremely difficult to allow themselves to accept something good, such as a caring relationship, a compliment or some success at work.

We now need to take a careful look at the underlying social and psychological dynamics which are being so powerfully dramatised in women's eating problems. It is certainly true to say that in our society, women experience much more difficulty and conflict about meeting their needs and having their needs met than men do. Very many women find it hard to ask for what they want, and feel confused and guilty when they experience their own needs for care and nurturance. Jane Flax (1981) suggests that the nature of the mother-daughter relationship itself makes nurturing baby girls a much more difficult and conflictual task for mothers than caring for baby boys. The closer identification of the mother with the baby girl means that a girl is likely to stir up in her mother all the mother's unresolved conflict about her own needs and how or whether she gets them met.

Eichenbaum and Orbach (1985) suggest that mothers unconsciously know that one of the things they have to teach their daughters is not to expect too much. The mother 'prepares' her daughter for the fact that as an adult woman she will not receive very much care and nurturance by limiting the amount of care she receives as a baby. They suggest that the mother's own unmet needs may add an extra complication. The mother may unconsciously believe that the baby daughter can meet some of her own need and longing for care. Thus, at least in fantasy, there is a reversal of the nurturing role or at any rate an expectation of reciprocity of caring. This might mean that the baby girl will not be allowed to have an adequate amount of emotional care within the earliest symbiotic relationship. It may well be that this very early withholding of a certain amount of care from baby girls is, even at this stage, symbolised in terms of food. It seems likely that the mother will not encourage her daughter to be 'greedy' with food, while she may delight in the 'healthy' appetite of her baby boy. In this way, the links between emotional nurturing and the taking in of food to meet bodily needs are being made for the little girl.

In adult life we find that women are attuned to meeting the needs of others and often perceive their own needs in terms of other people. But still the 'food' symbolisation remains powerful. Hilary Graham (1984) gives many examples of the ways in which women put their families' needs before their own in present day Britain if there is not enough food to go round. She quotes a woman from Marsden's study, *Mothers Alone* (1973), for example, who says that 'I'd rather the children had the food than I did. It seems to satisfy me more.'

Here we see again that physical and emotional satisfaction are being confused – or rather that they are experienced as inseparable. Clearly, the mother's *hunger* is not being satisfied by feeding her children, but something which overrides her hunger may be.

What we have been suggesting here is that women's problems with food and eating are the symptoms by which women express difficulties in the area of meeting their emotional needs. We have every reason to believe that the socialisation of women as carers, the ways in which women are encouraged from an early age to care for others rather than themselves, will make women much more likely than men to suffer from difficulties in this area. It also seems likely that women learn when they are quite young to symbolise these difficulties in the relatively 'safe' arena of their relationship to food. This means that instead of a woman taking the risky step of telling those who are close to her that she needs more emotional support, more signs of their care and concern, more attention to her as an individual, she is likely to keep all this to herself and to 'play out' the problem in her relationship to food.

The metaphor of bulimia

We can now look at the special case of bulimia. Until quite recently, bulimia was usually considered to be a variant of either compulsive eating or anorexia. It was thought to be merely a way of controlling weight in the face of overeating. Often, in fact, bulimia was and still is regarded by practitioners as a kind of 'failed' anorexia. The woman is deemed to be unable any longer to control her weight by abstinence and resorts instead to self-induced vomiting. The attitudes of professionals to anorexic and bulimic women is discussed and analysed by Troy Cooper (1987). Many bulimic women also feel that they would much prefer to be able to resist food altogether. It is only when they begin to unlock the symbolic meanings of the symptom that they begin to understand why they have chosen their particular way of expressing distress and what this 'choice' says about their internal world. Unlike compulsive eating, bulimia does not usually result in the woman becoming fat. It differs from anorexia in that nourishment is actually taken in and there is none of the reward to be gained from self-denial, the feelings of strength and control. On the contrary, the overwhelming feeling is of loss of control. But unlike the women who eats compulsively without making herself sick, the bulimic woman does not *show* that she is out of control. Her guilt and shame are not visible in terms of her fat. Rather, she passes as normal, yet she always has the sense that her normality is a fraud and a sham.

It is the hidden nature of the symptom which gives the first clues as to what is being stated symbolically. The symptom says that although the woman is thought to be normal, attractive, well-organised and successful at what she does, she herself knows that really she is lonely and starving. It may appear that she can deal with her needs openly and realistically, that she can express them and get them met. In fact though, underneath it all, she is a greedy baby; her needs are too huge ever to be met, too destructive to even allow other people to see. She cannot eat, but only, as she would call it, 'binge'. Bingeing is an important concept in our understanding of how the bulimic woman sees herself. Bingeing is not eating; to binge is not to nourish oneself. On the contrary, it is to make a mockery out of the whole process of self nourishment. Bingeing is 'sick' eating. And it is followed by quite literally being sick.

Unlike the anorexic woman, the woman whose symptom is bulimia knows that she has needs. They are not always suppressed or denied, but she perceives her own neediness as a great monstrous sickness, entirely out of keeping with the rest of her life. It is quite clear that for bulimic women, the throwing-out part of the symptom, the vomiting, is just as important as the taking in. They are twin aspects of the same problem, and if we are to understand the metaphor, we have to understand the symptom as a whole. The symptom as a whole represents the ambivalence towards nourishing herself, towards finding a way of getting what she needs. When she takes in good things, she can only do so in a way which is violent and self destructive. She takes them in in such a way that she is overcome by guilt and horror at her own neediness and can only find relief by giving up the nourishment and returning to a state of emptiness and isolation. The shame and agony involved in vomiting up the food is a compensation, a suitable punishment, for having greedily swallowed it in the first place. It is not just that too much food has been eaten and the fear of becoming fat makes vomiting inevitable. That is too simple an explanation. It is that needs have been perceived which are so terrifying that they must simultaneously be denied.

Perhaps we can now look more closely at the actual behaviour of the bulimic woman and the contradictions it embodies. She consumes an enormous amount of food. She eats whatever is in sight. She might eat raw food which should be cooked, frozen food without waiting for it to thaw, food intended for the dog or cat – we have encountered all of these in our work with bulimic women. She eats without any control over how much, what, where or when. Then she goes to the bathroom, locks herself in and in secret she vomits it all up, throws it all out. Then she cleans herself up, cleans the mess up and goes out relieved and empty of all the food which has become so bad and poisonous inside her. Some women spend hours cleaning up after themselves so that others will not discover the secret messy part of them.

The contradictions embodied by bulimia can be summarised in the following way:

The eating behaviour is all about ambivalence.

There is an obsession with food and an obsession with vomiting.

The eating of massive amounts of food – much more than she can handle – and then throwing it *all* up. The good, nourishing food gets thrown out along with the excess. The baby goes with the bathwater.

She fills herself up and empties herself out immediately afterwards.

She desperately seeks nourishment, yet harms her body at the same time.

She deadens her emotions and at the same time enlivens her physical sensations with the pain of the vomiting.

Bulimia is compulsive consumption, but at the same time, the inability to hold anything in.

It is desperately wanting, but at the same time violently rejecting.

It is submitting to the urge, but at the same time controlling its consequences.

Pulling and pushing.

All or nothing.

If we begin to translate some of these conflicts and contradictions and to look for the meaning of the symptom in the woman's inner world, we can see that the essence of the conflict is the good versus the bad inside herself. It is about having a clean, neat, good, unneedy appearance, which conceals behind it a messy, needy, bad part which must be kept secret. Another aspect of this conflict is shown in the way in which the food itself, once consumed, becomes bad and poisonous and must be thrown out and rejected.

The good and the bad

All of us as human beings have to live with the reality of the existence of good and bad things and feelings, both inside us and in the external world. All of us want to have good, positive, pleasurable feelings about ourselves and our environment. In our fantasy, we long for a situation where only good feelings exist; in reality, we have to reconcile the good and the bad. One of the ways to deal with our bad felings is to split them off from the good ones and to put them aside in a well-defined corner of our lives. This corner we then label 'bad' and we can choose to ignore the feelings there which would be in the way of or mess up the rest of life. This is what the bulimic woman does. If we look at the action of locking herself in the bathroom and throwing up her binge, we see that she is getting rid of the bad food she has just consumed, or that which has turned bad inside her. At a symbolic level, we see that the mess, the badness, is kept in one room in the house, one part of her life, the bulimia. It is the bulimic behaviour which deals with all her feelings of badness.

The function of the bulimia can then be seen as to encapsulate the messy, dirty and disgusting part of her in the hidden scene in the bathroom, behind locked doors and in secret. It is a way of diverting unpleasant and painful feelings which are the result of hurtful interactions with the external world on to an internal object which is familiar and safe. This enables the woman to maintain the pleasant, cheerful front which she so values and which she believes others like her for.

We believe that it is extremely important for women who have eating problems and for their counsellors, caseworkers or therapists to understand the implications of the symbolic nature of their symptoms. Casework or therapy can itself be thought of as a nurturing experience. A feminist therapy in particular is likely to offer to women a relationship which is caring and which in many ways replicates the kind of relationship which may or may not have been provided at a much earlier stage of development. The nature of this relationship is such that for the woman, the therapist will come to represent the care-giver, the nurturer, the mother. For the woman with an eating disorder, this is likely to present a problem. The woman who has difficulties in being nurtured, with getting her needs met, with allowing anyone to give her nourishment or with taking in good things when they are offered, is likely to find a therapeutic relationship initially difficult. In spite of the difficulties and just because it parallels a nurturing situation, psychotherapy is the most suitable form of treatment in which some of the issues to do with caring and being cared for can be resolved.

It is therefore both interesting and disturbing that, within the British National Health Service, psychotherapy is very rarely offered to women with eating disorders. Specialists working with anorexic women will very often delay offering psychotherapy until there has been some gain in weight. What they fail to understand is that weight cannot be maintained or increased until something has changed in the woman's capacity to take in nourishment. Similarly, in the case of bulimic women, behavioural treatments aimed at maintaining a balanced food intake are the most usual treatments offered ignoring the meaning and significance of the symptom the woman has adopted. This failure to use psychotherapy in the treatment of eating problems is in part the result of a recognition that women with problems of this sort can find psychotherapy difficult and can therefore present problems to the therapist. Women with eating problems may find therapy difficult precisely because their difficulties lie in the area of taking in and making use of good things. But we should not assume that the woman who finds it difficult to use therapy is unsuitable for it. The woman with problems in the area of food and eating is, through therapy, offered the opportunity to experience a kind of nurturing, a caring relationship which may help her to resolve some of these very difficulties.

Working with women who eat compulsively

Although a good deal has been written on the subject of therapy with compulsive eaters, we would like to look briefly at the implications of what we have said so far for this group of women. Women who eat in a compulsive way eat more than they are hungry for, yet they have a constant sense of still being empty. Unlike women in an anorexic phase, compulsive eaters do acknowledge their need for food, together with other basic needs they have in their lives. Unlike bulimic women, they experience no relief from emptying themselves of what they have consumed; as much as they take in, there is always the sense of being empty, of not having had enough. The nourishment has disappeared somewhere, as though it had never been taken in.

Although she may eat and eat, at the end of it all she still feels hungry. This is not hunger in the physical sense: physically she may feel stuffed with food. But she has a sense of still being hungry for whatever it was she yearned before the binge began. She is left with a sense of being unsatisfied with what has been taken in, as though it is not enough. Of course, it will never be enough, because usually when she reaches for food, it is not food but something else that she is needing. As it is not possible to satisfy her emotional hunger with food, she is always left unsatisfied, empty. The suggestion of a restrictive diet to deal with a problem of compulsive eating is not only unhelpful because it ignores the real issues – but it is positively harmful too. Her initial feelings of emptiness are not attended to, and the fear of feeling empty, which is what drives her to overeat, is magnified by stopping her from eating what she wants. Any treatment which tries to control the eating behaviour without understanding its meaning and significance is bound to fail.

Working with women in an anorexic phase

The major difficulty in working with anorexic women is that very little can be taken in, either from therapy or from anywhere else. The anorexic goal is self-sufficiency, the achievement of a steady state within a closed system. Nothing can change, nothing must enter. The problem is of course that a persistent refusal to eat does bring with it very dramatic changes. The end result is the outcome which is so terrifying and yet so mysteriously seductive to the anorexic woman: force feeding. The challenge in psychotherapy is to enable the woman to take something in because she feels able to do so without the therapist resorting to force feeding. Where the therapist indulges in 'force feeding' in the sense of pushing interpretations or insisting on certain therapeutic goals this also misses the point. It fails to address the real issue, which is the difficulty the woman has in feeding and nourishing herself.

There is a real sense in which a traditional psychoanalytic technique is not suitable for working with an anorexic or bulimic woman, relying as it does on the capacity of the woman to regulate how much help she needs and is able to take in. Psychoanalysis tends to give to the client a great deal of responsibility for the amount of help which can be 'ingested', allowing the analyst little more than the power to comment on or interpret the client's capacity to take in what she needs from therapy. The kind of therapy which we have in mind will make the therapist a much more active and responsible partner. Understanding the situation and the difficulties of the client, she will atempt to offer what is needed at the kind of rate at which it can be used. Although this has been asserted by a number of writers over the past decade (e.g. Bruch, 1978; Lawrence, 1984), we still come across therapists who insist on treating anorexic women lying on a couch, failing to appreciate how important it is that she can see what she is eating.

Frequency of sessions is another issue in working with anorexic women. Therapists who are accustomed to working analytically may be tempted to offer to see their anorexic clients several times a week. Indeed, we have heard of child psychotherapy clinics where it is customary to offer therapy four times a week to young people with anorexia. These therapists very often complain that their clients are difficult to keep in treatment. It is our experience that a woman in an acutely anorexic phase may find an hour a week a very long time. She may only manage to engage in therapeutic work for a part of her session. The rest of the time may be given over to a diary of weekly events or else devoted to a defensive monologue on the symptom, leaving no space for the therapist to intervene. We need to remember that women in an anorexic phase, as well as surviving on very small amounts of food, also thrive on small amounts of therapy. What for other clients might feel quite unsatisfying, produces for the anorexic a sensation of fullness. It is pointless to try to persuade her to binge; to offer too much therapy too soon is to awaken in her the terrifying recognition that if she allows herself to acknowledge her needs, she will experience them as insatiable. Until she has experienced in therapy the distinction between autonomy and self-sufficiency, she will be unable to allow herself to be nourished. Self-sufficiency is a denial of any needs which have to be met by someone outside the self; it is the assertion, 'I have everything I need within myself.' Autonomy, on the other hand, is the experience of being truly different from and separate from other people, able to act according to internal rather than external demands. But autonomy is based upon the experience of having had needs met, of having got enough from other people in terms of care and concern in order to be able to take care of oneself.

It is only as she begins to experience the therapeutic relationship as helpful and supportive of her attempts at autonomy that she will begin to feel safe about taking in both help and food.

Working with bulimic women

The bulimic woman comes seeking help with her symptoms. She comes in desperation about her patterns of eating, not yet able to fully acknowledge that she may need help with other issues in her life. Initially, she will concentrate very much on her bulimia. Sometimes the worker may be the first, the only person to know about it, the only person with whom she can talk freely about her secret, messy corner. She will need some time to share this knowledge, to get things off her chest and to see if the therapist can be trusted with that part of herself which she hates to acknowledge. This first period will be spent talking about food, about her binges and how horrible and disgusting she feels about what she does. The therapist will want to help her to move gradually on from this total preoccupation with food and eating as the only problem she has. To allow her to concentrate for too long merely on her eating problem is to do to her what she does to herself by her eating and vomiting. She is diverting attention from the more painful and serious conflicts in her life and in her inner world. By moving away from the idea of food and eating as the only problems, the worker allows her to see her life as a whole in a way which is more real. This does not mean that she should not talk about food, her eating and vomiting at all; but rather that these will become a part of her world rather than the centre of it; they will become one expression of her 'badness, her incompetence, her self-hatred, but not the encapsulation of it.

Therapy itself embodies her contradiction: how is she to take in good things from the therapist when she throws up every good thing she takes in? So she comes for help terrified that the other person will be overwhelmed by her needs, her bad feelings and the demands she wants to make. She wants to keep her rubbish, her needs, her baby-self (as she feels it to be), locked away from herself and from the therapist. Her hope is that she will be able to share these needs as well as her terror of what will happen if she does. Her fear is that she will overwhelm and frighten the therapist, who could not possibly like her and want to help her if she saw that part of her which is so needy and baby-like – or worse, that the therapist will perhaps mock and abuse that vulnerable side if she allows it to be seen.

We might say that the central characteristic of the bulimic woman in therapy is her ambivalence. Anorexic women also show a very high degree of ambivalence about giving up the symptom. This ambivalence has to be acknowledged and worked with if it is not to be acted out in the form of missed appointments or the seeking of other forms of treatment (Lawrence, 1984). If the ambivalence can be acknowledged, the anorexic woman will generally take what she wants and leave the rest. At times, this will not be enough and the worker will have to 'tempt her appetite'. The bulimic woman, on the other hand, can often appear very greedy in therapy. Sometimes she will exhaust the therapist with her despair, with her demands which can seem impossible to satisfy. Then she may go off and manage her life in her customarily efficient manner. It is as though her despair and desperation have been thrown up with the therapist, leaving her free to carry on – until the next time. In this way, none of the sadness and despair which are so apparent in her inner world and in the therapy is allowed to intrude into her outer world. In spite of her obvious and acknowledged neediness, the bulimic woman in therapy is often very frightened to hold on to the care and attention which the worker is able to offer, and it is very important that these ambivalent feelings are acknowledged and worked with. The bulimic client is likely to experience towards the worker the strong ambivalent feelings of which she is so afraid; sometimes she will feel warmth, love and gratitude for the care which is being offered; sometimes she will feel hurt and rejected because the therapist cannot meet all her needs; then again she may experience the care and nurturing which is being offered as poisonous and will want to vomit it out.

The aims of therapy with a woman in a bulimic episode

The bulimic woman becomes trapped in the idea of all or nothing. She must either eat everything or she must vomit it all up. Either she must not allow herself to have any needs, or else she must turn into a needy baby. To her, 'good' means thin, self-contained, always coping, never complaining. 'Bad' means fat, ugly, lazy, greedy, demanding and falling apart. There is no possibility of the good and bad being mixed and combined as part of each human being's nature.

She has the same feelings and misperceptions about the help she is offered. Either it must be totally good, the caseworker or therapist must be perfect and able to meet all her needs, be there for her whenever she needs her. Or if therapy does not give her everything she wants and has always wanted, it will be useless to her and must be got rid of. For the bulimic woman, the principal aim of therapy is to experience that although it is not perfect, although she will continue to have some needs which it cannot meet, it is still good – it can be held onto and it is nourishing.

If help is to be offered to bulimic women, it is important that it is consistent, even if it cannot always be long-term. Under these conditions both social worker and client need to recognise that some time for herself is better than none, even though not all her needs will be able to be met. It is therefore important that these issues are talked about within the relationship, to put into words the recognition that something is better than nothing.

In some cases however, the symptom covers up quite a lot of distress. Sometimes a short-term relationship with a social worker might prove insufficient and the woman might be left with unresolved needs and feelings. In these cases, recognition of her continuing need would make referral to another agency appropriate.

Being so frightened of her own aggression, because she feels that her negative feelings are so bad and dangerous, the bulimic woman will have great difficulty in talking about the fact that the therapy frustrates her with its imperfections. She will find it easier to stop coming or to stay away until she feels better. In this way she will keep her bad feelings locked away inside her and will not allow them to intrude into the therapy. She sees these feelings as separate from and not belonging to the therapy. Her aggression needs not only to be explored in the therapy, but also to be made real in the therapy. It allows her the freedom she may never have had before to express her negative, aggressive feelings overtly and without fear of retaliation. The aggression needs to be expressed in words rather than through her eating. She is terrified that if expressed it will destroy the therapist, make her run away and bring forth a hateful response. It is important for her to learn that her feelings of hate for the therapist are not overwhelming and will not destroy all the good in the relationship.

Intervention strategies: therapy, self help and social action

The understanding of bulimia which we have outlined here together with the principles of therapy are, in our opinion, applicable not only within a range of work settings, but also to a number of different intervention strategies. We have used a terminology deriving from one-to-one therapy, and our model often implies long-term work. However, we would also advocate the consideration of group work with women with this particular problem. We have offered groups for a number of years at the Women's Therapy Centre, run on analytic lines and lasting for about ten months. These offer the same opportunities for women to work through issues to do with good and bad feelings and the clear boundaries which are set up in such groups often provide a useful place for women to think about the actual limitations of nurturing which is available to them. Such groups, if they do nothing else, often provide women with what they can eventually experience as a good, solid meal – though not a binge. In addition the cohesiveness of a group can help to overcome the resistance and the ambivalent feelings which sometimes make it difficult for women to persist with therapy.

The Women's Therapy Centre has a tradition of encouraging and facilitating self-help groups for women with eating problems (cf. Orbach 1978; Ernst & Goodison, 1981). Bulimic women gain greatly from being able to talk to other women with the same 'guilty secret' and in spite of the difficulties which some leaderless groups have in dealing with their internal dynamics, we have still had some encouraging results. It is our view that whatever kind of intervention is attempted, the same basic understanding of the problem can be applied. The guidelines for self-help groups available from the Centre encourage women to tackle the same issues in a leaderless group (cf. Dana & Lawrence, 1983). We are currently undertaking a research project, as part of the Centre's programme of community care for women with eating disorders, to set up and evaluate a series of intensive two-day workshops followed by self-help groups, which we hope might combine some of the advantages of a led group with the support of a self-help group.

In summary, we would take the view that although our understanding is one that has been developed through therapeutic involvements with women with eating disorders and within the specific traditions of work developed at the Women's Therapy Centre, it is one which can be adapted for use by social workers, counsellors, occupational therapists, doctors and nurses – in fact anyone who might be involved in work with bulimic women. Our approach, as we have already said, is one which attends to both the inner psychological world of women as well as the social contexts of women's experience. This attention to the 'inner' and 'outer', to both unconscious phantasy and also real life experience, is often typical of what is increasingly known as 'feminist therapy'. However, it would be wrong to think of 'feminist therapy' as being represented by a unified line of theory and practice; rather it is part of an ongoing debate within which it is not uncommon to find both innovation and uncertainty. As Sheila Ernst and Marie Maguire have shown in their introduction to *Living with the Sphinx*, a collection of essays from the work of the Women's Therapy Centre, the question of where to place the emphasis between the 'internal' and the 'external' is still a matter open to considerable dispute. As they describe it, the ambitions of feminist therapy pose serious dilemmas in that our work as therapists constantly brings us up against the need to understand the economic and political situation of our women clients (cf. Ernst & Maguire, 1987). Therapeutic group interventions, for example, designed to allow women who have had an abortion to explore their feelings about pregnancy and abortion, which are often deeply troubling and ambivalent, simply cannot be separated off from the wider political significance of the right of access to abortion facilities (cf. Dana, 1987). In these ways, the approaches adopted by feminist therapists (and also the debates that have emerged between different schools of thought) are not at all dissimilar from the manner in which social workers, who by the nature of their work must also attend to both the 'inner' and the 'outer', have sometimes adapted psychoanalytic ideas within their work.

Note

1. This chapter is a version of an argument which originally appeared under the title ' "Poison is the Nourishment that makes one Ill": The Metaphor of Bulimia', in Marilyn Lawrence (ed.), *Fed Up and Hungry: Women, Oppression and Food* (Women's Press, 1987). A fuller discussion of the subject can be found in Mira Dana and Marilyn Lawrence, *Women's Secret Disorder: A New Understanding of Bulimia* (Grafton, 1988).

7 Casework as Dialogue: A Story of Incest[1]

Laurence Spurling

there is no speech without a reply, even if it is met only with silence, provided that it has an auditor; this is the heart of its function in analysis (Lacan, 1977, p. 40).

In a profession which seems more and more concerned about visibly and efficiently *doing* things to or with our clients, it can be easily forgotten that both speaking and listening are also actions (Searle, 1969). To be sure they are not separate activities but imply each other, although in any particular situation there may be more weight attached to the one or to the other. In social work this weighting has the classical form of the client speaking and the worker listening. But to what, or for what is the worker listening? What is the speech of the client which Lacan refers to and which requires the worker to hear in order for it to become present?

Consider what the client is doing in speaking to the worker, in telling her[2] story. She is undoubtedly conveying information about herself, she can specify what it is that is troubling her and give a precise and detailed history of herself and her problems. Furthermore in speaking she is also communicating, she is displaying some of her preoccupations, feelings and thoughts, and she is also, tacitly or otherwise, evoking certain responses in the worker. This all seems clear enough: the more she tells us about her problem and expresses something about what is troubling her in her speech, the better we will be able to respond with an appropriate intervention.

Yet there is something missing in this account. This something else is, for example, what is lacking in the story told by what we might call the 'professional' client, who can reel off her case history, who knows all the relevant facts about herself, who can effectively communicate her distress, anger, paranoia or whatever to whoever might happen to be in range, who can evoke all kinds of interesting responses in the worker, and yet, when all is said and done, remains quite unmoved by what she has to say. Nothing changes after she has spoken; her speech, if you like, has nothing to say.

What I am getting at is that speech can be more than exchanging information and more than communicating something to someone. It contains also the possibility of *experiencing*, of having an experience in language. Speech can make things real, can bring one's world alive. An event or experience can, by being put into words, crystallise itself into a certain insight or emotion. A thought or a feeling, if articulated for the first time, or expressed in a new way, might become tangible and thus find its place in the configuration of one's thinking or emotional life. Our experience can thus become embodied in speech and, once clothed in words, it can take on form and substance (Heidegger, 1971; see also Spurling, 1977, p. 48–75).

Although speech in this sense might not seem to be explicitly directed to another, some 'other' is always being addressed, and the participation of a listener (who may and may not be the other being addressed) is required, even if that participation is at times wordless. Speech in this sense is a *dialogue*. This dialogue between client and worker is difficult to achieve and sustain, and might never happen. Speaking can easily remain at the level of monologue, which shows us nothing new about ourselves and gives us only a reflection of ourselves, as when we catch a glimpse of ourselves in the mirror. Hence the social worker is called upon to listen to his client in such a way that she can begin to speak not so much *about* herself as *for* herself. This paradox – that to find one's own speech requires another as auditor – is similar to what Winnicott calls the paradox of the capacity to be alone, and which lies at the heart of the practice of casework: 'the basis of the capacity to be alone is the experience of being alone *in the presence of someone*' (1958b, p. 36, italics added).

To be present in this sense, as witness and listener, requires attentiveness. It is hard, however, to spell out precisely to what the worker should attend. Sometimes, for instance, what is *not* said can be more important than what is said. Sometimes what is glossed over or merely touched upon can say more to an attentive ear than what is actually uttered. Speech, by its nature, is ambiguous. One word or meaning alludes to another so that we always mean more than we can say.

It is true that this way of putting things is out of tune with the language of much of contemporary social work. The talk today is of clearly defined working contracts, objectives spelled out in detail, goals that are operational. All should be above-board, unambiguous and transparently clear to both worker and client. Such ideals are not without merit. Attempting to put them into practice can expose the deviousness and behind-closed-doors nature of some social work, especially where statutory powers are involved. Such ideals also remind us that there needs to be some sort of basic agreement between client and worker for effective work to begin. But the ideal of an unambiguous and transparent language of social work belongs to the realm of natural science and logic, not to that of ordinary speech. It is the language of monologue, the monologue of the client side by side with the monologue of the worker, whereas casework is the attempt to establish and maintain a dialogue between the two.

I would like to illustrate these remarks of mine by now presenting some aspects of my work with one particular client, work which extended over a period of three years, and which has perhaps taught me the most about the potency of speech in those encounters between client and worker.

The case of Wendy: initial contact

Wendy, when I first met her for an initial interview, was a young woman of 25. She wore drab and shapeless clothes, looked tired and anxious and spoke nervously and with difficulty. She told me she had been advised by a friend of the family to come to the social work agency where I was working, and said she was coming for help because she couldn't cope, she was depressed and worried about everything.

At times, she said, there was so much on her mind that she couldn't get to sleep at night. For instance she couldn't stop thinking about her mother, who had died about nine years ago. She cried for her mother because she missed her, but when she remembered her mother she often thought only of 'bad things' that had happened to her (she gave an example of her mother rushing to get on a bus but falling off and hurting herself; she stressed that no one had come to her assistance). She had little information about her father, who had left when Wendy was nine. She didn't know why he had left or where he had gone to. She had never seen him since and he was never talked about in the family. She did say he used to drink and also that he had 'interfered' with her when she was much younger. She refused to elaborate on this or discuss further what she meant.

Wendy was the youngest of four children and lived with her eldest sister in a council flat (all names and some details of events of family history have been changed in order to preserve confidentiality). Her brother (whom she described as 'nice') was married and lived some distance away, as did her other sister. She worried about her family, particularly about her sister Elizabeth, who was nervous and had no friends. Wendy had a boy-friend, John, about whom she also worried (she said he drank too much, which reminded her of her father). Although not really close to her sisters or brother and in spite of having a life outside of her family (she spent time with John and also worked part-time in an office) her life appeared bounded by the horizon of her family as though she felt she could not get free of them.

As well as her worries about her family, which were generalised and unspecific, she also had some very concrete fears, of small, enclosed rooms or spaces, such as cupboards or small lifts, which she would not go into under any circumstances. Although these fears bothered her she made it plain they were not the reason she was coming for help and that, although she wanted to be free of them, she would not let anyone try and make her give them up. What she did want was to cope better with her life and be able to stand up for herself with other people; 'to be myself and not someone else'.

My initial impression was of a very troubled young woman who, although managing to hang on to the threads of her life, was quietly desperate. Her life was hemmed in by her phobias as well as by her more generalised anxiety. She was stuck in a state of chronic grief over her mother's death and was drawing attention to other past events which were playing on her mind. The story of no one having come to her mother's assistance alluded perhaps to some guilt concerning her mother, but very likely also to Wendy's own sense that no one had come to her aid when she had needed them, and that people were not to be trusted.

To be sure, her whole manner of seeking help was markedly ambivalent. She said she had been 'sent' by the friend of the family (who had, in fact, persuaded Wendy to refer herself previously, when she had seen another worker but had attended only sporadically), and spoke of herself being 'in two minds' about coming. Nevertheless her ambivalence was out in the open and its very upfrontness – for instance in refusing to elaborate on certain matters which she had herself raised in the first place – seemed to be a tacit invitation for us to go further.

Wendy spoke of the relief of having someone she could talk to without having to feel guilty that she was burdening them with her worries. Although shy and very guarded with me, I felt she was able to make room for me in her manner of presenting herself and was prepared, in spite of her doubts, to put some trust in me, at least provisionally. I detected a determination in her to see something through, and there was also an honesty which I liked, a desire to get things straight. All of these boded well for future work since in casework the outcome depends crucially on the co-operation and active participation of the client; in Freud's words, it depends on '. . . his own conduct, his understanding, his adaptability and his perseverance' (Freud, 1916–17, p. 39).

By the end of the first session I already felt we had engaged with each other and we agreed I would see her at my office once a week for an hour. The contract was left open-ended; there was no mention of a finishing date.

The virtue of trying not to know in advance

My preference, where possible, is not to set a time limit in advance with a client, even when it turns out, as it often does, that no more than a few sessions are required. The time I have available for a client depends on at least three factors. One is simply to do with the demands and requirements of the agency in which I am working. When I saw Wendy I was employed by a social work agency with a commitment to the 'counselling' aspect of social work and a belief in allowing work with clients to develop at its own pace, and over a long period if necessary. However there were always pressures from crises or from statutory work which meant that for any particular client the time I had available for them depended on how busy I was. In practice at any one time I had room for no more than a handful of 'longer-term' cases. Wendy was one of them. Where I know that I have no more than, say a few sessions, or a limited period to work with a client, I make that clear at the beginning, so that we both then have to accommodate to this time schedule.

The second factor is the needs of the client. Although to speak of what the client needs can sometimes be tendentious – it can be a way of justifying what a worker or agency does for a client by imputing internal 'needs' to the client which are then deemed to have been 'met' by the worker's actions – it is clear that the worker is called upon to make an assessment about what is likely to be helpful to a particular client. In Wendy's case there were several indications that a 'brief intervention' would probably not be appropriate. She presented with no clearly defined problem. Although she mentioned specific phobias, her concern was with her more generalised unhappiness and unease. In speaking of having been 'interfered' with she was referring to something of importance but which she was not likely to reveal unless given time for trust to develop. The fact she had made a previous contact but not kept it up, as well as her fear and anxiety about speaking, all pointed to the desirability of giving her time to find her own way of telling her story instead of having to fit into a pre-arranged and inevitably arbitrary time-scale.

Thirdly there is the worker's own motivation and interest in working with a particular client. As I have said I felt that Wendy was worth spending time with. This way of putting it may sound odd, even suspect, as the language of social work focuses almost exclusively on what clients need and rarely makes mention of what workers need in order to sustain both their commitment and their imagination. It is well known, however, that a worker's commitment to and belief in a particular client are essential elements in the helping process.

One difficulty I have with this question of how much time to give to a client is that I find the very language in which this debate is conducted – 'short-term' versus 'long-term' work – to be problematic. The point is: *for whom* is the work short or long? The terms 'short-term' and 'long-term' refer to *the worker's* concept of time, not the client's. A few sessions with a client where profound and perhaps disturbing material comes to light can be, in terms of the client's sense of time, of immensely long duration. On the other hand to spend several years seeing someone (I am thinking particularly of very disturbed people) can be scarcely enough to get to know them. Each person has their own temporality, their own sense of timeliness and readiness for understanding and experiencing, and which, where possible, can be respected by not determining *in advance* to what time scale that timeliness must accommodate. Of course this may not be possible because of the demands on our time as workers, so that we may have to time-limit our work in advance, but I do not believe in making a virtue out of this. I suspect that pre-arranged time-limits are more to do with the worker's anxieties than the supposed needs of the client. As long as one is alert to the dangers of what Hutton has called 'compulsive care-taking' (1977, p. 3), and is prepared openly to discuss with the client if and when the work becomes no longer productive, and to face the concomitant anxieties, then I can see no merit in trying to know in advance at what pace the work must proceed.

Transference and counter-transference

As it was, I found the early stages of our work together difficult enough and soon found myself bogged down, sometimes having little clear idea of what was happening in the sessions. To be sure, progress was made on some fronts. Wendy moved out of her sister's flat and went to live with a girl-friend, and her relationship with John started to show some promise. She began to make efforts, with my encouragement, to stand up for herself with other people. But I found the work slow, frustrating and sometimes boring. Wendy would miss appointments, cancel others and sometimes arrive late for those she did attend. She would invariably begin each session with a lengthy and tedious blow-by-blow account of the week's events and which, even if interrupted by a question or comment of mine, would then be laboriously resumed. Even if a particular problem appeared to admit of some resolution, a new one immediately arose to take its place.

There were, however, glimpses of other, more profound concerns. When the flood of chat about contemporary events and difficulties began to dry up, usually around two-thirds of the way through a session, there were sometimes memories or reflections about the past. Then her manner and tone would change; she would become more solemn, speak with hesitation and care as though she had to struggle to find the right words. At such times she talked with evident feeling, unlike her usual chatter which I felt was largely a distraction from what was really preoccupying her, and which tended to send me to sleep. It was not that I was only interested in her past, but rather the way she talked of her present life seemed to lead nowhere, it foreclosed reflection or exploration, whereas when she found herself speaking of the past her present life was illuminated. She spoke about how much she missed her mother, how she had not looked after her mother enough while she was dying and so blamed herself in part for her mother's death. She hardly spoke of her father but did tell me that 'once or twice' her brother had also 'interfered' with her when she was young (she had described him as 'nice' in the first session). She refused to elaborate. There were also memories of her early family life which she found puzzling as they contained unaccountable absences. For example she sometimes couldn't remember her mother being around even though she 'knew' her mother had been there. And she had nightmares about being chased by men or about people dying.

It required great effort on my part to extract such nuggets from the avalanche of Wendy's words, and patience to hold back in the hope they may emerge of their own accord. Nevertheless I did not confront Wendy with any consistency or real conviction about the missed and cancelled sessions, about why she could only allude to some of her more preoccupying concerns after a slow and careful build-up of rather compulsive chatter. Looking back over that period of work it seems to me that my tentativeness and proneness to boredom were largely counter-transference reactions of which I should have taken more heed.

The notions of transference and counter-transference are crucial to any attempt to understand what happens in casework between client and worker. Transference is a common enough phenomenon. We are all led to transfer feelings and attitudes that derive from one person onto another; we say, for example, that so-and-so 'reminds' us of someone else. Transference simply means that present experiences are coloured by past ones. In psychoanalytic usage the term refers more specifically to the process by which a client displaces onto the worker feelings, attitudes, etc., which derive from previous figures or experiences in her life (Rycroft, 1972, pp. 168–9). In Wendy's case her father and brother had 'interfered' with her. This made her wary and distrustful of them, and she extended such an attitude, to a greater or lesser extent, to all men. 'All men are pigs' she once told me, although she then qualified this by adding that John and I weren't, but sometimes we were. Hence she could not help but experience me as interfering (or at least potentially so) and consequently be wary and distrustful of me. The missed sessions, her unwillingness at times to let me get a word in edgeways, all seemed designed, in part at least, to keep me at a safe distance and herself well out of harm's way.

This was not the only aspect of Wendy's transference to me. There was a more 'positive' side to her emotional attitude to me in which I was seen as someone with whom she might perhaps be safe, and who might even, in some way, be able to take care of her. Otherwise she could not have kept coming. But, as far as I can now see, it was her 'negative' transference that produced a more farreaching response in me as a way of dealing – or rather not dealing – with her transference to me. That is, my counter to Wendy's transference was to try *not* to be interfering, and it was this that resulted in my tentativeness about addressing what was going on. I responded to her fear that all men become like her father by working hard not to be like him. But this only led me to become over-protective, backing off from confrontation in case it was experienced by Wendy as interference, and taking refuge from my resulting frustration in boredom.

So instead of becoming aware of Wendy's transference to me and taking its effect on me into account, or even thinking of bringing it to her attention, I chose instead to try and avoid it, and ended up by simply colluding with it. That is, my very efforts to try *not* to be whom she took me for had the effect of unwittingly confirming her experience of me as interfering. But it was this very prejudice, this transference on her part that needed to be held in suspension in the course of our work so that Wendy could become aware of it and see what it comprised. My counter-transference meant that, in Winnicott's words, my professional attitude was spoilt; the thoughtfulness, consistency and relative detachment called for in casework, which create a certain distance between client and worker so that experiences that affect the work can come into play and be recognised, had become disturbed (Winnicott, 1960).

Although, strictly speaking, one cannot know one's own counter-transference as it is unconscious, one can catch glimpses of it in retrospect. The boredom I was sometimes subject to was a sure sign that something had gone amiss in my ability to be receptive to Wendy and I was beginning to become aware of this and to consider taking some initiative. But Wendy beat me to it. One day, some nine months or so after our work had begun, she arrived for a session distressed and highly agitated.

She told me that a few days earlier she had 'made herself' watch a play on television about a woman who, as a child, had been sexually assaulted by her father and who now, as an adult, had hallucinations of her now dead father coming for her while she lay in bed with her husband. Since watching this play Wendy said she had been nervous and close to tears all week. She then went on to tell me that her father had 'done things', the same kind of things as in the play, to her from when she was about five or six until he left. These things might be done once a week or even more often. They always occurred when her mother was at work or out of the house.

Wendy had told no one (and subsequently given only John an idea of what her father had done to her). She felt no one would have believed her. She didn't even know whether any of her family knew what had happened, although she herself had been told by Elizabeth that she (Elizabeth) had been raped when she was young, although Wendy did not know by whom. Wendy felt 'dirty' because of what had happened, felt in some way she was to blame for it, and was unsure whether she had done the right thing in telling me of it. She agreed with a comment of mine that it felt like she was disloyal in having now spoken to someone outside the family about what had happened.

She had always tried to 'block off' this part of her childhood but she couldn't forget it. But to think of it made both her father and mother seem bad. In spite of what he had done to her she could still cry for her father. She told me she hated him – but then added there were things about him she liked, for example he would protect her if other children tried to bully her. She said little about her mother. Near the end of the session she also spoke for the first time of sexual difficulties with John, of how bad she felt that sometimes she didn't want sex with him.

We had now clearly crossed a threshold from which there was no going back. For some reason – perhaps because my growing awareness of some of my counter-transference enabled me to become more empathic, and this somehow conveyed to Wendy that it was safe to confide in me – Wendy now had enough confidence to begin to reveal what she had kept hidden for so long. But once her secret was out in the open it became impossible to predict or control what else might be unearthed and subjected to scrutiny. Thus although in this session she spoke principally of her father and what he had done to her, I felt she was even more disturbed by the person whom she hardly mentioned, namely her mother. The ambivalence towards her father – her holding side by side contradictory and mutually incompatible attitudes towards him, hating him and liking him at the same time – now threatened to engulf her mother as well. Wendy had striven hard to preserve the good memory of her mother from any 'bad thoughts' she might have about her, but her mother's stark failure to protect her from her father now showed up her idealisation of her mother as an attempt to ward off her feelings of having been let down and even betrayed by her.

Some remarks of Peter Dale's, based on his work with seriously abusing families at Rochdale's NSPCC's unit, are apposite. He writes:

> Our experience is that fatal and serious child abuse is invariably a triangular relationship. A distorted, enmeshed relationship between the two parent figures occurs, where their respective individual identities appear to become blurred or even merged.

The couple act as one in the abuse of the child who may have been perceived as being persecutory to the parents. The 'failure to protect' behaviour of the partner with the passive role is at least as crucial and pathological as the role of the aggressor (Dale, 1984, p. 21).

But Wendy preferred to interrogate herself about why she had told no one at the time rather than have to give consideration to how and why her mother had failed to know something about something that had gone on systematically over a period of years.

Transference and resistance

The opening up of such lines of enquiry, as well as the new and unfamiliar intimacy of our relationship now that Wendy had confided in me, were propelling her into a crisis. In the subsequent session she reported that she had felt nervous all week and shaky in the pit of her stomach. In the next few weeks she seemed to calm down. But then, having thrown her hat into the ring, she made an ambivalent attempt to retrieve it.

This came in the form of a letter sent to me a few weeks later. Wendy wrote that she had been thinking about things and didn't want to come to see me anymore. 'I would like to try on my own for a little while.' She went on that she still felt 'a little bit depressed' and also 'lost', but she felt as if no one could help her but herself. She then qualified this by adding, 'I am really not sure what I want to do' and she ended by asking me to write back 'to let me know'.

This letter, stating her wish to go it alone but at the same time leaving it up to me, showed how Wendy was both driven to speak to me about her past life and was also terrified to do so. I wrote back that it might be a good idea for her to try on her own for a while (the fact that her wish to leave can be seen as a manifestation of resistance does not mean it should not be taken seriously) but that we needed to talk about it first, and I suggested she keep the appointment she already had.

In that session she repeated that she thought she wanted to have a go on her own, but wasn't sure. It had been very helpful to come and let out all her problems, it took the pressure off her. But she wasn't sure how much it had really helped her. I replied that was because she wasn't allowing it to, she was keeping me at a distance because she didn't trust me. Things had changed, she said, since she had told me about her father. She hadn't wanted to tell me, it had been John's idea. I asked her whether, in putting questions to her about her father, it felt to her as though I was dragging things out of her, and whether this made me, in some way like her father, so that in her mind we got mixed up together. She conceded this and said she had felt angry with me about it, but had taken it out on John. At first she refused to consider why she hadn't told me about being angry with me, but when I persisted she finally said I might be hurt or embarrassed. She was also afraid I might get fed up with her and refuse to see her anymore. After her mother's death she had told Elizabeth some of the things on her mind, but Elizabeth had got fed up with her, saying that listening to Wendy made her depressed.

I told Wendy that I thought her wish to stop coming here was not just a desire to become more independent but also a way of running away from me. [I might have said it was also a way of running away from herself]. That really she had been in control all the time in our work. She replied she could never relax in my presence. She often felt tense in the pit of her stomach before she came and when she was with me. She found it hard to relax with any man. The session ended with an agreement that she would come again next week, when she would reach a final decision about whether she wished to continue. In fact it took her two more weeks to resolve to carry on.

This session marked a turning-point as, for the first time, Wendy's resistance to the work was on the table and could thus be dealt with. It was fuelled by her fear of what she might be doing to me by putting her trust in me, that she might be burdening me with something I might not be able or willing to cope with. She disclosed she was also fearful of the effect her anger might have on me, her anger towards me because I was a man and therefore in some way like her father. All of this might prompt me to reject her or leave her in the lurch. I think it was my ability to finally confront her with her fears and her resistance which demonstrated to her that I was strong enough to tolerate whatever she had to show of herself, and therefore someone who could be trusted. Hence her decision to carry on.

My confrontation of her with what she was doing in wanting to finish was itself provoked by her letter. In a way, then, I was being put to the test; Wendy was showing me how I needed to be in order to help her. It was not enough for me to be consistently there for her – same time, same place as far as was possible, my mood not wildly different from week to week – although it was also essential that I was (as neither parent, nor anyone in the family, had been for her). I also had to be someone to whom she could tell all sorts of terrible, intimate and 'dirty' things without my falling to pieces (as her sister Elizabeth had done, and as Wendy probably feared her mother would have done if she had dared to confide in her). I had to show her that I could be firm without being sadistic or abusive (as her father and brother had been). She needed to feel safe with me, to be held in an emotional sense, so that she could risk experiencing for the first time what she had for so long suppressed. To experience her distress, guilt, hatred, grief etc. in the protected space made available to her gave her the opportunity of not being overwhelmed or destroyed by such experiences but of surviving them, and hence finding them less disturbing and frightening. She could then discover that her pain could be contained (Salzberger-Wittenberg, 1970, pp. 142–55).

In casework it is the client who has the answers. It is she who shows the worker by her manner of speaking and relating to him, what is manifestly in play and what is latent and hence in need of being addressed. For his part the worker might well be deaf to the signs, or misread the cues, but it is the particular, indeed peculiar, nature of this style of working that it is the client who teaches the worker what needs to be done, and when the time is ripe, rather than the other way round.

After this Wendy missed no more sessions. Although the rhythm of the work continued to be slow and sometimes ponderous, punctuated with only brief spells where the pace quickened, as in these sessions, it was evident that she was now determined to see things through. In subsequent weeks and months she characterized her whole life as running away, but having no one to run to. She felt no one had listened to her in her life, no one had really cared for her. She had had thoughts in the past of doing away with herself and sometimes she thought it would have been better if she had not been born.

Her sense of guilt

Now that she had told me, at least in outline, of the events in the past she was trying to come to terms with, she was faced with the question of what part she had played in them, whether she was in any way responsible for what had happened. This question of guilt, however, was mixed up with her ignorance about many aspects of her family life which, up until now, she had never discussed with anyone in the family for fear of what she might find out. I therefore encouraged her to speak to one of her sisters and after much equivocating – 'part of me wants to know what happened and part of me doesn't' – she rang me one day to say she had to see me that day as she had finally spoken to Elizabeth. In the course of their two-hour conversation Wendy had discovered that before she was born her father had 'done something terrible' to her brother Robert, as a result of which he went away (to prison?) for some years. But when he returned her mother took pity on him and had him back. She also discovered that when her sister Frances was young her father had 'interfered' with her and that he had raped Elizabeth and made her pregnant so that she had to have an abortion. Her mother 'hadn't known' about Frances, nor that it had been their father who had made Elizabeth pregnant. Because of all this both Frances and Elizabeth had tried to keep an eye on Wendy as they were worried what their father might do to her (although it seemed both Frances and Elizabeth spent periods away from home, their singular failure to protect Wendy, and their decision not to tell their mother or, apparently, anyone else, were not explained).

Wendy still felt in a state of shock after learning all this. She told me, 'I don't feel sorry for myself or guilty anymore, I just feel uneasy.' She was uneasy about what had happened to Robert and Elizabeth, whom Wendy felt had been even more abused than she had. In fact a certain embarrassment and estrangement set in between Elizabeth and Wendy after their conversation, which I do not think was referred to subsequently, as though a family rule had been broken forbidding family members to talk to each other about what had occurred in the past, or to even acknowledge that anything had occurred at all. Wendy was more uneasy about her mother, as she was now not only faced with her mother's failure to protect her siblings as well as herself, but also with the knowledge that her own suffering – but also her very existence – were a consequence of her mother having taken her father back. And she could not stop thinking about her father. What he had done to her brother and sisters only seemed to highlight what he had done to her, as though she could only allow herself to experience its horror once she knew she had not been alone in her degradation. She was now telling me her dreams, which were more real to her than her waking life and which made her terrified of going to sleep (I took her dreams not necessarily or even primarily as steps on 'the royal road to her unconscious', as the gateway to what lay hidden, but more simply as a way of her showing what was pre-occupying her at that moment). They were monotonously on the same theme: a man, or men – sometimes she recognised them as her father, or John's father – were chasing her and 'doing things' to her. Her terror of her father seemed to reach a climax when, for three consecutive nights, she felt as though he was in her bedroom with her. When this feeling went it was replaced for a time by a feeling that a man was following her.

In spite of all her attempts to 'block him off' Wendy found she could not escape from a sense of her father's presence nor free herself from memories and dreams of him. She could not let go of him in part because of an obscure but pervasive sense of guilt (although she had said, after her conversation with Elizabeth, that she no longer felt guilty, only uneasy, she might have meant she felt less guilty in the eyes of her family, as they had also not escaped her father's attention; what she called her uneasiness seemed to be a restlessness suffused with guilt). This became evident in a session later, some 21 months after we had begun working together.

Wendy was talking about how things were not good sexually with John. In reply to a question of mine she admitted that while she was having intercourse with John she would think of her father. She said that she would think that the thing she was doing with John (i.e. having intercourse with him) was something her father would have done with her if he had not gone away. This rather odd way of putting it made it clear to me that she was indicating not just that she was disgusted and frightened by what her father had done to her, but, in some sense, she had wanted it to continue, that she had got some kind of pleasure out of it. I said this to her and she agreed; this was the first time she had admitted this to anybody. She had to confess that she had liked some of the things her father had done to her. She felt very confused about it. She felt there was something wrong with her and blamed herself for that. This was one reason she hadn't told her mother. Her mother might not have believed her; but, even worse, her mother might have blamed her for having led her father on, as she blamed herself, even though she couldn't say how she had led him on and that she 'really' knew that she hadn't. Wendy's confusion was to do with her having taken on what Ferenczi (1932) has called 'the confusion of tongues between adults and the child', where a child's wish for tenderness from her father (which may take on erotic forms but is primarily at the level of playfulness)

becomes confounded and perverted by the actions of her father into
the language of sexual desire. This left no space for Wendy to see
through what might be called her ordinary oedipal desire for her
father, her wish to love him and be loved by him, because, in Freud's
notion of the oedipus complex, these incestuous desires remain at the
level of fantasy and are not acted upon precisely because they
presuppose a father who has *not* seduced his daughter into premature
sexual development (Bettelheim, 1983, pp. 20–30). But because her
father did act out his own erotic (and hateful) feelings towards
Wendy, she found her own oedipal wishes towards him had also
become reality, causing her to recoil in horror and guilt from her own
budding sexuality and to remain tied up, in fantasy at least, with her
father.

Her guilt also gave some sort of answer to her persistent and
anguished question: why me? And the more she blamed herself the
less she had to consider who else might be to blame. Intimidated by
her father, cut off from her mother, both terrified of but also yearning
for attention, she had little choice but to collude with her father in
having to accept and make the best of the perverted form of attention
she got from him.

This acknowledgement, indeed confession, of her guilt resulted in
a dramatic improvement. Wendy said she felt much better and in fact
started to look better. She became less preoccupied with thoughts
and memories of her father and more concerned with her current life.
Her attempt at letting go of some of her past allowed more of a future
to come into view. She and John began to make plans to get married.
She also spoke of her wish to have children as she wanted an
opportunity to do things better than her own parents had done.

Wendy made a further attempt to find out more of what she didn't
know about her early family life by plucking up the courage to ask her
sister Frances. But Frances made it clear that she would not talk
about what had happened in the past and Wendy was left feeling
angry and let down. Indeed her depression was dissolving more and
more into anger and she frequently complained of 'having the hump'
with everyone around her.

Speaking the truth

Such an attempt to find out more exactly what had gone on in her
family served to highlight for both of us that Wendy had not yet

spelled out to me precisely what her father had done to her. The nearest we got were comments like 'he made me hold his thing', or 'I couldn't say he raped me, but I couldn't say he didn't'. Although I believed that she needed to tell me specifically what had occurred in order to allow her, as far as it could ever be possible, to lay the ghost of her father, I was too easily dissuaded from pressing her by her adamant refusals to go into detail. However Wendy was being propelled by her own logic into finally speaking to me about precisely what had taken place. 'If you can't talk to someone in the family you shouldn't talk to someone ouside', she said to me once. But she was beginning to realise that her ideal of her family was largely a product of her wishful thinking. She said it felt like she had never had a father or a mother. She was having to acknowledge what she had known but had preferred not to see, namely that her siblings had not only failed to protect her, but were still cowering behind the wall of silence that had been erected. Wendy thus felt pushed to transcend her sense of loyalty to her family by taking the risk of disclosure to an outsider.

Over a period of several sessions, and this was now two and a half years after we had started, Wendy finally spoke some of what she had held back for so long. She began one session by saying she had recently found herself walking through a playground where her father used to take her, and this led her – via several detours – to tell me what had transpired in the playground. She remembered going there with her father and another little girl. She wasn't sure who this little girl was, but thought she might have played with her once or twice. It was in the day. Her father took Wendy and the little girl to an area nearby surrounded by trees. He then made Wendy sit on a bench and watch while he raped the little girl. The girl screamed but no one came. Wendy tried to look away but her father told her to keep looking. When it was over he threatened that if she told anyone what had happened he would rape her himself and have her sent away.

Wendy thought she had been about 7 at the time. The little girl had been about the same age. Wendy had been too terrified of her father to tell anyone and she now blamed herself for her silence. She said she used to take it out on herself, she remembered sitting and scratching herself until she was bleeding while being made to watch.

Another session began with Wendy's reluctance to tell me the worst that her father had done to her. She spoke of imagining she could hear a voice, her father's saying 'don't tell, don't tell'. Eventually she said it would be easier for her if I asked her some questions [this made me realize, rather belatedly, how much she needed me to actively take part in the telling of her story]. In this fashion she told me what used to happen when she had to spend some time with her father when he worked as a kitchen assistant in a hotel. She used to beg her mother not to take her to where her father worked, but she had to go as her mother went out to work herself and there was no one at home to look after Wendy. Her father would take her to a small pantry at the back of the kitchen and lock the door. Then he would take his 'thing' out and make her hold it, and then make her kneel down. I spelt it out for her: he would make her hold his penis and then make her take it into her mouth. She was now staring fixedly past me, speaking with the intensity of suppressed emotion, tears in her eyes. I asked whether he came in her mouth, she said no, over her head. When she got home he made her wash the sperm out of her hair (an edge of sarcasm to her voice). Sometimes he would hit her as well, at times so hard that she would 'bounce off the walls' and come home black and blue. He told her to tell her mother she had fallen over. Wendy wondered bitterly how her mother could have believed it. These events took place many times, from the time Wendy was 5 until her father left.

In the weeks that followed her telling me of these, and other events Wendy spoke of feeling great relief. But her initial reaction was to go into a state of shock which she described as like being in a trance. She said she couldn't concentrate on what she was doing at home. She had dropped so many cups while washing up she had had to go out and buy herself a new set. She told me on one occasion, while crossing the road after coming out of a session, her mind had been so transfixed by what she had recounted that she had been completely oblivious of the traffic and nearly got knocked over. She couldn't be bothered with anyone, she wanted to be left alone. She felt 'gutted, empty, drained'. She said, 'I'm not thinking but I'm feeling how I used to feel as a child.' And, indeed, it was now possible to link some of her present fears and phobias to the past. Going into one of the cupboards at home was frightening not only because of what it reminded her of, but also because even to think about going in it meant, in her mind, that in some way she would be giving in to her father. She spoke in one session of finding it hard to eat as she felt sick when she put something into her mouth, and again it was not difficult to link this with what her father had made her do to him. We were also able to tie in her frequent difficulties in going to sleep with her childhood memories of lying awake at night in case her father came into her bedroom.

Gradually she emerged from her state of shock. She told John some of what she had told me and was relieved that he proved to be sympathetic and understanding. Her sex life with him began to improve, although this awakening of her sexuality brought other possibilities and conflicts into play as she now found herself fancying an old boyfriend of hers who was still around. And her dreams were changing. For example one dream began, as usual, with a 'horrible' man chasing her and getting into her flat, but now John protected her by punching the man in the face. In another dream one of her sisters saved a child from drowning in a river. Her dreams showed that for the first time there was a possibility of protection from danger and that other people might be relied on for help.

Conclusion: the potency of words

The primary medium of psychoanalytic casework is words. Just words. But how could simply putting into words what had taken place between Wendy and her father make such a difference? Sometimes, however, words can embody such potency, have such an impact, that when something is spoken for the first time in the presence of another things can never remain the same again.

> Words were originally magic and to this day words have retained much of their ancient magical power. By words one person can make another blissfully happy or drive him to despair. By words the teacher conveys his knowledge to his pupils, by words the orator carries his audience with him and determines their judgement and decisions. Words provoke affects and are in general the means of mutual influence among men (Freud, 1916– 17, p. 41).

The putting into words, in my presence, of her traumatic experiences made them powerfully and dramatically real – and hence events that could be faced, survived, even in some way laid to rest. Finding her tongue, discovering her own speech made Wendy's history her own, in which she could find her place. What had happened in her childhood was then no longer to be lived out as cruel and arbitrary destiny, as a curse condemning her to eke out her existence forever in its shadow, but as events, however terrible, that had happened to *her*. Once she had claimed her past the possibility arose of being able to let it go. In fact in the weeks and months following the climaxes to her narration Wendy reported that she had hardly thought of her father. Although at different times her relationship to her father had, according to the rhythm of the work, become a preoccupation, only then to fade into the background, each time this happened subsequent to her narration he retreated further into the background, leaving Wendy freer to live more fully in the present.

It is true that Wendy's relationship to her dead mother was still left unsettled. Despite the fact that she had been forced to consider her mother's complicity in what had happened Wendy was not prepared to jettison her grimly held belief in her mother as the only good one in the family – even though she 'knew' that her belief was no more than a false hope. But in casework, as in life, nothing is ever completely resolved. Indeed it is not clear that what her father did and her mother failed to do admitted of a resolution, perhaps more of a forebearance was the most that could be hoped for.

Telling me her story had been for Wendy not only a recounting of what was already known, but became more of a *discovery* of what it was that she did know, for what is spoken is already different from what is not yet spoken or what cannot be put into words. Discovering one's history, however, is not the same as inventing it. What she recounted of her past, and her difficulty in actually speaking of it, gave what she said an unmistakable stamp of authenticity, so that it never even crossed my mind that what I was listening to were inventions, day-dreams or fantasies (fantasying has a quite different quality to remembering (Winnicott, 1974) although her fantasies, thoughts and feelings about what occurred determined how it came to be experienced and understood by her). Her overwhelming relief when she managed to speak to me of that which she had for so long been silent was, I think, not only a relief at letting out what she had held on to, but also that she had finally experienced the truth of what she was saying. In the telling of her tale private obsession had become transmuted into communal truth.

Casework is often characterised, even by some of its practitioners, as an emphasis on the 'inner world' as opposed to the 'outer world', or as making the world of feelings – conceived of as some sort of internal states, a refuge from the world outside – as the particular focus or even property of casework. But feelings, although of paramount importance, are only one aspect of a person's relationship to himself and to others. To elevate feelings into the domain of what is most personal is to fall into sentimentality, an attitude tellingly depicted by Martin Buber, in which 'the spectrum of the emotions swings before the interested eye; here one enjoys one's inclinations and one's hatred, pleasure and, if it is not too bad, pain. Here one is at home and relaxes in one's rocking chair.' And, he adds, even despair at the unreality of feelings will not open one to the world, 'after all, despair is also a feeling and quite interesting' (Buber, 1970, pp. 93–4).

Wendy's struggle was not with her 'inner world' of feelings rather than the 'outer world' of events but with the radical disconnection between the two. She was existing in the present but, in a sense, had been actually living in the past. She was wanting to get married to John but, even if she were to go through the ceremony of marrying him, she could not *feel* married to him until she could 'divorce' her father. Although these splits define the lives of all of us, clients and workers, Wendy has had the courage and determination to try and find a way through to a kind of connection or re-connection, however partial, incomplete and unstable it must be, between her present and her past, her feelings and her actions and between herself and her world.

As I am writing this we have reached the third anniversary of our work together. Wendy is now making plans to get married. This may lead to a natural and fitting end to our work, as her fixation onto the past is transformed into a growing concern for the future. Although there are still events that she refuses to speak about we cannot go on for ever, and it may even be appropriate that she keeps some secrets. Wendy has grown attached to me (as I have to her) and committed to our work, so that the way we finally part company, the manner in which she can carry with her what she has so bravely invested in me and our work together, will leave an indelible mark on the whole experience. But that story, like this chapter, must remain unfinished.[3]

184   *Casework as Dialogue*

Notes

1. Although there are far too many acknowledgements to mention, I would like to record my special thanks to Walter Finn, Roger Weissman and Paul Zeal.
2. For the sake of convenience, and also because it fits the case history which is to follow, I shall refer to the client as 'she' and to the worker as 'he'.
3. Our work together lasted another year, by which time Wendy had married her boyfriend and become pregnant. She felt less uneasy and less constricted by her fears, some of which had almost vanished. She has since given birth to a daughter.

8 Counter-Transference in a Case Conference: Resistance and Rejection in Work with Abusing Families and their Children[1]

Roger Bacon

Introduction

In this chapter I want to look at the process whereby a group of concerned professionals, who have met to discuss the best way of helping a child and its family, end up by seeming to reject the family and child in their distress and pathology and to resist allowing themselves to get too closely involved with them. I will be looking at some of the processes involved from a psychoanalytic point of view.

What I shall be describing is a case conference – and individual professionals – getting into a mess with a family. The point I will try to make is *not* that getting into a mess is a necessarily bad thing which should be avoided. Rather, I want to emphasise that the form of the mess, its content, the emotional experience of it, is the way in which the family enters into the professional group and becomes psychologically real to it. Recognition and acceptance of this can therefore provide the professionals with a most valuable guide to both an understanding of the nature of the family's problems and as to how they may best be helped. Rejection, on the other hand, of these feelings and attempts to expel them from consciousness, can lead to efforts to punish the family and to view them as dangerous, bad or mad – in analytic language, what is called the 'talionic' response. I will suggest that this resistance and rejection by the professionals constitutes a form of distorted, sado-masochistic, identification with the child – an identification which develops from a failure by the professionals to allow themselves consciousness of their counter-transference feelings towards the child and family, and to use these feelings as a guide to their actions and involvement.

The bulk of this chapter will consist of an extended case description. But I will begin by giving a brief description of some key changes in analytic thought and practice which have brought the concept of counter-transference to prominence.

Object relations and counter-transference

The last forty years have witnessed a number of radical changes in psychoanalytic theorising which have, in their turn, had important effects on certain aspects of therapeutic practice. In Britain, the major theoretical changes are associated with the work of therapists like Fairbairn, Winnicott, Little and Guntrip, all of whom have been loosely grouped together under the name of the British Object Relations school (cf. Fairbairn, 1954; Guntrip, 1961; Little, 1981; Winnicott, 1965; Kohon, 1986).

While the development of their thinking owed a lot to the earlier revolution in theory and practice of Melanie Klein, what distinguished the object relations theorists was their interest not so much in inner fantasy and instinct, but in the world of outer relationships – especially the early mother–child relationship – and how these relationships in outer reality met with and became transformed into inner psychological reality, the development of an internal object-world, and a sense of self and identity.

Theoretically, these developments have allowed for a wider understanding of the course and vicissitudes of psychological development than was possible with either the classical, Freudian, instinct-based model centred on predominantly Oedipal concerns (Freud, 1915); or with the ornately over-elaborated attempts of Klein and her followers to push the implications of the Freudian model back into earliest infancy. For what in essence the object relations theorists were concerned to do was to bring into theoretical account the social and psychological experience of the infant and child in interaction with the environment – the breast, the mother, the father, the family, the outside world – and to look at the complex interaction of inner world and outer reality as they continuously produce and transform each other.

What, however, I want to concentrate on here is not so much the impact on theory or metapsychology of these ideas, but their effect on actual therapeutic practice. There are two, interlinked, points which seem particularly important. First, by emphasising the interplay of inner world and outer reality, they brought into renewed focus the importance of the relationship between the therapist and the patient. However, this relationship was not just the transference relationship as emphasised in Freud or Klein; nor was it what the American analyst Leo Stone (1961) called the therapeutic alliance – the meeting of two adult egos. Rather, the object relations theorists concentrated on the relationship as the creative medium within which therapy – regression, dependence, change – took place. What became central was the use which both therapist and patient could make of this relationship – in play, in fantasy and in reality – as the therapeutic process unfolded.

Second, the involvement of the therapist as an object – inner and outer – for the patient to make use of in interaction led to increased attention on the presence and function of the therapists' own feelings, fantasies and reactions to the patient; that is, to the nature of the therapists' psychological involvement with the patient or counter-transference. In orthodox theory and practice counter-transference was (and is) considered to be an obstacle, something that therapists should be analysed out of. What the object relations theorists did was to reverse this and postulate the importance of counter-transference, made conscious, for guiding the therapist in the task of managing and interpreting the therapeutic relationship. What is crucial here is the therapists' capacity both to allow such feelings into consciousness, and to contain them, reflect upon them and make them available to the patient in such a way as to allow the patient to come to terms with his or her own unconscious forces.

Transference and counter-transference are not phenomena confined to psychoanalytic consulting rooms, but are met within all helping relationships. What seems critical is the extent to which one party to such a relationship is able to make these feelings conscious and to manage and interpret them for both parties. Failure to do so can result in blind retaliation – an effort to expel the feelings from consciousness and to punish their source, and I will suggest that this expulsion takes the form of a confused sado-masochistic identification between the helper and the helped.

I now want to give an extended case example of the phenomenon. I have chosen this particular case conference for two reasons. First, while in this conference the ostensible focus of resistance was to placing the family on the child abuse register, I want to suggest that the issue of registration became symbolic of a deeper-seated resistance to the family and its problems.

Second, it was a conference that involved a case of severe emotional abuse centering on the distress and anger of one child who had become the locus of the disturbed dynamic of the family. What this brought into clear relief was the flight from the child by both other family-members and the professional group within a context of both depending upon and identifying with the child.

This conference was a very long one – over two hours – of which well over an hour was taken up with a lengthy argument as to (a) the form that intervention and treatment of the family should take; and (b) whether or not the family should go on the Register. These two issues were not clearly separated but led into each other. At the end of the conference no firm conclusion was reached, and in fact a further conference was held a few months later to resolve the argument. I will follow the basic plan of the conference by giving first the actual information on the family and then the way in which this information was discussed and dealt with.

The case conference: (1) information and evidence

Mr and Mrs M were in their mid-twenties and had three children: Trina, a girl of 6, Robert, a boy of 5 and Scott, a boy of 3. Both parents worked fulltime and the children were looked after by a childminder from before they went to school in the morning and again after school till the parents came home in the evening.

The family were being helped by the health visitor because of Robert's incontinence. She decided that there were obviously other problems in the family and referred them for social work support. The social worker was welcomed by the family but it was made clear to him that they only wanted help with their financial problems and with finding childminders. In the nine months of his involvement the social worker had paid about six visits. It was decided to call a case conference because of repeated complaints from the various childminders about how difficult the children were to manage and how little affection Mrs M gave to Robert. The school was also expressing increasing concern about Robert. The conference was attended by the social worker, team leader, senior social worker, child minder, health visitor, general practitioner, educational welfare officer, school doctor, headmistress and child abuse co-ordinator.

At the conference the main information was given by the childminder, the GP and the headmistress. In outline the information was as follows:

(i) From the Childminder: Her opening words were 'You can't play with Scott like you can with other three-year olds. When you try to get him to play he screams.' She described him as being aggressive with other children, and as withdrawn and sitting by himself and playing on his own.

Robert she described as

Very difficult, miserable, he always has a bad cough. It seems to me he really gets depressed. When he comes with his mother he often just goes and flops down on the sofa and just lies there. He needs more food than I can actually give him. He wets his bed every night. I'm very close to him and he needs lots of love.... Irina is jealous of Robert, she calls him smelly and taunts him about his bed wetting. This really upsets Robert and leads him to be very aggressive towards her. She says that 'Mummy, Daddy and I don't like you because you are wicked and I hate you and you smell all the time.

Robert confides to the childminder that they all play tricks on him at home:

He told me once that his father had said that he was going to belt him and made him stand in the middle of the living-room and take down his trousers in front of everyone and then they all laughed and he said it was just a joke and that he wasn't going to belt him. He says that his parents fight a lot and hit each other.

Mrs. M has told me that she finds Robert very difficult. When I described to her what I thought about Robert being depressed she said 'Oh, that's no problem, he is like that all the time at home'.... She says that I make her feel inadequate as a mother because I seem to manage to stay with the children all the time. I think that she is really asking for help and she keeps asking me what to do.

After the childminder had finished it was confirmed that her descriptions were the same as those of the previous two childminders for the family.

(ii) From the GP: He had had one long talk with Mrs M which is worth quoting in some detail:

She told me that she didn't like Robert and that she never had done; she had never had anything but a bad time with him.... Robert was born about 8 months after the birth of Trina at about 30 weeks gestation. He was small for dates and because of his prematurity he was transferred from C. to O. and he was in a Special Care Unit for about two weeks during which time he was not seen by his mother at all. He was then transferred back to the hospital in C. and then he was seen only once or twice by his mother. So for about the first two months of his life he had really negligible contact with his mother. He then came back home and his mother found it impossible to love him or to care for him as she had done with the others. While she was telling me this she was weeping, she felt very guilty about Robert.... She says that she finds Robert physically and emotionally unattractive and that he is the one who is always getting sick.... She takes everything out on Robert.... I hoped that after she had told me all this in our first long talk that she might come back and see me again but she didn't and she felt that she had resolved her problems because she had got a job.... I think that she felt better after we had had a talk. She said that she thought Robert was bed-wetting deliberately to punish her because she knew that he knew that she didn't like him. I think I helped her with this by telling her about enuresis and by pointing out to her that Robert wasn't doing this deliberately just to punish her.

(iii) From the head mistress: Robert was admitted early to the school because Mr M had turned up with him saying that his wife had left, leaving him alone with Robert and he didn't know what to do with him.

When I first talked with Mr M he said how much they both disliked Robert. They both complained about Robert. Also, Mrs M on her own has told me how hard it is to be nice to Robert because he is so horrible.... Two weeks prior to the conference Mrs M came to the school very distressed about the whole day she had spent alone with Robert. She described what had gone on in the home and said that she was now getting frightened of what Robert was going to do. Robert said that he hated all grown-ups and wanted to kill them.... The class-teacher noticed that Robert was really going downhill fast. He was extremely disturbed, he was difficult to control, he was looking very white ... he is a very sad

little boy. Robert made an unsolicited comment saying that he
hoped he would get a machine gun for Christmas because then he
would be able to kill his mother and father.

The head mistress also presented to the conference a record
sheet of the school's observations on Robert which concluded:

He has been looking increasingly worse all this term. At times he
looks quite ill. He is very pale and has black shadows under his
eyes. Rarely co-operates in the classroom unless on a one-to-one
basis which is pretty near impossible. Usually a sad silent figure
sitting still – but interrupted by great bouts of aggression. In the
playground he is aggressive all the time. His speech has regressed.
At one time we could understand everything that he said but at
times now this is not possible. Robert is not achieving in any way –
in fact he is in a regressive situation; a sad figure.

The case conference: (2) what to do

At the end of the giving of evidence the child abuse co-ordinator
reminded the conference that 'when we are talking about child abuse
we are not just talking about physical abuse and here we have what
looks like major emotional abuse.' It was then agreed that so far very
little attempt had been made by the agencies to rectify the rejection
of Robert by his family which led to the following interchange:

Team leader:
Mrs M has never expressed her feelings to the social worker; she
defined her problem to the social worker as being one of debts.
Co-ordinator:
One can't really assess this relationship with the social worker
because Social Services haven't yet been honest with Mrs M and told
her what we now know.
Social worker:
Mrs M is now saying to the child minder that she feels inadequate.
Are we just going to make this worse by putting in more people?

The discussion then turned to the issue of who should approach
Mrs M, who should be open with her. As the GP put it: 'I think that
Mrs M is beginning to sense interference so we will now place our

cards on the table. None of us have really behaved as baddies to the family; we have all shown our concern for the family and for the children.'

The team leader agreed that social services should be honest with the family but was worried because they did not have the permission of the other agencies to be so and 'without it we haven't really got any kind of entrée into the family'. The senior social worker backed this up with the fear that if social services were honest with the family it would break the faith of the family in the GP and the school. The head mistress said that she did not think that the family liked her very much and that the GP ought to be the one who was honest with the parents. The GP agreed but the team leader was still worried that this might lead the family to sever their links with the GP and the school.

This then developed into a second issue, introduced by the social worker: 'I think that if we offer them a lot of support it could lead to the marriage breaking up because there is a lot of violence and friction there and if we help Mrs M with the children so that she gets a better relationship with them this could lead to a break-up of the marriage.'

The co-ordinator agreed that this was a risk but it had to be weighed against the real needs of Robert. She raised the possibility of direct work with Robert. Both the senior social worker and GP objected, on the grounds that 'we should work with the parents first and if that breaks down then we can work with Robert'. The co-ordinator continued to press for details of the work that would be done, and obtained no real reply. The issue seemed to revolve round both the potentially destructive nature of working with them, and whether they should be worked with as individuals, as separate groups or as a family. As the team leader summed it up: 'I think that looking at the long-term goals for a moment I think that we can't decide at the moment but we do need to decide at a later stage after we have seen how they have reacted, whether to work with them as a family group or to work with them just as parents.'

At this point the discussion about the management and intervention plans for the family formally came to an end with the appointment of the social worker as key worker for the family. The discussions then moved on to consider the question of registration. At this point it is worth describing what seem to be some of the main features of the discussion so far as they are taken up again in a different form when considering the Register.

The first thing to note is the perception of the professionals of how explosive or dangerous the knowledge is that each of them contains. The fear seems to be that if this knowledge is made open to the family it will shatter their relationship with the professionals. It is interesting to note that the GP is chosen, and chooses himself, to be the messenger because, of all the professionals 'the doctor does have the edge here because of course they do have to keep coming to see me'. It would appear then that this knowledge about the family, what is really happening inside it, is both exclusive knowledge and excluding knowledge. Quite clearly, the professional group feel that they are in danger of fragmenting themselves if they come clean with the family.

It is worth noting here how this use of dangerous knowledge reflects the behaviour of the family. It could be objected that the whole difficulty of talking to the family is a nonsense – after all, they will not be telling the family anything that the family, quite explicitly, do not already know. The family have already made it bluntly clear to the various professionals what they feel about Robert; and he has been pretty blunt about what he feels about his parents. However, two things stand out. First, again with the exception of what is said by the child and seen of his behaviour, these revelations have been one-off, isolated occurrences. They have not been followed-up by either the professionals or the family, but rather have been left hanging in mid-air. Second, that the one agency professional who has not overtly been made party to these confessions – Social Services – is precisely the agency which possesses the statutory power to intervene. What is being described therefore indicates a high degree of collusion between the family and the professionals, particularly in the case of the Social Services who, it appears, must have worked quite hard not to notice, not to hear and not to talk.

The picture then, is of a family split into warring, jealous, damaged and damaging parts. The professionals, too, are split off from each other, each containing hidden and dangerous 'bits' of the family and their difficulties which somehow have to be brought together. The act itself of bringing these facts together then causes the anxiety of whether they are capable, either collectively or individually, of withstanding the impact of this task; whether it will not turn them against each other in the same way as it has the family.

There is however a complementary but opposite way in which this dangerous knowledge is used, and that is to create a sense of identity between the professionals which holds them together. One can see it in the recognition of the social worker that the family itself is also being held together by its own pathology. As the social worker says, putting in more workers, trying to heal the relationship between the mother and her child, may well cause an outburst of violence which will split the family apart by breaking up the marriage. Bringing out into the open what has been successfully kept hidden may cause great disruption. It would seem to me that the major dynamic here concerns the relationship between the professionals and the child, and in particular the fantasy – shared perhaps between the professionals and the child – of being omnipotently destructive. I will come on to this later through the issue of registration.

One further point worth noting at this stage is the concern of the professionals about being 'good', both in their eyes and in those of the family. As the GP said, 'None of us have really behaved as baddies to the family; we have all shown our concern for the family and for the childen.' It is unclear in this context as to what 'being bad' might consist of other than being angry, failing to show concern, etc. But the concern that has been shown has been such as to hide both the professionals and the family from the open recognition of the difficulties they are experiencing. That is, it has consisted of rejection as much as acceptance. There is a corollary to this, which is the extent to which the professionals can let the family be 'bad' – that is angry and hateful towards each other.

In my experience of case conferences and social work the problem of badness is usually coped with in one of two ways: either by expulsion and punishment of the 'bad' person; or by employment of a quite sophisticated vocabulary of compassion to retranslate hate, anger and destructiveness into more acceptable categories of guilt, despair, deprivation and 'cries for help', etc. There seems to be a small class of emotions which are very difficult to accept openly as being an often central and painful part of clients' experience of themselves. An example of this retranslation is given by the GP when he reassured the mother that Robert's bed-wetting was not a deliberate attempt to punish her because she did not like him. Sch reassurance may not only be factually wrong – the child *may* be deliberately trying to punish the mother – but it also cuts off and denies a significant attempt by the mother to express an honest but painful emotional truth about her relationship with her son. Implicitly she is being told that she does not possess the bad, destructive feelings towards her son she feels she possesses. I will come back to this point in connection with the discussion of the child.

The case conference: (3) registration?

I want to move on now to look at the discussion of registration. At the conference, my impression was that there would be relatively little problem over this. It seemed to be, in terms of the criteria for abuse in the guidance booklet, an absolutely clear-cut case of emotional abuse. There were also indications of both physical abuse and of neglect. What happened was quite different.

The co-ordinator raised the question of registration and whether it would be appropriate to tell the family about the Register. The team leader said he wanted to wait and see what response the family made; the GP said that the family would interpret it 'that they are seen by us as a bad family and they will see us just as negative and destructive'; the senior social worker said they should not be on the Register because the Register is about putting extra resources into the family and 'Social Services are already going to put in resources so there is no real point in them going on the register'. The team leader and the GP then said that they should be placed on the Register if they failed to cooperate with the helping agencies; the health visitor thought that perhaps they ought to go on the Register for the sake of information, 'but as everybody does seem to know already that seems to be rather unnecessary'; the head mistress said she had little experience of the Register and 'I would tend to agree with everyone else'.

That was the end of what could be called Round 1. The co-ordinator then read out the relevant criteria from the booklet. With the exception of the senior social worker, everyone agreed that Robert was subject to parental rejection and neglect and that he was a candidate for the register. The senior social worker maintained that (i) there were lots of parents in the division who neglected/rejected their children and they didn't want them all on the register; (ii) that the rejection and abuse was not serious; and (iii) that a comma was missing in the text of the booklet which completely altered all the meanings. The team leader said that Robert was definitely a candidate but registration was not appropriate because there were no advantages to it. The social worker said bluntly: 'By the criteria you have read out he is definitely a candidate, but I don't want him on the Register.' That was the subject matter of Round 2. Round 3 was characterised by a move of great subtlety on the part of the social worker. The head mistress asked the question whether the family had to be told about registration and was told that it was not mandatory. She then said:

Why is it such a bad thing to put them on? I am disturbed, I am very disturbed about this child at the moment. He is being emotionally abused. I think that they should go on the register and the family should not be told.'
Co-ordinator:
At a very basic level placing them on the register is an expression of our professional concern. It's a separate issue of how and why they are actually told about this.
Social worker:
If they're placed on the register they must be told. I couldn't visit if I wasn't able to be completely honest with them.... I really don't want to put them on the register. I can't see it acting in any way as a benefit for the family if they go on the register, but I agree that severe emotional abuse is taking place.

With this statement, the discussion virtually came to an end. Everyone, with the exception of the co-ordinator, agreeing that the family should not go on the Register. As the educational welfare officer said: 'With this family in particular, how can the social worker work if he's not being truthful with them?'

Discussion and conclusion

The problem then is to try to decode what is going on here; why it is that, in the face of such a clear-cut case, a case which all the professionals recognise as being one of emotional abuse, there is such hostility to registration? It would seem as if, in a condensed form, registration has become the focus for a whole series of issues around the perception, management and understanding of the family. In particular, I want to argue that the issue of registration is concerned with the relationship between the significant professionals – social services in particular – and the child. By rejecting registration they are in effect rejecting the child.

I shall approach this issue in two ways. First by re-examining the stated reasons for rejecting registration and asking what difference would it make to the professionals if registration took place. What changes would it occasion in either their actions or their attitudes or both? Second, I shall look at the image of the child, the way it has been described and the way that description is being used by the professionals and by the family.

Re-examining the arguments against registration then, one can see that essentially there are three – or rather two, one of which has two aspects. The first argument is that registration will not do anything. On a practical level this is quite correct. No additional services will be provided to this family as a result of registration. On the level, however, of a communication to the family and to the professionals themselves, quite the opposite is the case. For the second major argument against registration is that: 'If we say that they are on the register they are going to take it that they are seen by us as a bad family and they will see us just as negative and destructive.' This is then taken up as the third major argument – that the social worker couldn't work with the family if he was not able to be completely honest with them. That would mean he would have to tell them they were on the register, and that in turn would be damaging to the family. So, one can say that registration would make a big difference to the professionals because they would be causing the family a double deprivation. On the one hand, they would be confirming the family in its own negative self-image – reinforcing it in fact. On the other hand, by so doing they would be depriving the family of the opportunity of making use of the help offered by the professionals because the family would only be able to see the professionals as bad. Registration therefore would be a sadistic act causing pain to the family.

There is however an irony to this in that if the family subsequently show themselves to be bad – that is, fail to cooperate with the professionals and change – then they should be placed on the Register. Again, this reinforces the image of the Register as a punishment, and symbolises it as something very powerful that the professionals could do but have, temporarily, chosen not to.

There are, however, two sets of strong arguments for saying that not only is this line of argument quite wrong, but also that it constitutes a defensive rationalisation by the professionals in order, on the one hand to avoid a painful reality about the family, and on the other hand, to maintain a collusive identification with the parents and a masochistic identification with the child. And that it is these two aspects that the professionals want to keep out of consciousness.

The first line of argument would be that registration is not just as the co-ordinator said, 'an expression of our professional concern', but is also a way of fixing in the mind that what is going on in the family is abuse, and that it is a child who is being abused. That is, registration makes it harder to avoid bringing into the centre of consciousness what had hitherto been kept on the periphery and sealed up in each of the workers individually. In effect, therefore, registration closes a gap between what the professionals all 'knew' was going on in the family but which was cut off from what they did with the family and what they expressed to the family.

Further, there is the stress on the fact that it is a child who is being abused. Registration implies a concentration on the child; bringing the child to the centre of the stage, having to confront it and to work with it. This, it will be remembered, was something that was very quickly glossed over when treatment was being discussed. Although the co-ordinator raised the issue of direct work with Robert, this was objected to on the grounds that he should only be worked with if the work with the parents broke down. The General Practitioner puts it neatly:

> Isn't the first thing to try and lay our cards on the table with the parents to see how they react and then if things go badly then we would perhaps have to get in something like Child and Family Psychiatry to work with Robert. The trouble with the set-up here [i.e. the Child and Family Psychiatry] is that they are very child-orientated and not really family orientated.

The case is marked by the fact that no one with the exception of the childminder and the school teacher have really got near to Robert at all. What should be noticed, however, is that getting near to him sounds like a nasty and potentially damaging task. He has been described as smelly, depressed, aggressive, possessing murderous rage towards caretakers, orally dependent and very demanding. He is described as a fool, a buffoon who is mocked by his siblings and parents but who is also central to the family. All in all, a child to be avoided like the plague as he is unloved, unlovable and, what is perhaps most anxiety provoking of all, seemingly undefended against his own feelings and acting them out to the terror of his mother and the childminder. Avoiding registration avoids this nasty reality. Theoretically, it can be recognised that he exists and abuse exists but this must not be explicitly named.

This leads to the second set of arguments – the collusive identification with the parents and the masochistic identification with the child. To understand this means accepting a paradox that these two modes of identification rest on a rejection. Failing to register and failing to communicate the fact of registration to the family withholds from the family an open recognition by the professionals of the nature of their pain and pathology. That is, it constitutes a collusion with the parents to defend them against a central part of their acting and feeling. This in turn radically denies the parents and the whole family access to both what is healthy inside themselves and what is therapeutic in the professionals. First, by failing to be honest with them about their failure at the parenting task. For failing openly to accept and confirm their messages of aggression, rage, rejection and despair is to strike at what is a fundamentally honest and moral part of their awareness of themselves. Precisely that part of themselves which will have to be mobilised if any therapeutic work is to be successful. Moreover, it locks them into a sense of failure and despair by in effect telling them that what they are experiencing about themselves is not real but is a fantasy. That is, they are being told that to succeed, to become 'good' parents, they must deny one important part of their feelings. That part which is, in all probability, their significant articulation and protest about the deprivations and hurt they have also experienced, and are continuing to experience through the child.

Second, this failure withholds from them a crucial message that what is most 'bad' – i.e. destructive, damaging and damaged – about them can be held contained and modified. First by the professionals and then, through identification, by themselves. The professionals' retreat from this aspect of the parents' behaviour mirrors their own worst fantasy which is that such self-knowledge is too devastating to contain; it cannot be made compatible with a sense of a functioning identity, and that therefore it has to be dealt with by repression and projection.

Thirdly, therefore, the professionals are colluding with the central family dynamic whereby the badness is projected onto the child who is rejected and punished and thus becomes the reality of the projections: he becomes the evil, destructive, depressed and unlovable part of the family. The retreat from the reality of the child by both the parents and the professionals locks the child into identification with its own worst omnipotent destructive fantasies, while depriving it of the knowledge in reality that its parents have rejected and hated it. The professionals, in turn, by colluding with this dynamic, are also defending themselves against the anxiety generated by their own central fantasy of their malevolent omnipotence – that is, their ability to blow up themselves and the family if they expose themselves and the family to what is going on. The paradox here is that they defend themselves against the sadistic nature of their withholding from the family by perceiving such withholding as a defence against their sadism. However, as Freud would agree, 'While the pains are being inflicted on other people, they are enjoyed masochistically by the subject through his identification of himself with the suffering object.'

As was made clear in the discussion of how best to intervene in the family, Robert is central to its survival as a (pathologically) functioning unit, and it is this mode of functioning that the professionals seem concerned to preserve. I would suggest that one fundamental reason for this is that they, like the parents, have become bound up in a masochistic identification with the child; that, like the family, they have not been able to face up to either their own aggressive feelings, or their feelings of having been hurt and damaged by contact with this family. In effect, that is, they have not found a way of adequately parenting themselves in order to pass this on to these clients.

My concern here has been simply to point to some possible dynamics of child abuse case conferences, in trying to understand why certain kinds of decisions are taken. I have wanted to make clear two paradoxes which I think are central to the operation of such conferences. The first is that the apparent form of resistance and rejection which I have been pointing to is based upon a deeper form of identification of a collusive and sado-masochistic nature; and that sado-masochistic relationships can best be understood as a defensive regression from the pain of reality-based relationships. I think that this makes sense of the famous, if enigmatic, statement by Kempe that where, in child abuse cases, a worker, two parents and child meet, four sick individuals are involved.

The second paradox is that, while ostensibly the child is supposed to be the main focus of attention and discussion at child abuse case conferences, in practice many conferences and much of the work done with abusing families are organised as a defence against such attention and discussion and in fact take the form of a professional flight from the child.

Note

1.   The datum on which this chapter is based is derived from a research
      study into social work decision-making and management practices in
      cases of child abuse. The study, which was funded by the Department of
      Health and Social Security, was carried out between 1978 and 1982 by
      the author and Dr Iain Farquhar at the Child Care and Development
      Group, University of Cambridge. Among other aspects, the study
      involved the detailed observation and recording of 90 case conferences
      called to decide whether or not a child should be placed on the Child
      Abuse Register.

9 Thinking about Feelings in Group Care

John Simmonds

The influence of psychoanalytic theory on social work practice has declined dramatically over the past 15–20 years. While playing a more important part in social work theory and training than in actual practice, doubts have always existed about the alliance of social work with a fundamentally intrapsychic theory with a predominantly therapeutic mode. The powerful sociological and political critiques of the late 1960s and early 1970s have indeed argued that, so formulated, social work becomes a part of the state apparatus that makes a positive contribution to the maintenance of inequality and social injustice. The equally powerful arguments of the new right have made their own mark in the late 1970s and early 1980s (Brewer & Lait, 1980). Even the therapeutic mode itself has moved away from a psychoanalytic base, with alternative theories that seem to offer more readily accessible explanations of human behaviour and more easily acquired techniques of intervention. Poor teaching and supervision have played their part as well. The effect of all of this seems to have driven psychoanalytic thought very much into the background and history of social work. This has been accompanied by an exodus of those with a continuing interest in its application out of social work and into the analytic and therapeutic professions.

If this is so in casework practice, then apart from a minute number of distinguished exceptions, such as Peper Harrow and the Mulberry Bush, psychoanalysis has barely had a foothold in the residential and day care sector at all (cf. Miller, 1964; Docker-Drysdale, 1968). Yet some of the developments in psychoanalytic theory itself since Freud have a significant contribution to make to social work in this area. The plan of this chapter is therefore to explore a number of the key points in these developments and then to relate them to some of the problems faced by residential workers in their work.

The capacity to think about what one feels and to learn from experience has been one of major interests and developments in psychoanalytic thought since Freud. Stripped of some of its jargon it might be thought of as the use of intuition. However, given the powerful human capacity to defend against emotional pain, this is an intuition of a special kind based on the ability to be receptive to feelings in oneself or in others which because of their painful nature might ordinarily be defended against.

Much of the development of this line of thinking has resulted from the work of Bion (1962) in his concern to link the development of thought with the development of the emotions. Based as his work is on the analysis of psychotic patients, the primitive processes he explores are complex. However, what is relevant here derives from the model he developed to formulate the mental processes by which individuals learn from experience. One of the critical components in this is the mother's capacity to transform the baby's emotional experience of, for example, being hungry or wet through the care she gives the baby. The act of feeding or changing Bion argues is more then than just a bodily or physical transformation of hunger into satisfaction or a wet bottom into a dry one. For each physical act there is a qualitative change in the baby's accompanying emotional experience of the time. Hunger or discomfort are felt as an attack inside the baby which it attempts to deal with by expulsion into its mother. The mother's capacity to respond with a physical act of a quite different emotional content to the discomfort and pain originally present in her baby has the effect of, as it were, detoxifying these feelings. What the baby communicates to its mother at one level is transformed and returned to the baby at another. The significance of the disjunction between two different emotional values can be seen in adults, e.g. the feeling of wanting to retaliate when attacked or to panic when the atmosphere is one of panic is very strong. Emotional values of one kind seem to produce a corresponding instinctive response in many situations. However, in normal circumstances, parents are able to hold on to their own feelings of panic when their babies get into a panic. Similarly they do not retaliate to the feeling of being attacked by the baby's sense of being attacked from inside by hunger pains. In Bion's view, it is this capacity to contain these feelings that brings about the qualitative change that forms the foundation for the development of the capacity to think and for learning based on experience.

Building on the work of Freud and Klein, Bion has developed this complex argument to describe the fundamental elements of mental functioning and the corresponding processes which enable raw experience to be used as building blocks for the development of the mind.[1] Primitive emotional experiences must be processed not just in order to tidy them away as some kind of psychological sewage but because they are the means by which individuals learn to relate to their own and in turn other people's psychic reality. Avoidance and evasion of feeling not only lead to pathological emotional development but to disordered thinking.

Bion's work along with others has given new meaning to the terms transference and particularly counter-transference.[2] Counter-transference as it was first written about was considered to be a dangerous intrusion into the analyst's capacity to understand the patient objectively. The analyst's emotional response to the patient was not to be allowed to interfere with the analytic work. However, later developments in the use of the term emphasise that the analyst's capacity to be emotionally receptive to what the patient is feeling is one of the principle elements by which the patient's difficulties are understood. It is the analyst's capacity to engage in thinking about the significance of the denied and unwanted parts of the patient that are projected as experience into the analyst that transforms them into something that the patient can take back in a modified and less threatening form inside himself. At the same time the danger remains that in its raw state what the patient projects into the analyst becomes the source of acting out in the analyst rather than of understanding. Just as a feeling can be painful to the patient and evacuated, so it can evoke painful feelings in the analyst and be defended against. Given the complexity and subtlety of these processes this is probably one of the most taxing difficulties that analysts have to struggle with.

Bain discusses this issue further in a different context by considering the role of the social scientist in an action research project. He draws attention to the importance of the social scientist not only being clear about the task of the project and his role within it but also of his experience of the evolving emotional reality of that role. This is important he says because social scientists can be used by members of a social system as an object into which they can unconsciously project feelings about themselves in that social system which they find anxiety provoking. A proper appreciation of these projected elements can help the social scientist to understand crucial parts of that social system which might not be otherwise available. In so doing, such understanding can be a source of important unblocking in the social system itself and therefore the source of organisational change (cf. Bain & Barnett, 1980).

Bain gives an interesting example of this in his analysis of the working of a local authority day nursery. He states that the original conception by the nursery staff of the research team's role was that of expert with immediate solutions to their many problems. Given the strong social expectations associated with 'expertness' this is not surprising and given some of the real problems the staff were facing it is not difficult to imagine how easy it would have been for the research team to have fallen into this role. However, Bain argues that by resisting this temptation it gave his team a deeper insight into the workings of the nursery – in particular the staff's denial of their own knowledge and experience of the children they were working with. The staff's denial of their expertise not only resulted in the staff acting irresponsibly, it served the function of defending them against the anxiety of forming intimate relationships with the children. By taking back inside themselves what they knew, the staff were able to think about the needs of the children and particularly the emotional needs of the children in a more realistic way. In turn this helped them to develop closer relationships with the children they were working with.

While important in what it says about day nurseries, Bain demonstrates that not only are parents and analysts the objects of projection, but that social systems are too. He also demonstrates with considerable clarity that understanding and working with these projections is a source of learning and development both in individuals and social systems. This view contrasts sharply with many of the accepted views on organisations and organisational change.

Although there are many schools of organisation theory and much controversy about the nature of organisations, we normally think of them as being rationally conceived with explicit aims and a structure designed to execute those aims. The subjective and emotions are an anathema to much thinking about organisations, preference being given to thinking of them as being firmly rooted in an objective reality even if it is suggested that the actions they sometimes engage in seems far removed from this. What goes on inside people is not a comfortable subject of study for most organisational theorists and rarely is the concern of management consultants or senior managers. What happens between people in organisational life may figure more prominently but even then it is not uncommon for theory to de-personalise the uncomfortable subjective element by talking in terms of organisational role. What people bring of themselves apart from their capacity to fulfill their formal work tasks is seen therefore as an unfortunate encumbrance to the efficient and proper working of the organisation. Some sociological and organisational debate has centred around the relevant merits of theories and their positions over the subjective, but the thrust of much of what is actually applied in organisational design and taught and expected of managers rests largely on formal theory and the exclusion of the subjective and the emotions. In social work this trend can be seen in some of the work of the Brunel Institute and some of the current management trends in Social Services Departments (cf. Rowbottom *et al*; 1974; Billis *et al.*, 1980). The recent policy of 'general management' in the NHS is based on similar assumptions about organisational processes and change. The significance of this school of thought on organisational thought and change is profound. Under it for instance, it might be argued that the change brought about by Bain in the day nursery could be as well accomplished by management simply identifying an objective like – 'create closer relationships between staff and children' as a working hypothesis. All then that would be required is for this objective to be implemented hierarchically through the nursery's formal supervisory system. However, while the objective might appear the same under both approaches, the greater advantage of Bain is that he takes into account the part played by the organisationally-structured avoidance of closeness in the work of the nursery. Failure to appreciate unconscious defences in organisational matters can make many well intentioned changes simply the object of powerful resistance and in consequence fruitless work.

There are two theoretical and practical traditions that have most tried to evolve a psychoanalytic view that combines both organisational structure and of the individual with an inner unconscious world. The first not surprisingly is associated with a specific movement in the mental health field – that of the democratic therapeutic community (Jones, 1955, 1976). The second has had a more general application to commercial, industrial as well as human service agencies and is exemplified in the work of the Tavistock Institute of Human Relations and more particularly that of A. K. Rice (cf. Rice & Miller, 1967).

One of the main arguments of organisational analysts like Rice and psychoanalysts like Jaques and Menzies is that the importance of objective and rationally conceived notions of task and structure, must be complemented by an understanding of the place of emotions and particularly unconscious motivation in organisational life. This is unambiguously put by Jaques (1955) when he says, 'One of the primary cohesive elements binding individuals into institutionalised human association is that of defence against psychotic anxiety. In this sense individuals may be thought of as externalising those impulses and internal objects that would otherwise give rise to psychotic anxiety, and pooling them in the life of the social institutions in which they associate.' He goes on to say, 'Many social problems – economic and political – which are often laid at the door of human ignorance, stupidity, wrong attitudes, selfishness, or power seeking, may become more understandable if seen as containing unconsciously motivated attempts by human beings to defend themselves ... against the experience of anxieties whose sources could not be consciously controlled'. In comparison to the model of organisations which starts with task and derives structure from a rational appraisal of that task, this picture of organisational functioning is inside out. However, it is important in understanding the psychoanalytically informed model of organisations, that this does not of itself reduce task and structure to a secondary position in such a theory but that task and structure cannot be fully understood without also being aware of what these come to represent to members of the organisation. When Menzies (1960) traces the structural problems of the nursing service in a teaching hospital back to institutional methods of dealing with individual nurse anxiety, it does not place the objective need for nurses or a structure to deliver their services in a secondary place. However, it does draw attention when looking at the concepts of task and structure to the deeper and dynamic significance of these terms. It also demands that we consider these dynamic aspects when looking at the processes which interfere with an organisation's successful pursuit of its task.

Britton (1981) adds another dimension to this theme when he explores the Freudian concept of repetition and re-enactment not just in relation to individual or family dynamics but also in relation to the way that professionals handle these dynamics both inside and among themselves. He is concerned therefore to demonstrate the way in which patterns of relationships in one situation can be transferred into a different situation 'in which new participants become the vehicles for the reiterated expression of the underlying dynamic. . . . The basic situation remains unrealised and unchanged whilst new versions of it proliferate. The cast changes but the plot remains the same, (p. 49). This adds a new if not unexpected dimension to the concept of transference and counter-transference, for not only does the possibility exist of individual analysts 'acting out' in the transference but groups of professionals too can become dramatis personæ to the client's unconscious world. Britton suggests that 'the intensity of feeling aroused by a case; the degree of dogmatism evoked; of the pressure to take drastic and urgent measures' together with inappropriate unconcern, surprising ignorance, undue complacency, uncharacteristic insensitivity or professional inertia (p. 48) are all possible indicators that such is happening. The uncontained and unwanted feelings in a case therefore come to dominate and dictate professional thinking and consequent action in that case. It is a clear example of Bion's argument for the fusion of thought and feeling. When thinking is divorced from the painful emotional reality to which it relates then unhealthy and inappropriate action can result. However, this is not only a possibility in individual cases and therefore peculiar and confined to individual instances for, as Menzies makes clear, the actual structure and practices of the professions and organisations themselves may take on these unconsciously determined themes. This is discussed by Miller and Gwynne (1972) in their study of long-term residential establishments for the physically handicapped. Here defences against the emotional and social anxiety of the primary task give rise to what they call humanitarian and liberal defenses. From this they derive two models of residential care – warehousing and horticultural – both of which seek to deny some important aspect of the reality of the task of these establishments. Bain and Barnett (1980) make a similar point in their description of the domestic culture of a day nursery for children.

What I am arguing therefore is that developments in psychoanalytic thought suggest that every aspect of organisational life from task, structure and culture to individual decision-making and case management can express the basic problem human beings have in facing emotional pain and learning from experience. In so doing not only are there socially-structured mechanisms for the defence against anxiety but each situation has the potential for expressing an underlying and unconsciously determined emotional dynamic. Menzies' description of institutional defenses clearly implies this but she does not make explicit the dynamic processes by which these defenses are built up.

However, rather than this theory being a negative expression of the potential of organisational life, it opens up the possibility of organisations becoming more sensitive to the emotional reality of human problems. In so doing they can develop descriptions of their tasks and corresponding structures and work practices that relate to the necessity of understanding and working with the underlying anxiety and dynamics of the task.

This is exemplified in a residential establishment that helped young people who had been in long-term local authority care to establish themselves independently. A crisis had occurred in the establishment over staffing and shift rotas. While on paper there were adequate people to cover shifts in the establishment itself, it was difficult when preparing rotas to allow staff to have the time necessary to support those residents who had actually left. Because of these difficulties, the quality of the after-care work had in fact diminished and those staff who were following up on residents were largely doing it in their own time. The crisis had also deepened recently as the management group had tried to deal with this problem by quantifying present demand for after-care and also anticipating future needs for those residents about to leave. These figures showed that an increase of some 30 per cent would be required to meet this demand. This figure was not only rejected by the senior managers of the organisation but started a questioning of the necessity of doing after-care work at all. This was greeted by considerable anger in the staff and over time a marked drop in morale.

In discussing after-care with the staff of the establishment, it became apparent that the issue as presented – staffing – was in fact only one aspect of a problem that there was considerable feeling about. Not only were staff concerned about what happened to residents when they left, they were also worried about what was happening to residents while they were actually resident. After some time, it became clear that the principal issue that linked both areas of concern was the question of separation – separation for the young people from an uncertain past into for many an uncertain future. For the staff this was also important as it meant the breaking of important relationships with residents which had been built up over time and with considerable effort. As this was discussed in more detail, it became clear that many staff found the aims of the establishment difficult to relate to in that so many of the young people that were referred and accepted had needs and problems that were far deeper than two years' stay could deal with. The staff felt that for many of the young people, it could take two years to build up any kind of trusting relationship. The focus on this aspect of the work tended therefore to push the other aspect of the work – preparation for leaving – into the background. While, therefore, it was not absent from discussions during a person's stay, it was something that was discussed with considerable ambivalence on the staff's part. I had the impression that for some young people there may well have been an air of some unreality about the plans for the future and their need actively to engage in work on it. The point at which it was actively discussed could therefore be only weeks and in one instance three days before the move to a flat was planned. In that time, the emotional atmosphere could easily be dominated by panic in the resident and guilt on the part of the staff. Preparation itself was often focused on practical matters with little consideration being given to the feeling content of what was happening. A culture seemed to have developed in the establishment based on the difficulty of both being in a close relationship and at the same time dealing with the complex issues of separation and independence. The residents' anxiety about this latter issue caused many of them to deny completely the reality of what they were facing and forced them into expressing a powerful and oftan a negative dependency on the staff. As a consequence of this, the period of after-care was at its best often used to deal with some the issues which might more usefully have been focused on during the period of residence. It was at these times that the demands of after-care on staff resources became particularly acute but even then the anxiety of bringing the work to an end and transferring the responsibility elsewhere caused the work to go on for longer than appropriate. In a number of instances where after-care was not used to recoup the lost work during residency, the young person's previous poor experiences of separation was re-enacted in a mixture of rejection and neglect. It was often these young people that had the most difficulty in coping with independence and over time of needing a further period of residential care – although this time it could be in a mental hospital or prison.

The focus of the work with both management and staff group was in the first instance not so much in finding a way of increasing staff resources. Rather they needed help in developing their own emotional resources in order to understand the emotional content of the task and the corresponding culture that had developed in order to cope with the anxiety of that task. In so doing, the staff's deepened understanding of this task and of their own subjective responses to it became the most significant point in the development in the original problem and the work of the establishment. By both experiencing and reflecting on the pain of separation, and it was quite clear that at the point of deepest understanding the staff most directly experienced this pain inside themselves, the staff found a way of becoming more openly sensitive and receptive to the problems and anxieties of the residents. This in turn enabled the staff to help the residents confront more directly and in a more helpful way both their past and future while they were in residence and as a preparation for leaving.

The second example also demonstrates the way in which anxiety prevents a thorough discussion of a resident's problems with subsequent difficulties for both parties. However, it also demonstrates the way in which organisational practices can unwittingly become a part of the problem they were designed to solve.

In a weekly meeting in an adolescent unit, the staff group wanted to discuss a particularly difficult problem with a girl resident named Tracy who was 17. During the week before the discussion, Tracy had been the object of quite a lot of talk and hushed rumour from other residents and this seemed to centre around some speculation that she had been engaging in some peculiar behaviour in the toilets. The group found it difficult to actually say what this was but it finally emerged that she had been seen by other residents with her head inside the toilet bowl and as a result had been the subject of much ridicule and humiliation. The staff were clearly disgusted and perplexed by this and feeling rather out of their depth. What they found particularly difficult about the problem was Tracy's apparant lack of concern. When they had tried to discuss the incident with her she had reacted abusively and said that it didn't matter – if other people were worried then it was their problem. The staff had found this very provocative. The staff group felt themselves to be quite out of their depth with Tracy – the incident and her lack of concern about it being the final straw. They didn't feel they had the knowledge, skill or experience to deal with her problems and also felt unclear as to whether their agency was set up to be dealing with her anyway. I felt very sympathetic to this problem – a great deal was expected of them, given the kinds of referrals they were getting from social workers. Yet while there was much good will and common sense in the staff, this was objectively not enough to enable them to sufficiently get to grips with the kinds of problems they were being presented with.

The group went on to discuss Tracy in a bit more detail. It emerged that she had had longstanding problems with boy friends. She was sexually promiscuous and had a poor sense of the integrity and value of her own body and feelings. Some months before, the persistence of these difficulties had led, after discussion in a case conference, to Tracy being referred to a sex counsellor. Tracy had been accompanied to the first session by her key worker who reported that the counsellor had encouraged Tracy to explore some of her feelings about sexuality and particularly masturbation. The key worker found the intimate detail in this first session rather an uncomfortable experience but afterwards Tracy herself seemed to feel unconcerned about it. The sessions became rather erratic in their frequency after this and Tracy became increasingly resistant to going to them. At the point we were discussing it, the counsellor had not reappeared after a long holiday and nobody was clear what was happening.

There seemed to be quite a lot of anger in the staff group about the way that the counsellor had acted. It was clear that she was felt to be unhelpfully invasive in her approach and failed to appreciate the importance of consistency in arranging both the times and dates of sessions and her holidays. While the anger did not seem inappropriate in the circumstances (although I imagined the details about the counselling were more complex) I was struck on further questioning about how little the staff group knew or had found out about the counsellor, and with what haste and lack of planning the sessions had been arranged. I was also struck by how little Tracy had been consulted and prepared for them. From what I knew of the staff group this didn't arise because of a lack of genuine feeling for or desire to help her.

During the course of subsequent discussion with the staff, it became clear that Tracy's insistence that her actions had little meaning and that she was freely available sexually to anybody who showed the slightest interest in her clearly had stirred up some very strong feelings in the staff. On the one hand there was a common and shared concern for her vulnerability and fear for her safety and her future. There was also some very strongly expressed indignation from women in the group about the general sexual exploitation of women by men, a subject that caused the men in the group to become increasingly silent. After I made this observation to the group, one of the men admitted how threatening he had found this discussion. Not only did he feel uncomfortable that he was being identified with the men that had so freely taken advantage of Tracy, he had always found himself quite disturbingly intrigued by some of the detail of her sexual exploits. His anxiety about saying any of this had always made it difficult for him to discuss Tracy's problems very thoroughly in the group. These very frank admissions were greeted in the group by enormous relief and led on to a general discussion about the difficulties of handling sexual issues in the group.

In the course of subsequent discussions in the group the impact of this inhibition on the way Tracy had been handled became much clearer. At the time of her referral to the counsellor the lack of any full discussion of Tracy's needs with herself or in the staff group could clearly be related to its unacknowledged discomfort over sexual issues. The action the group took therefore was as much determined by its anxiety over this as it was over finding an appropriate way of coping with Tracy and her difficulties. It was also as though they believed sexual counselling by an outsider would act as some kind of cold shower to Tracy's actual promiscuity and their feared sexual interest. It was also clear that there was some considerable anxiety about the reaction of management to the discussion we were having especially in the light of recent public outrage about sexual scandals in residential care.

In not thoroughly discussing the problem between themselves and most particularly with Tracy herself the problem was compounded. For not only were her needs not properly assessed, the group acted as though her psyche belonged to them and that they could do as they wished with it. At this level, there is an uncomfortable similarity to the way Tracy allowed herself to become the possession of the men she came into contact with, to be used sexually as they wished. Accustomed as she had become to decisions being taken about her by a substantial history in the very care system that was supposed to respect her, one more decision taken on her behalf to 'therapeutically poke and prod her' evoked no conscious protest. She acted as though both her body and mind were an unbearable and anxiety provoking responsibility that she could not tolerate. Her attitude and behaviour for that reason led to her either her being exploited or abused. In this light, the original incident might be understood as both an unconscious protest at the way she felt she was being treated by others as well as a way of her further degrading and humiliating herself.

However, while understanding the nature of this girl's psychopathology is important in planning appropriate intervention, in the context of the issues discussed above the organisational issues are at least as important in identifying how she might be helped in the long run. While in this case there was a procedure for reviewing Tracy's problems as they developed, they were not enough in themselves to prevent the organisation from becoming caught up in and re-enacting underlying dynamic processes. As such, it is not just Tracy's problem in setting limits to the way that either she or others uses and abuses herself. The staff group also seemed to have problems in understanding and using its own anxieties about sexuality and in haste attempted to seek reassurance from an outsider rather than using the feelings generated by a complex issue to guide the thinking about what to do about it.

If the staff did not feel comfortable or could not work with their own or with each other's feelings about sexuality, then they could not work with Tracy's. In particular, they could not communicate a sense of structure and boundary that might act as the basis for providing the psychological security she needed to work on her problems. Menzies makes this point when she says, 'An aspect of healthy development in the individual is the establishment of a firm boundary for the self and others across which realistic and effective relationships and transactions can take place (Menzies Lyth, 1985).

This issue is of considerable importance throughout the field of social work. Given the high levels of stress and anxiety inherent in many social work cases, the potential for re-enacting the dynamics in the case between worker and client, worker and supervisor, different parts of the Department and between different organisations is enormous (cf. Fineman, 1985; Britton, 1981; Mattinson & Sinclair, 1979; Mattinson, 1975). It is this factor that can make the current demands to tighten up on procedure in child abuse cases very dangerous for there is nothing in procedures themselves that can prevent them from becoming the object of powerful projections and from there the means by which these problems become perpetuated by the very agencies who have responsibility to sort them out. While clear guidelines and procedures are important as a way of helping contain anxiety in high risk and complex situations, in themselves they cannot take the place of the capacity to think based on what is felt inside. Whether in group care settings or in fieldwork, considerable attention needs to be given to the kinds of organisational structures and practices that allow workers to understand and use what they have been made to feel by the clients that they come into contact with. In enabling worker's fears to be used diagnostically and therapeutically, managers will have to recognise that this means workers exposing themselves to feelings that are not normally thought to be at all admissible in a work setting.

Organisational structures and practices seem more typically to have the effect of making workers feel more insecure and more guilty about such feelings when such anxiety provoking situations are encountered. Rather than enabling these feelings to be worked with, the response is to control them. Rather than understanding and using what is being experienced, the feelings are repressed.

In the current debate in social work, therefore, much more thought needs to be given to the impact of the very powerful feelings that I have discussed than currently seem to be in vogue. Whether in theory or in practice, what we feel and often want to ignore may be the basis for building a social work less dominated by the present climate of insecurity, guilt and tragedy.

Notes

1. It might be noted that in contrast to the accepted view that it is the capacity to think that gives rise to thought, in Bion's model it is the existence of the raw emotional elements of thoughts which leads to the development of an apparatus for thinking.

2. Analysts apart from Bion have approached the problem of transference and counter-transference from different perspectives although there are many similarities in the ideas that they developed about the subject. See Racker (1968) and Winnicott (1949).

Bibliography

Ackerman N. W. (1958) *The Psychodynamics of Family Life* (New York: Basic Books).

Ackerman N. W. *et al.* (eds) (1961) *Exploring the Base for Family Therapy* (New York: Family Service Association of America).

Addison C. (1982) 'A Defence Against the Public? Aspects of Intake in a Social Services Departments', *British Journal of Social Work*, vol. 12, no. 6.

Adorno T. W. *et al.* (1950) *The Authoritarian Personality* (New York: Harper & Row).

Adorno T. W. (1951) 'Freudian Theory and the Pattern of Fascist Propaganda', in A. Arato and E. Gebhardt (eds), *The Essential Frankfurt School Reader* (Oxford: Blackwell, 1978).

Adorno T. W. (1967) 'Sociology and Psychology, I', *New Left Review*, no. 46.

―― (1968) 'Sociology and Psychology, II', *New Left Review*, no. 47.

Althusser L. (1971) 'Freud and Lacan', in *Lenin and Philosophy and Other Essays* (London: New Left Books).

Bacon R. (1977) 'Child Abuse and Child Care: Connections and Implications', *Adoption and Fostering*, vol. 90, no. 4.

―― (1982) 'Background Notes for a Discussion of Family Violence', in A. Bernecker, W. Merten and R. Wolff (eds), *Ohnmachtige Gewalt* (Rowolt).

Bailey R. and P. Lee (eds) (1982) *Theory and Practice in Social Work* (Oxford: Blackwell).

Bain A. and L. Barnett (1980) *The Design of a Day Care System in a Nursery Setting for Children Under Five* (London: Tavistock Institute of Human Relations).

Baker Miller J. (ed.) (1973) *Psychoanalysis and Women* (Harmondsworth: Penguin).

Baker Miller J. (1978) *Towards a New Psychology of Women* (Harmondsworth: Penguin).

Balint E. (1973) 'Technical Problems Found in the Analysis of Women by a Woman Analyst: A Contribution to the Question "What Does a Woman Want?"', *International Journal of Psychoanalysis*, vol. 54 [repr. in G. Kohon (ed.) *The British School of Psychoanalysis: The Independent Tradition* (London: Free Association, 1986).]

Balint M., P. H. Ornstein and E. Balint (1972) *Focal Psychotherapy: An Example of Applied Psychoanalysis* (London: Tavistock).

Banton R., P. Clifford, S. Frosh, J. Lousada and J. Rosenthal (1985) *The Politics of Mental Health* (London: Macmillan).

Barham P. (1984) *Schizophrenia and Human Value* (Oxford: Blackwell).

Barker M. (1982) 'Through Experience Towards Theory: a Psychodynamic Contribution to Social Work Education', *Issues in Social Work Education*, vol. 2, no. 2.

216

Beck A. (1979) *Cognitive Theory of Depression* (New York: Wiley).

Bernheimer C. and C. Kahane (eds) (1985) *In Dora's Case: Freud, Hysteria, Feminism* (London: Virago).

Bettleheim B. (1983) *Freud and Man's Soul* (London: Chatto & Windus).

Billig M. (1982) *Ideology and Psychology: Extremism, Moderation and Contradiction* (Oxford: Blackwell).

Billis D., G. Bromley, A. Hey and R. Rowbottom (1980) *Organising Social Services Departments* (London: Heinemann).

Bion W. R. (1962) *Learning from Experience* (London: Heinemann).

____ (1968) *Experiences in Groups* (London: Tavistock).

____ (1973) *Brazilian Lectures* (Sao Paulo: Imago Editora).

____ (1977) *Seven Servants* (New York: Aronson).

De Board R. (1978) *The Psychoanalysis of Organisations* (London: Tavistock).

Bocock R. (1976) *Freud and Modern Society* (London: Van Nostrand Reinhold).

____ (1977) 'Freud and the Centrality of Instincts in Psychoanalytic Sociology', *British Journal of Sociology*, vol. 28, no. 4.

Boszormenyi-Nagy I. and G. Spark (1973) *Invisible Loyalties* (New York: Harper & Row).

Bottomore T. (1984) *The Frankfurt School* (London: Tavistock).

Bowen M. (1978) *Family Therapy in Clinical Practice* (New York: Aronson).

Bowlby J. (1951) *Maternal Care and Mental Health* (Geneva: World Health Organisation).

____ (1965) *Child Care and the Growth of Love* (Harmondsworth: Penguin).

____ (1969) *Attachment and Loss, vol I: Attachment* (London: Hogarth Press).

____ (1973) *Attachment and Loss, Vol II: Separation* (London: Hogarth Press).

____ (1979) *The Making and Breaking of Affectional Bonds* (London: Tavistock).

____ (1980) *Attachment and Loss, Vol III: Loss* (London: Hogarth Press).

Bowlby, J., K. Figlio and R. M. Young (1986) 'An Interview with John Bowlby on the Origins and Reception of His Work', *Free Associations*, no. 6.

Box S., B. Copley, J. Magana and E. Moustaki (eds) (1981) *Psychotherapy with Families* (London: Routledge).

Breton A. (1978) *What is Surrealism? Selected Writings* (London: Pluto).

Breuer J. and S. Freud (1985) *Studies on Hysteria*, in *The Standard Edition of the Complete Psychological Works of Sigmund Freud*, vol. 2 (London: Hogarth Press, 1955) [also in *Pelican Freud Library*, vol. 3 (Harmondsworth: Penguin, 1974).]

Brewer C. and J. Lait (1980) *Can Social Work Survive?* (London: Temple Smith).

Britton R. (1981) 'Re-Enactment as an Unwitting Professional Response to Family Dynamics', in S. Box *et al.* (eds) *Psychotherapy with Families*, (London: Routledge).

Brown G. W. (1978) 'Depression: A Sociological View', in D. Tuckett and J. M. Kaufert (eds) *Basic Readings in Medical Sociology* (London: Tavistock).

218   *Bibliography*

Brown, G. W. and T. Harris (1978) *Social Origins of Depression: A Study of Psychiatric Disorder in Women* (London: Tavistock).

Brown N. O. (1959) *Life Against Death: The Psychoanalytical Meaning of History* (London: Routledge).

_____ (1966) *Love's Body* (New York: Vintage Books).

Brownmiller S. (1976) *Against Our Will: Men, Women and Rape* (Harmondsworth: Penguin).

Bruch H. (1974) *Eating Disorders: Obesity, Anorexia Nervosa and the Person Within* (London: Routledge).

_____ (1978) *The Golden Cage: The Enigma of Anorexia Nervosa* (London: Open Books).

Bunyan A. (1987) 'Help! I Can't Cope with my child. A Behavioural Approach to the Treatment of a Conduct Disordered Child within the Natural Homesetting', *British Journal of Social Work*, vol. 17, no. 3.

Buber M. (1970) *I and Thou* (Edinburgh: T & T Clark).

Burlingham D. and A. Freud (1942) *Children in War-Time* (London: Allen & Unwin).

_____ (1944) *Infants Without Families* (London: Allen & Unwin).

Caplan G. (1969) *An Approach to Community Mental Health* (London: Tavistock).

Carlen P. (1976) *Magistrates' Justice* (London: Martin Robertson).

Carpenter P. (1979) 'The Real World of Social Work', Proceedings of Oxford Conference on 'Change and Renewal in Psychodynamic Social Work'.

Castel R., F. Castel and A. Lovell (1982) *The Psychiatric Society* (New York: Columbia University Press).

Caudwell C. (1965) *Studies in a Dying Culture*, in *The Concept of Freedom* (London: Lawrence & Wishart).

Chasseguet-Smirgel J. (1985a) *Creativity and Perversion* (London: Free Association).

_____ (1985b) *The Ego Ideal* (London: Free Association).

Chasseguet-Smirgel J. *et al.* (1985) *Female Sexuality: New Psychoanalytic Views* (London: Maresfield Library).

Chasseguet-Smirgel J. and B. Grunberger (1986) *Freud or Reich? Psychoanalysis and Illusion* (London: Free Association).

Chodorow N. (1978) *The Reproduction of Mothering: Psychoanalysis and the Sociology of Gender* (Berkeley: University of California).

Cooklin A. (1979) 'A Psychoanalytical Framework for a Systemic Approach to Family Therapy', *Journal of Family Therapy*, vol. 1, no. 2.

Cooper M. (1983) 'Community Social Work', in B. Jordan and M. Parton (eds) *The Political Dimension of Social Work* (Oxford: Blackwell).

Cooper T. (1987) 'Anorexia and Bulimia: The Personal and the Political', in M. Lawrence (ed.) *Fed Up and Hungry: Women, Oppression and Food* (London: Women's Press).

Cosin B. R.,C. F. Freeman and N. H. Freeman (1982) 'Critical Empiricism Criticised: The Case of Freud', in R. Wollheim and J. Hopkins (eds) *Philosophical Essays on Freud* (London: Cambridge University Press).

Coward R. and J. Ellis (1977) *Language and Materialism* (London: Routledge).

Crisp A. H. (1980) *Anorexia Nervosa: Let Me Be* (London: Academic Press).
Crowe M. J. (1978) 'Conjoint Marital Therapy: A Controlled Outcome Study', *Psychological Medicine*, Vol. 8.
Dalbiez, P. (1941) *Psychoanalytical Method and the Doctrine of Freud*, 2 vols (London: Longman).
Dale P. (1984) 'The Danger Within Ourselves', *Community Care*, 1 March 1984.
Dally P. and J. Gomez (1979) *Anorexia Nervosa* (London: Heinemann).
Dana M. (1987) 'Abortion: A Woman's Right to Feel', in S. Ernst and M. Maguire (eds) *Living with the Sphinx* (London: Women's Press).
Dana M. and M. Lawrence (1986) *Bulimia: An Information Sheet for Self-Help Groups* (London: Women's Therapy Centre).
Dare C. (1979) 'Psychoanalysis and Systems in Family Therapy', *Journal of Family Therapy*, vol. 1, no. 2.
—— (1981) 'Psychoanalysis and Family Therapy', in S. Walrond-Skinner (ed.) *Developments in Family Therapy* (London: Routledge).
—— (1985) 'Family Therapy', in M. L. Rutter and L. Hersov (eds) *Child and Adolescent Psychiatry: Modern Approaches* (Oxford: Blackwell).
de Beauvoir S. (1974) *The Second Sex* (Harmondsworth: Penguin).
Deleuze G. and F. Guattari (1972) *L'Anti-Oedipe: Capitalisme et Schizophrénie* (Paris: Les Éditions de Minuit).
—— (1977) *Anti-Oedipus: Capitalism and Schizophrenia* (New York: Viking).
Descombes V. (1980) *Modern French Philosophy* (London: Cambridge University Press).
Deutsch H. (1944, 1945) *Psychology of Women*, 2 vols (New York: Grune & Stratton).
Dicks H. V. (1967) *Marital Tensions* (London: Routledge).
Dinnerstein D. (1978) *The Rocking of the Cradle* (London: Souvenir Press).
Docker-Drysdale B. E. (1968) *Therapy in Child Care* (London: Longman).
Dollard J. and N. E. Miller (1950) *Personality and Psychotherapy* (New York: McGraw-Hill).
Downes C. and S. M. Hall (1977) 'Consultation within Social Work', *Social Work Today*, vol. 8, no. 17.
Eagleton T. (1983) *Literary Theory* (Oxford: Blackwell).
Eichenbaum L. and S. Orbach (1982) *Outside In . . . Inside Out* (Harmondsworth: Penguin).
—— (1985) *Understanding Women* (Harmondsworth: Penguin).
Ellenberger H. F. (1970) *The Discovery of the Unconscious: The History and Evolution of Dynamic Psychiatry* (London: Allen Lane).
Ellis A. and R. Grieger (eds) (1977) *Handbook of Rational Emotive Therapy* (New York: Springer).
Erikson E. H. (1950) *Childhood and Society* (New York: Norton).
—— (1958) *Young Man Luther* (New York: Norton).
—— (1959) *Identity and the Life Cycle* (New York: International Universities Press).
Ernst S. and L. Goodison (1981) *In Our Own Hands: A Book of Self-Help Therapy* (London: Women's Press).
Ernst S. and M. Maguire (eds) (1987) *Living with the Sphinx* (London: Women's Press).

Evans-Pritchard E. E. (1965) *Theories of Primitive Religion* (London: Oxford University Press).

Eysenck H. J. (1986) *Decline and Fall of the Freudian Empire* (Harmondsworth: Penguin).

Fairbairn W. R. D. (1952) *Psychoanalytical Studies of the Personality* (London: Tavistock).

_____ (1954) *An Object Relations Theory of Personality* (New York: Basic Books).

Family Discussion Bureau (1955) *Social Casework in Marital Problems: The Development of a Psychodynamic Approach* (London: Tavistock).

_____ (1962) *The Marital Relationship as a Focus for Casework* (Hitchin, Herts: Codicote Press).

Fanon F. (1967) *Black Skin, White Masks* (New York: Grove Press).

Ferard M. L. and N. K. Hunnybun (1962) *The Caseworker's Use of Relationships* (London: Tavistock).

Ferenczi S. (1932) 'Confusion of Tongues Between Adults and the Child', in J. M. Masson, *The Assault on Truth: Freud's Suppression of the Seduction Theory* (Harmondsworth: Penguin).

Feyerabend P. (1975) *Against Method* (London: New Left Books).

Fineman S. (1985) *Social Work Stress and Intervention* (Aldershot: Gower).

Firestone S. (1971) *The Dialectic of Sex: The Case for Feminist Revolution* (New York: Bantam).

Fischer J. (1978) *Effective Casework Practice* (New York: McGraw Hill).

Fisher J. and R. Greenburg (1977) *The Scientific Credibility of Freud's Theories and Therapies (Brighton: Harvester).*

Flax J. (1981) 'The Conflict Between Nurturance and Autonomy in Mother-Daughter Relationships and Within Feminism', in E. Howell and M. Bayes (eds) *Women and Mental Health* (New York: Basic Books).

Foucault M. (1967) *Madness and Civilisation* (London: Tavistock).

_____ (1976) *The History of Sexuality, Vol I: An Introduction* (London: Allen Lane, 1979 ed).

_____ (1980) 'Confessions of the Flesh', in C. Gordon (ed.) *Power/Knowledge: Selected Interviews and Other Writings 1972–1977* (Brighton: Harvester).

_____ (1984a) *L'Usage des Plaisirs. Histoire de la Sexualité 2* (Paris: Gallimard).

_____ (1984b) *Le Souci de Soi. Histoire de la Sexualité 3* (Paris: Gallimard).

Freidson E. (1970) *Profession of Medicine: A Study in the Sociology of Applied Knowledge* (New York: Dodd, Mead).

Freud A. (1937) *The Ego and the Mechanisms of Defence* (London: Hogarth Press).

_____ (1965) *Normality and Pathology in Childhood* (New York: International Universities Press).

Freud S. (1984) 'On the Ground for Detaching a Particular Syndrome from Neurasthenia under the Description "Anxiety Neurosis"', in *The Standard Edition of the Complete Psychological Works of Sigmund Freud* (24 vols), vol 3 (London: Hogarth Press). And in *The Pelican Freud Library* (15 vols), vol 10 (Harmondsworth: Penguin).

Freud S. (1985) 'Project for a Scientific Psychology', in *Standard Edition*, 1.

____ (1900) *The Interpretation of Dreams* (London: Allen & Unwin, 1954 ed). Also *Standard Edition*, vols 4–5 and *Pelican Freud*, vol. 4.

____ (1901) *The Psychopathology of Everyday Life* (London: Ernest Benn, 1914 ed). Also *Standard Edition*, vol. 6 and *Pelican Freud*, vol. 5.

____ (1905a) *Three Essays on the Theory of Sexuality*, in *Standard Edition*, vol. 7 and *Pelican Freud*, vol. 7.

____ (1905b) 'Fragment of an Analysis of a Case of Hysteria', in *Standard Edition*, vol. 7 and *Pelican Freud*, vol. 8.

____ (1905c) Jokes and their Relation to the Unconscious, in *Standard Edition*, vol. 8 and *Pelican Freud*, vol. 6.

____ (1909) 'Analysis of a Phobia in a Five Year Old Boy', in *Standard Edition*, vol. 10 and *Pelican Freud*, vol. 8.

____ (1910) *Leonardo Da Vinci* (Harmondsworth: Penguin, 1963 edn). Also in *Standard Edition*, vol. 11 and *Pelican Freud*, vol. 14.

____ (1911a) 'Psychoanalytical Notes on An Autobiographical Account of a Case of Paranoia (Dementia Paranoides)', in *Standard Edition*, vol. 12 and *Pelican Freud*, vol. 9.

____ (1911b) 'Formulations on the Two Principles of Mental Functioning', in *Standard Edition*, vol. 12 and *Pelican Freud*, vol. 11.

____ (1913) *Totem and Taboo: Some Points of Agreement between the Mental Lives of Savages and Neurotics*, in *Standard Edition*, vol. 13 and *Pelican Freud*, vol. 13.

____ (1914) 'Remembering, Repeating and Working Through', in *Standard Edition*, vol. 12.

____ (1915a) 'The Unconscious', in *Standard Edition*, vol. 14 and *Pelican Freud*, vol. 11.

____ (1915b) 'Instincts and Their Vicissitudes', in *Standard Edition*, vol. 14 and *Pelican Freud*, vol. 11.

____ (1916–17) *Introductory Lectures on Psychoanalysis*, in *Standard Edition*, vol. 15–16 and *Pelican Freud*, vol. 1.

____ (1917a) 'A Difficulty in the Path of Psychoanalysis', in *Standard Edition*, vol. 17.

____ (1917b) 'Mourning and Melancholia', in *Standard Edition*, vol. 14 and *Pelican Freud* vol. 11.

____ (1921) *Group Psychology and the Analysis of the Ego*, in *Standard Edition*, vol. 18 and *Pelican Freud*, vol. 12.

____ (1923) *The Ego and the Id*, in *Standard Edition*, vol. 19 and *Pelican Freud*, vol. 11.

____ (1927a) *The Future of an Illusion*, in *Standard Edition*, vol. 21 and *Pelican Freud*, vol. 12.

____ (1927b) 'Postscript to *The Question of Lay Analysis*', in *Standard Edition*, vol. 20 and *Pelican Freud*, vol. 15.

____ (1930) *Civilisation and Its Discontents*, in *Standard Edition*, vol. 21 and *Pelican Freud*, vol. 12.

____ (1933a) *New Introductory Lectures on Psychoanalysis*, in *Standard Edition*, vol. 22 and *Pelican Freud*, vol. 2.

____ (1933b) 'Femininity', in *New Introductory Lectures*, ibid.

____ (1933c) 'Why War?', in *Standard Edition*, vol. 22 and *Pelican Freud*, vol. 12.

____ (1962) *The Question of Lay Analysis*, in *Two Short Accounts of Psychoanalysis* (Harmondsworth: Penguin).

____ (1974) *The Freud/Jung Letters* (London: Hogarth Press).

Fromm E. (1932) 'The Method and Function of an Analytic Social Psychology', in *The Crisis of Psychoanalysis: Essays on Freud, Marx and Social Psychology* (London: Cape, 1971 edn).

____ (1934) 'The Theory of Mother Right and its Relevance for Social Psychology', in *The Crisis of Psychoanalysis*, ibid. (London: Cape, 1971 edn).

____ (1942) *Fear of Freedom* (London: Routledge, 1960 edn).

____ (1962) *The Art of Loving* (London: Allen & Unwin).

____ (1963) 'Psychoanalysis: Science or Party Line?', in *The Dogma of Christ* (London: Routledge).

____ (1968) *The Revolution of Hope* (New York: Harper & Row).

____ (1980) *Greatness and Limitations of Freud's Thought* (London: Cape).

Gallop J. (1982) *The Daughter's Seduction: Feminism and Psychoanalysis* (London: Macmillan).

Gellner E. (1985) *The Psychoanalytical Movement* (London: Paladin).

Giddens A. (1979) *Central Problems in Social Theory* (London: Macmillan).

Goldberg E. M. (1953) 'The Function and Use of Relationship in Psychiatric Social Work', *British Journal of Psychiatric Social Work*, vol. 2, no. 8. [Repr. in E. Younghusband (ed.) *New Developments in Casework* (London: Allen & Unwin, 1966).]

Goldberg E. M. (1958) *Family Influences and Psychosomatic Illness: An Inquiry into the Social and Psychological Background of Duodenal Ulcer* (London: Tavistock).

Gordon R. (1973) 'Symbols: Content and Process', in Fordsham *et al.* (eds) *Analytic Psychology: A Modern Science* (London: Academic Press).

Graham H. (1984) *Women, Health and the Family* (Brighton: Wheatsheaf).

Greer G. (1971) *The Female Eunuch* (London: Paladin).

Guattari F. (1984) *Molecular Revolution: Psychiatry and Politics* (Harmondsworth: Penguin).

Guntrip H. (1961) *Personality Structure and Human Interaction* (London: Hogarth Press).

____ (1968) *Schizoid Phenomena, Object Relations and the Self* (London: Hogarth Press).

Habermas J. (1972) *Knowledge and Human Interests* (London: Heinemann).

Haley J. (1973) *Uncommon Therapy: The Psychiatric Techniques of Milton H. Erikson* (New York: Norton).

____ (1976) *Problem Solving Therapy* (New York: Harper & Row).

Halmos P. (1965) *The Faith of the Counsellors* (London: Constable).

Hamilton P. (1982) *Talcott Parsons* (London: Tavistock).

Hardiker P. and M. Barker (eds) (1981) *Theories of Practice in Social Work* (London: Academic Press).

Heidegger M. (1971) *On the Way to Language* (New York: Harper & Row).

Heimann P. (1969) 'Counter-Transference', *British Journal of Medical Psychology*, vol. 33.

Held D. (1980) *Introduction to Critical Theory* (London: Hutchinson).

Herbert M. (1981) *Psychology for Social Workers* (London: Macmillan).

Hirst P. (1979) *On Law and Ideology* (London: Macmillan).

Hocquenghem G. (1978) *Homosexual Desire* (London: Allison & Busby).

Hoggett P. and J. Lousada (1985) 'Therapeutic Interventions in Working Class Communities', *Free Associations*, no. 1.

Holland S. and R. Holland (1984) 'Depressed Women: Outposts of Empire and Castles of Skin', in B. Richards (ed.) *Capitalism and Infancy: Essays on Psychoanalysis and Politics* (London: Free Association).

Holmes J. (1983) 'Psychoanalysis and Family Therapy: Freud's Dora Case Re-Considered', *Journal of Family Therapy*, vol. 5, no. 3.

Horney K. (1939) *New Ways in Psychoanalysis* (New York: Norton).

Horney K. (1967) *Feminine Psychology* (New York: Norton).

Horkheimer M. (1947) *Eclipse of Reason* (New York: Seabury Press, 1974 edn).

Howell E. and M. Bayes (eds) (1981) *Women and Mental Health* (New York: Basic Books).

Hudson B. L. and G. Macdonald (1986) *Behavioural Social Work: An Introduction* (London: Macmillan).

Hunter P. (1969) 'A Survey of Psychiatric Social Workers Working in Mental Hospitals', *British Journal of Psychiatric Social Work*, vol. 10, no. 1.

Hutton J. (1977) *Short-Term Contracts in Social Work* (London: Routledge).

Irvine E. E. (1952) 'The Function and Use of Relationship between Client and Psychiatric Social Worker', *British Journal of Psychiatric Social Work*, vol. 2, no. 6. [Repr. in E. Younghusband (ed.) *New Developments in Casework* (London: Allen & Unwin, 1966).]

____ (1956) 'Transference and Reality in the Casework Relationship', *British Journal of Psychiatric Social Work*, vol. 3, no. 4. [Repr. in Younghusband, ibid.]

Iwaniec D., M. Herbert and A. S. McNeish (1985) 'Social Work with Failure-to-Thrive Children and their Families', *British Journal of Social Work*, vol. 15, no. 3 and vol. 15, no. 4.

Jackson D. D. (ed.) (1968) *Human Communication*, 2 vols (Palo Alto: Science & Behavior Books).

Jacoby R. (1975) *Social Amnesia: A Critique of Conformist Psychology from Adler to Laing* (Boston: Beacon Press).

Jaques E. (1955) 'Social Systems as a Defence against Persecutory and Depressive Anxiety', in M. Klein, P. Heimann and R. E. Money-Kyrle (eds) *New Directions in Psychoanalysis* (London: Tavistock).

____ (1970) *Work, Creativity and Social Justice* (London: Heinemann).

Jay M. (1973) *The Dialectical Imagination: A History of the Frankfurt School and the Institute of Social Research 1923–1950* (London: Heinemann).

Jeffreys S. (1985) *The Spinster and Her Enemies: Feminism and Sexuality 1880–1930* (London: Pandora).

Jones E. (1925) 'Mother-Right and the Sexual Ignorance of Savages', *International Journal of Psychoanalysis*, vol. 6, no. 2.

____ (1961) *The Life and Work of Sigmund Freud* (London: Hogarth Press).

Jones J. (1978) *Responses to Child Abuse: Implications for Social Work Practice* (Unpublished MSW Dissertation, University of York).

Jones M. (1955) *The Therapeutic Community: A New Treatment Method in Psychiatry* (New York: Basic Books).

——— (1976) *Maturation of the Therapeutic Community* (New York: Human Sciences Press).

Jung C. J. (1953) 'Two Essays on Analytic Psychology', in *Collected Works* vol. 7 (London: Routledge).

Jung C. G. (1954) 'The Aims of Psychotherapy' and 'The Practice of Psychotherapy', in *Collected Works*, vol. 16 (London: Routledge).

Kasius C. (ed.) (1950) *A Comparison of Diagnostic and Functional Casework Concepts* (New York: Family Service Association of America).

Kazdin A. E. and G. T. Wilson (1978) *Evaluation of Behaviour Therapy: Issues, Evidence and Research* (Nebraska: University of Nebraska Press).

Kermode F. (1985) 'Freud and Interpretation', *International Review of Psychoanalysis*, vol. 44.

Klein M. (1929) 'Personification in the Play of Children', in *Love, Guilt and Reparation* (London: Hogarth Press, 1975 edn).

——— (1932) 'An Obsessional Neurosis in a Six Year Old Girl', in *The Psychoanalysis of Children* (London: Hogarth Press, 1975 edn).

——— (1946) 'Notes on Severe Schizoid Mechanisms', in *Envy and Gratitude* (London: Hogarth Press, 1975 edn).

——— (1948) *Contributions to Psychoanalysis, 1921–1945* (London: Hogarth Press).

——— (1955) 'On Identification', in M. Klein, P. Heimann and R. E. Money-Kyrle (eds.) *New Directions in Psychoanalysis* (London: Tavistock).

Kohon G. (ed.) (1986) *The British School of Psychoanalysis: The Independent Tradition* (London: Free Association).

Kolvin I. *et al.* (1981) *Help Starts Here: The Maladjusted Child in the Ordinary School* (London: Tavistock).

Krüll M. (1986) *Freud and His Father* (London: Hutchinson).

Kutek A. (1986) *Group for the Advancement of Psychotherapy in Social Work: Chairman's Report.*

Lacan J. (1977) 'The Function and Field of Speech and Language in Psychoanalysis', in *Écrits: A Selection* (London: Tavistock).

Lacan J. (1979) *The Four Fundamental Concepts of Psychoanalysis* (Harmondsworth: Penguin).

Laing R. D. (1965) *The Divided Self* (Harmondsworth: Penguin).

——— (1967) *The Politics of Experience* (Harmondsworth: Penguin).

——— (1969) *Self and Others*, 2nd edn (Harmondsworth: Penguin).

Laing R. D. and A. Esterson (1964) *Sanity, Madness and the Family* (London: Tavistock).

Langer S. (1942) *Philosophy in a New Key* (Cambridge, Mass.: Harvard University Press).

Lasch C. (1979) *The Culture of Narcissism* (New York: Norton).

——— (1985) *The Minimal Self: Psychic Survival in Troubled Times* (London: Picador).

Lawrence M. (1984) *The Anorexic Experience* (London: Women's Press).

Lawrence M. (ed.) (1987) *Fed Up and Hungry: Women, Oppression and Food* (London: Women's Press).

Ledwidge B. (1978) 'Cognitive Behaviour Modification: A Step in the

Wrong Direction?', *Psychological Bulletin*, vol. 85, pp. 353–73.

Lee S. G. M. and M. Herbert (eds) (1970) *Freud and Psychology: Selected Readings* (Harmondsworth: Penguin).

Leonard P. (1984) *Personality and Ideology* (London: Macmillan).

Lidz T., S. Fleck and A. R. Cornelison (1965) *Schizophrenia and the Family* (New York: International Universities Press).

Lipshitz S. (1978) ' "The Personal is the Political": The Problem of Feminist Therapy', *m/f*, no. 2.

Little M. (1981) *Transference Neurosis and Transference Psychosis* (New York: Aronson).

MacCabe C. (ed.) (1981) *The Talking Cure: Essays in Psychoanalysis and Language* (London: Macmillan).

McBarnet D. (1981) *Conviction: Law, the State and the Construction of Justice* (London: Macmillan).

McCaughan N. (1967) 'Social Work with Three Men Suffering from a Loss of Limb, Parts I & II', *Medical Social Work*, vol. 20, nos. 5, 6.

MacDonald M. (1981) *Mystical Bedlam: Madness, Anxiety and Healing in Seventeenth Century England* (London: Cambridge University Press).

MacLeod S. (1981) *The Art of Starvation* (London: Virago).

McGuire W. (ed.) (1979) *The Freud/Jung Letters* (London: Picador).

Mahler M. S. (1968) *On Human Symbiosis and the Vicissitudes of Individuation* (New York: International Universities Press).

Malcolm J. (1986) *In the Freud Archives* (London: Flamingo).

Malinowski B. (1927) *Sex and Repression in Savage Society* (London: Routledge).

Marcuse H. (1955) *Eros and Civilisation* (Boston: Beacon Press).

_____ (1970) *Five Lectures: Psychoanalysis, Politics and Utopia* (Boston: Beacon Press).

Marsden D. (1973) *Mothers Alone: Poverty and the Fatherless Family* (Harmondsworth: Penguin).

Masson J. M. (1985a) *The Assault on Truth: Freud's Suppression of the Seduction Theory* (Harmondsworth: Penguin).

_____ (1985b) *The Complete Letters of Sigmund Freud to Wilhelm Fleiss, 1887–1904* (Cambridge, Mass.: Harvard University Press).

Mattinson J. (1975) *The Reflection Process in Casework Supervision* (London: Institute of Martial Studies).

Mattinson J. and I. Sinclair (1979) *Mate and Stalemate* (Oxford: Blackwell).

Matson F. W. (1964) *The Broken Image: Man, Science and Society* (New York: Braziller).

Mayer J. E. and N. Timms (1970) *The Client Speaks* (London: Routledge).

Medawar P. (1975) 'Victims of Psychiatry', *New York Review of Books*, 23 January 1975.

Meichenbaum D. (1977) *Cognitive Behaviour Modification* (New York: Plenum).

Meltzer D. (1973) *Sexual States of Mind* (Perth: Roland Harris Trust, Clunie Press).

_____ (1975) *The Kleinian Development* (Perth: Roland Harris Trust, Clunie Press).

_____ (1984) *Dream Life: A Re-Examination of the Psychoanalytical Theory and Technique* (Perth: Roland Harris Trust, Clunie Press).

Menzies I. E. P. (1960) 'A Case Study in the Functioning of Social Systems as a Defence Against Anxiety', *Human Relations*, vol. 13. [Repr. as *The Functioning of Social Systems as a Defence Against Anxiety: A Report on a Study of the Nursing Service of a General Hospital*, Tavistock Pamphlet no. 3, 1970.]

Menzies Lyth I. (1985) 'The Development of the Self in Children in Institutions', *Journal of Child Psychotherapy*, vol. 11, no. 2.

—— (1986) 'Psychoanalysis in Non-Clinical Contexts: The Art of Captaincy', *Free Associations*, no. 5.

Merleau-Ponty M. (1965) *The Structure of Behaviour* (London: Methuen).

Millett K. (1970) *Sexual Politics* (New York: Doubleday).

Miller A. (1983a) *The Drama of the Gifted Child* (London: Faber).

—— (1983b) *For Your Own Good: Hidden Cruelty in Child-Rearing and the Roots of Violence* (London: Faber).

—— (1985) *Thou Shalt Not Be Aware: Society's Betrayal of the Child* (London: Pluto).

Miller D. (1964) *Growth to Freedom* (London: Tavistock).

Miller E. J. and A. K. Rice (eds) (1967) *Systems of Organisation* (London: Tavistock).

Miller E. J. and G. V. Gwynne (1972) *A Life Apart* (London: Tavistock).

Minuchin S. (1974) *Families and Family Therapy* (Cambridge, Mass.: Harvard University Press).

Minuchin S., B. L. Rosman and L. Baker (1978) *Psychosomatic Families: Anorexia Nervosa in Context* (Cambridge, Mass.: Harvard University Press).

Minuchin S. and H. C. Fishman (1981) *Family Therapy Techniques* (Cambridge, Mass.: Harvard University Press).

Mitchell J. (1974) *Psychoanalysis and Feminism* (Harmondsworth: Penguin).

Mitchell J. (ed.) (1986) *The Selected Melanie Klein* (Harmondsworth: Penguin).

Mitzman A. (1977) 'Anarchism, Expressionism and Psychoanalysis', *New German Critique*, no. 10, Winter 1977.

Money-Kyrle R. (1956) 'The World of the Unconscious and the World of Common Sense', *British Journal of Philosophy of Science*, vol. 7.

Moretti F. (1983) *Signs Taken For Wonders: Essays in the Sociology of Literary Forms* (London: Verso).

Needleman J. (ed.) (1963) *Being-in-the-World: Selected Papers of Ludwig Binswanger* (New York: Basic Books).

North M. (1972) *The Secular Priests: Psychotherapists in Contemporary Society* (London: Allen & Unwin).

Orbach S. (1978) *Fat is a Feminist Issue* (London: Hamlyn).

—— (1986) *Hunger Strike* (London: Faber).

Palazzoli M. S., L. Boscold, G. Cecchin and G. Prata (1978) *Paradox and Counterparadox* (New York: Aronson).

Palmer R. L. (1980) *Anorexia Nervosa* (Harmondsworth: Penguin).

Parad H. J. (ed.) (1965) *Crisis Intervention: Selected Readings* (New York: Family Service Association of America).

Parkes C. M. (1972) *Bereavement: Studies of Grief in Adult Life* (London: Tavistock).

Parry-Cooke G. and J. Ryan (1986) *Evaluation of Self-Help Therapy Groups for Women with Compulsive Eating Problems* (Research Report no. 13. London: Health Education Council).
Parsons T. (1937) *The Structure of Social Action* (Glencoe, Ill.: Free Press).
____ (1951) *The Social System* (London: Routledge).
____ (1964) *Social Structure and Personality* (Glencoe, Ill.: Free Press).
Parsons T. and R. F. Bales (1956) *Family, Socialisation and Interaction Process* (London: Routledge).
Parton N. and T. Thomas (1983) 'Child Abuse and Citizenship', in B. Jordan and N. Parton (eds) *The Political Dimensions of Social Work* (Oxford: Blackwell).
Pearson G. (1974) 'Prisons of Love: The Reification of the Family in Family Therapy', in N. Armistead (ed.) *Reconstructing Social Psychology* (Harmondsworth: Penguin).
____ (1975) *The Deviant Imagination* (London: Macmillan).
____ (1988) 'Social Work and Unemployment', in M. Langan and P. Lee (eds) *Social Work in Recession* (London: Hutchinson).
Pincus L. (ed.) (1960) *Marriage: Studies in Emotional Conflict and Growth* (London: Methuen).
Pincus L. and C. Dare (1978) *Secrets in the Family* (London: Faber).
Polanyi M. (1958) *A Study of Man* (Chicago: University of Chicago Press).
Popay J., Y. Dhooge and C. Shipman (1986) *Unemployment and Health: What Role for Health and Social Services?*, Research Report no. 3. (London: Health Education Council).
Rachman S. (1983) 'Irrational Thinking with Special Reference to Cognitive Therapy', *Advances in Behaviour Research and Therapy*, vol. 5, no. 1.
Rachman S. and G. T. Wilson (1980) *The Effects of Psychological Therapy* (Oxford: Pergamon).
Racker H. (1968) *Transference and Counter-Transference* (New York: International Universities Press).
Rank O. (1945) *Will Therapy & Truth and Reality* (New York: Knopf).
Reich W. (1927) *The Function of the Orgasm* (London: Panther, 1968 edn).
____ (1929) *Dialectical Materialism and Psychoanalysis* (London: Socialist Reproduction, 1972 edn).
____ (1931) *The Sexual Struggle of Youth* (London: Socialist Reproduction, 1972 edn).
____ (1932) 'Politicizing the Sexual Problem of Youth', in *Sex-Pol* (New York: Random House, 1972 edn).
____ (1933a) *The Mass Psychology of Fascism* (London: Souvenir Press, 1972 edn).
____ (1933b) *What is Class Consciousness?* (London: Socialist Reproduction, 1971 edn).
____ (1948) *Listen, Little Man!* (London: Souvenir Press, 1972 edn).
____ (1949) *Character Analysis*, 3rd edn (New York: Farrar, Straus & Giroux).
Reich W. and K. Teschitz (1973) *Selected Sex-Pol Essays 1934–37* (London: Socialist Reproduction).
Reid W. J. and L. Epstein (1977) *Task-Centred Practice* (New York: Columbia University Press).

Rice A. K. (1965) *Learning for Leadership* (London: Tavistock).

Rich A. (1976) *Of Woman Born: Motherhood as Experience and Institution* (New York: Bantam).

Rieff P. (1959) *Freud: The Mind of the Moralist* (London: Gollancz).

——— (1966) *The Triumph of the Therapeutic: Uses of Faith After Freud* (London: Chatto & Windus).

Riley D. (1983) *War in the Nursery: Theories of the Child and Mother* (London: Virago).

Roazen P. (1970) *Freud: Political and Social Thought* (New York: Vintage Books).

Roazen P. (1985) *Helene Deutsch: A Psychoanalyst's Life* (New York: Meridian).

Robertson J. (1952) Film: *A Two Year Old Goes to Hospital* (London: Tavistock Child Development Research Unit).

——— (1958) Film: *Going to Hospital with Mother* (London: Tavistock Child Development Research Unit).

Robertson J. (ed.) (1962) *Hospitals and Children: A Parent's-Eye View* (London: Gollancz).

Robertson J. and J. Robertson (1967–1973) Film Series: *Young Children in Brief Separation*. No. 1 (1967): Kate, 2 years 5 months, in fostercare for 27 days; No 2 (1968): Jane, 17 months, in fostercare for 10 days; No 3 (1969): John, 17 months, 9 days in residential nursery; No 4 (1971): Thomas, 2 years 4 months, in fostercare for 10 days; No 5 (1973): Lucy, 21 months, in fostercare for 19 days (London: Tavistock Institute of Human Relations.

——— (1971) 'Young Children in Brief Separation: A Fresh Look', *Psychoanalytical Study of the Child*, vol. 26.

Robinson P. A. (1972) *The Sexual Radicals* (London: Paladin). [Originally publ. as *The Freudian Left*, 1969.]

Robinson V. P. (1930) *A Changing Psychology in Social Casework* (Chapel Hill: University of North Carolina).

Rocher G. (1974) *Talcott Parsons and American Sociology* (London: Nelson).

Roheim G. (1950) *Psychoanalysis and Anthropology* (New York: International Universities Press).

——— (1955) *Magic and Schizophrenia* (Bloomington: Indiana University Press).

Rorty R. (1979) *Philosophy and the Mirror of Nature* (Princeton, NJ: Princeton University Press).

Rorty R. (1982) 'Method, Social Science and Social Hope', in *Consequences of Pragmatism: Essays 1972–1980* (Brighton: Harvester).

Rose J. (1978) ' "Dora": Fragment of an Analysis', *m/f*, no 2. [Repr. in C. Bernheimer and C. Kahane (eds) *In Dora's Case: Freud, Hysteria, Feminism* (London: Virago, 1985).]

Rothman D. (1971) *The Discovery of the Asylum* (Boston: Little, Brown).

Rowbottom R., D. Billis and A. Hey (1974) *Social Services Departments* (London: Heinemann).

Ruesch J. and G. Bateson (1951) *Communication: The Social Matrix of Psychiatry* (New York: Norton).

Rushton A. and J. Treseder (1986) 'Developmental Recovery', *Adoption and Fostering*, vol. 10, no. 4.

Rutter M. L. and L. Hersov (eds) (1985) *Child and Adolescent Psychiatry: Modern Approaches* (Oxford: Blackwell).

Rycroft C. (1968) *A Critical Dictionary of Psychoanalysis* (London: Nelson; Penguin edn, 1972).

―― (1971) *Reich* (London: Fontana).

―― (1985) 'The Present State of Freudian Psychoanalysis' in *Psychoanalysis and Beyond* (London: Chatto & Windus).

Ryle G. (1949) *The Concept of Mind* (London: Hutchinson).

Salzberger-Wittenberg I. (1970) *Psychoanalytic Insight and Relationships: A Kleinian Approach* (London: Routledge).

Sandler J., C. Dare and A. Holder (1973) *The Patient and the Analyst* (London: Allen & Unwin).

Sayers J. (1982) *Biological Politics: Feminist and Anti-Feminist Perspectives* (London: Tavistock).

―― (1984) 'Feminism and Mothering: A Kleinian Perspective', *Women's Studies International Forum*, vol. 7, no. 4.

―― (1986) *Sexual Contradictions: Psychology, Psychoanalysis and Feminism* (London: Tavistock).

Schatzman M. (1973) *Soul Murder: Persecution in the Family* (London: Allen Lane).

Scheff T. J. (1968) 'Negotiating Reality: Notes on Power in the Assessment of Responsibility', *Social Problems*, vol. 16, no. 1.

Scull A. T. (1979) *Museums of Madness: The Social Organisation of Insanity in Nineteenth Century England* (London: Allen Lane).

Scull A. T. (ed.) (1981) *Madhouses, Mad-Doctors and Madmen: The Social History of Psychiatry in the Victorian Era* (Philadelphia: University of Pennsylvania Press).

Searle J. (1969) *Speech Acts: An Essay in the Philosophy of Language* (London: Cambridge University Press).

Sears R. R. (1943) 'A Survey of Objective Studies of Psychoanalytical Concepts', *Social Science Research Council Bulletin*, no. 51.

Sedgwick P. (1982) *Psycho Politics* (London: Pluto).

Segal H. (1973) *Introduction to the Work of Melanie Klein* (London: Hogarth Press).

―― (1979) *Klein* (London: Fontana).

Selvini Palazzoli M. (1974) *Self Starvation* (London: Chaucer).

Simmonds J. (1984) 'Crossing the Boundary: From Student to Qualified Social Worker', *Journal of Social Work Practice*, vol. 1, no. 2.

Smale G. (1983) 'Can We Afford Not to Develop Social Work Practice?' *British Journal of Social Work*, vol. 13, no. 3.

Snow C. P. (1959) *The Two Cultures and the Scientific Revolution* (London: Cambridge University Press, 1962 edn).

Spence D. (1982) *Narrative Truth and Historical Truth* (New York: Norton).

Spitz R. (1965) *The First Year of Life* (New York: International Universities Press).

Spurling L. (1977) *Phenomenology and the Social World* (London: Routledge).

Steele R. S. (1982) *Freud and Jung: Conflicts of Interpretation* (London: Routledge).

Stevenson O. *et al.* (1978) *Social Service Teams: The Practitioners' View* (London: HMSO).

Stierlin H. (1977) *Psychoanalysis and Family Therapy* (New York: Aronson).

Stone L. (1961) *The Psychoanalytical Situation* (New York: International Universities Press).

Strachey J. (1934) 'The Nature of the Therapeutic Action of Psychoanalysis', *International Journal of Psychoanalysis*, vol. 15.

Sulloway F. (1979) *Freud, Biologist of the Mind: Beyond the Psychoanalytic Legend* (London: Burnett).

Sussenwein F. & J. Treseder (1985) 'Psychiatric Social Work', in M. L. Rutter and L. Hersov (eds) *Child and Adolescent Psychiatry: Modern Approaches* (Oxford: Blackwell).

Sutherland J. D. (1956) 'Psychotherapy and Social Casework', in *The Boundaries of Casework* (London: Association of Psychiatric social Workers).

Szasz T. S. (1963) 'The Concept of Transference', *International Journal of Psychoanalysis*, vol. 44.

Taft J. (1933) *The Dynamics of Therapy in a Controlled Relationship* (New York: Macmillan).

Thomä H. (1967) *Anorexia Nervosa* (New York: International Universities Press).

Thompson C. M. (1964) *Interpersonal Psychoanalysis: The Selected Papers of Clara M. Thompson* (New York: Basic Books).

Thornton E. M. (1986) *The Freudian Fallacy: Freud and Cocaine* (London: Paladin).

Timpanaro S. (1976) *The Freudian Slip: Psychoanalysis and Textual Criticism* (London: New Left Books).

Trotsky L. (1927) 'Culture and Socialism', in I. Deutscher (ed.) *The Age of Permanent Revolution: A Trotsky Anthology* (New York: Dell, 1964).

Tseng W. S. and D. Y. H. Wu (eds) (1985) *Chinese Culture and Mental Health* (London: Academic Press).

Turkle S. (1978) *Psychoanalytical Politics: Freud's French Revolution* (New York: Basic Books).

Walrond-Skinner S. (1976) *Family Therapy: The Treatment of Natural Systems* (London: Routledge).

Watzlawick P., J. H. Beavin and D. D. Jackson (1968) *Pragmatics of Human Communication* (London: Faber).

Watzlawick P., J. Weakland and R. Fisch (1974) *Change: Principles of Problem Formation and Problem Resolution* (New York: Norton).

Whitaker C. (1983) Institute of Family Therapy, Conference, London.

White M. B. and W. C. White (1983) *Bulimarexia: The Binge/Purge Cycle* (New York: Norton).

Whitebook J. (1985) 'Reason and Happiness: Some Psychoanalytical Themes in Critical Theory', in R. J. Bernstein (ed.) *Habermas and Modernity* (Oxford: Blackwell).

Williams R. (1980) 'Problems of Materialism', in *Problems in Materialism and Culture* (London: Verso).

Wilson G.T. and I. M. Evans (1977) 'The Therapist-Client Relationship in Behaviour Therapy', in R. S. Gurman and A. M. Razin (eds), *Psychother-*

apy: An Empirical Approach (New York: Pergamon).

Winch P. (1958) *The Idea of a Social Science* (London: Routledge).

Winnicott D. W. (1949) 'Hate in the Counter-Transference', *International Journal of Psychoanalysis*, vol. 30 and *Collected Papers*, op. cit.

—— (1953) 'Transitional Objects and Transitional Phenomena', *International Journal of Psychoanalysis*, vol. 34 and *Collected Papers*, op. cit.

—— (1956) 'The Antisocial Tendency', in *Collected Papers*, op. cit.

—— (1958a) *Collected Papers: Through Paediatrics to Psychoanalysis* (London: Tavistock).

—— (1958b) 'The Capacity to Be Alone', in *Maturational Processes*, op. cit.

—— (1960) 'Counter-Transference', *British Journal* of *Medical Psychology*, vol. 33 and *Maturational Processes*, op. cit.

—— (1963a) 'The Mentally Ill in Your Caseload', in *New Thinking for Changing Needs* (London: Association of Social Workers) [Repr. in *Maturational Processes*, op. cit.]

—— (1963b) 'Psychiatric Disorder in Terms of Infantile Maturational Processes', in *Maturational Processes*, op. cit.

—— (1964a) 'The Value of Depression', *British Journal of Psychiatric Social Work*, vol. 7.

—— (1964b) *The Child, the Family, and the Outside World* (Harmondsworth: Penguin).

—— (1965) *The Maturational Processes and the Facilitating Environment: Studies in the Theory of Emotional Development* (London: Hogarth Press).

—— (1971a) *Therapeutic Consultations in Child Psychiatry* (London: Hogarth Press).

—— (1971b) *Playing and Reality* (London: Tavistock; Penguin edn, 1974).

—— (1974) 'Dreaming, Fantasying and Living: A Case History Describing a Primary Dissociation', in *Playing and Reality* (Harmondsworth: Penguin).

—— (1978) *The Piggle: An Account of the Psychoanalytic Treatment of a Little Girl* (London: Hogarth Press).

—— (1986) *Holding and Interpretation: Fragment of an Analysis* (London: Hogarth).

—— (1987) *The Spontaneous Gesture: Selected Letters of D. W. Winnicott*, ed. F. R. Rodman. Cambridge, Mass.: Harvard University Press.

Wisdom J. (1984) 'What is Left of Psychoanalytic Theory?', *International Review of Psychoanalysis*, vol. 11.

Wollheim R. (1971) *Freud* (London: Fontana).

Woodroofe K. (1962) *From Charity to Social Work* (London: Routledge).

Wrong D. (1961) 'The Oversocialised Conception of Man in Modern Sociology', *American Sociological Review*, vol. 26.

Wrong D. (1976) 'Postscript', in *Skeptical Sociology*, (New York: Columbia University Press).

Wynne L. C., I. M. Ryckoff, J. Day and S. I. Hirsch (1958) 'Pseudo-mutuality in the Family Relations of Schizophrenics', *Psychiatry*, vol. 21, no. 3. [Repr. in G. Handel (ed.) *The Psychosocial Interior of the Family* London: Allen & Unwin, 1968).]

Yelloly M. A. (1980) *Social Work Theory and Psychoanalysis* (London: Van Nostrand Reinhold).

Young R. M. (1986) 'Freud: Scientist and/or Humanist', *Free Associations*, no. 6.

Younghusband E. (1978) *Social Work in Britain, 1950–1975*, vol. II (London: Allen & Unwin).

Yule W. L. Hersov and J. Treseder (1980) 'Behavioural Treatment in School Refusal', in L. Hersov and I. Berg (eds) *Out of School* (New York: Wiley).

Index